INTRODUCTION

FOR THE RECORD: REPORT WRITING IN LAW ENFORCEMENT offers guidelines for writing at all levels of law enforcement. The book teaches and gives practice using guidelines for producing professional reports that reflect positively on the writer. It is designed to be equally effective for individual study by working law enforcement officers or for course work by police science students.

FOR THE RECORD presents the general features of law enforcement reports and the steps in producing them. It also covers principles of clear writing, grammar, spelling, and punctuation. Although the text focuses on investigative reports, the principles of effective writing apply to any written work.

The authors wish to thank the many students who worked through the developmental version of this text and offered suggestions for its improvement. Some of these students, as well as several law enforcement officers, have contributed their reports to be used (often in modified form) as samples in this text.

Kären M. Hess, PhD
Christine Hess Orthmann, MS

Most law enforcement officers submit their reports for prosecution with concern over the outcome, but without much thought about the wheels they've started in motion. This is understandable, for they've done their jobs and many more cases wait to be investigated. But what happens when they haven't really done their jobs— when their reports are distorted or incomplete (as many are) because of poor writing? The results not only cost the taxpayers in wasted officers' time, but they also breed disaster in the courtroom.

To cite an all-too-common example, in one criminal case, the reporting officer, using the passive voice, wrote the following in his report: "The weapon was found in the bushes where the suspect had thrown it." He did not clarify this statement elsewhere in his report. Expectedly, the prosecuting attorney subpoenaed the reporting officer to testify at the preliminary hearing. Unfortunately, the reporting officer's testimony revealed that his partner, not he, had observed the suspect's actions and had retrieved the weapon. The partner was unavailable to testify on short notice. Without his testimony the necessary elements of the crime could not be established. The case was dismissed and had to be refiled. The hours expended at the time of the dismissal—by witnesses, secretaries, clerks, attorneys, and the judge—were virtually wasted because the whole process had to be repeated. The reporting officer could have avoided the problem at the onset through use of the active voice, by writing, "Officer Jones found the weapon in the bushes." Sadly, this basic writing error is not an isolated example. Such errors slip through the system daily, causing delays in the judicial process and depleting dwindling budgets.

I've been told that, as action-oriented people, law enforcement officers tend to neglect what they consider to be the more mundane tasks, such as writing, but I don't think this is a major cause of poorly written reports. I think the cause is more basic. Like their counterparts in any industry, many law enforcement officers lack a firm foundation in basic English skills.

YOU can develop both a firm foundation in basic English skills and expertise in writing investigative narratives by diligently following the recommendations made throughout this text.

Floyd T. Stokes
Chief, Eureka Police Department

A Word about This Text

The purpose of this text is to improve your narrative writing skills—not to show you how to fill out forms. However, forms are important. Law enforcement report forms vary greatly in format. Keep in mind that the examples shown throughout the text are only a few of the variety of forms in use.

Report forms typically contain boxes or separate category sections, e.g., property loss section, for placement of descriptive information, addresses, and phone numbers of the persons involved. It is unnecessary to repeat this information in the narrative *unless it is needed for clarity* because it tends to interrupt the flow of words and clutter the narrative.

Conversely, narrative reports that are *not* contained within box-style law enforcement reports often include descriptive information, addresses, and phone numbers within the body of the narrative because no separate boxes exist for that data. Read the following excerpt from a narrative and note the underlined descriptive information:

> I talked to the victim, Harry Brown, 1925 West State St., Milwaukee, Wisconsin, phone: 555-4331. Brown told me that his diamond ring was taken during the burglary. The ring was a one-third carat diamond stone, 14-karat gold setting, with the initials R.S.G. inside the band, valued at $575.00.

Many of the sample narratives shown in this text would ordinarily be part of a completed law enforcement report form. Since they are not *shown* in that manner, descriptive information, addresses, and phone numbers of persons involved are included in the body of those narratives. If those same narratives were part of a completed box-style report form, the descriptive information, addresses, and phone numbers would be deleted *unless that information was needed for clarity*, as shown in the following excerpt:

> The victim, Harry Brown, told me that his diamond ring was taken during the burglary.

How to Use This Text

You learn to produce professional law enforcement reports by actually writing them. Throughout this text you will write reports, read background information, work through exercises, correct sentences, and refine final reports. And you will check your own work; answers follow each activity. To get the most out of this book, follow the directions carefully at each point. You will learn best by actually writing, wherever it is called for. Included within each chapter are practical exercises called "applications." Although the answers are provided for the applications within the text, it is important that you do *not* look at them until you have formulated your own answers. A series of 15 small, black boxes (■ ■ ■ ■ ■ ■ ■ ■ ■ ■ ■ ■ ■ ■ ■) indicates the end of an application and the beginning of the answers. Cover all material following these boxes until *after* you have written your answers.

At the end of each chapter you will be given the starting page of the self-test that will examine how well you have mastered the skills and principles of the chapter. After you have completed the self-test, correct it using the answers starting on p.238, and compare your score with the score that indicates mastery of the material. If your score is lower than the mastery level score, review the chapter, concentrating on the principles you were unable to apply in the self-test.

In addition, although we do not emphasize abbreviations, we have included a list of abbreviations commonly used in law enforcement notes (Appendix C). Finally, at the end of the Chapter-by-Chapter Review, we have included for your reference a checklist containing guidelines for evaluating every report you write (p.208).

If you follow the recommended procedures throughout this text, your writing should improve dramatically. You may even find that you enjoy writing!

CONTENTS

Chapter One

AN INTRODUCTION TO REPORTS AND REPORT WRITING

Do you know:

- What a report is?
- What types of reports exist?
- How reports are used?
- Who reads your reports?
- How to make your reports reader friendly?
- What common problems occur in many police reports?
- Why your reports should be well written?

Key terms: administrative report, operational report, report

Most people enter law enforcement for the activity and excitement it offers, for the challenge of solving crimes, and for the chance to help others. They often do not realize the amount of paperwork involved—they think of themselves as law enforcement officers, not "pencil-pushers." And then the rude awakening: For almost every official action law enforcement officers take, they must write a report. What's the point? Let's see. And remember to cover the answer below the line of boxes (▪ ▪ ▪ ▪ ▪) until you are finished devising your own answer.

REPORTS DEFINED

You probably have a general idea of what a report is, but your idea will depend on your past experience with spoken or written reports. As a point for beginning, how would you define the word *report*?

____

____

____

▪ ▪ ▪ ▪ ▪ ▪ ▪ ▪ ▪ ▪ ▪ ▪ ▪ ▪ ▪ ▪ ▪ ▪ ▪

There is no correct answer. Your response probably included something like "gives an account of," "tells about," "a statement," or "a record of." This text uses a more precise meaning of the word *report*.

A *report* is a permanent written record that communicates important facts to be used in the future.

Consider the outcome in the following example if the officer did not write a report:

> A police officer is called to the scene of a hit-and-run accident. After tending to the victim, she talks to all six onlookers. Ten months later, the case comes to court. Could the officer remember what each witness said? Could she remember the length of the skid marks? No. Police officers cannot rely on memory; they *must* write down what each witness says. They must also observe the scene carefully and record all important facts, such as skid marks and the victim's location.

➢ Application

Using the preceding definition of a report, check the statements below that accurately describe a law enforcement report.

_____ 1. It is a permanent record.

_____ 2. It may include a statement of an officer's opinion as to the suspect's guilt.

_____ 3. It may include a description of a suspect.

_____ 4. It may include what a witness said.

_____ 5. It may include what an officer observed at the scene of the crime.

_____ 6. It may be used by the prosecution in court.

_____ 7. It may include a statement of a police officer's activities.

_____ 8. It may be used by a supervisor to evaluate an officer's performance.

9. How would you now define the term *report*? ____

____

____

■■■■■■■■■■■■■■■■■

You should have checked all the statements except 2. A police report should *not* include an officer's opinion as to the suspect's guilt. It should be limited to facts.

9. A report is a written record that communicates important facts to be used in the future.

TYPES OF REPORTS

Law enforcement reports can be classified into two major groups: (1) administrative and (2) operational. Administrative reports deal with the routine functioning of the agency or department. Such reports may cover proper uniforms, reporting procedures, and grievances.

This text is primarily concerned with the second type of report—the operational report—which deals with the activities of law enforcement officers. The five primary types of operational reports are:

1. Incident/Miscellaneous Service Reports
2. Crime Reports
3. Arrest Reports
4. Crash Reports (or Traffic Accident Reports)
5. Supplemental Progress Reports/Follow-Up Reports

An *administrative report* deals with the routine functioning of the department or agency, whereas an *operational report* deals with the activities of law enforcement officers.

Each law enforcement agency has its own forms and procedures for completing operational reports, but most of these forms have some things in common. For example, the writers almost always have to clearly identify the type of report they are completing.

➢ Application

Identify the following reports as operational (O) or administrative (A) by placing the appropriate letter in the blank.

______ 1. assault

______ 2. arson

______ 3. homicide

______ 4. retirement benefits

______ 5. shoplifting

______ 6. injured person

______ 7. police training opportunities

______ 8. request for personal leave

______ 9. driving under the influence

■ ■ ■ ■ ■ ■ ■ ■ ■ ■ ■ ■ ■ ■ ■ ■

1.O, 2.O, 3.O, 4.A, 5.O, 6.O, 7.A, 8.A, 9.O

Operational reports include assault, arson, homicide, driving under the influence, injured person, and shoplifting. The other reports deal with *administrative* matters such as police training opportunities, retirement benefits, and requests for personal leave.

USES OF REPORTS

The definition of a report as a "permanent written record that communicates important facts to be used in the future" implies that reports *are used*, not simply filed away. If they weren't needed for the efficient operation of law enforcement activities, you wouldn't have to write them.

Reports are used to:

- **examine the past.**
- **keep other police officers informed.**
- **continue investigations.**
- **prepare court cases.**
- **provide the courts with relevant facts.**
- **coordinate law enforcement activities.**
- **plan for future law enforcement services.**
- **evaluate law enforcement officers' performance.**

Reports are permanent records of all important facts in a case—a stockpile of information to be drawn upon by all individuals on a law enforcement team. They are an aid to individual law enforcement officers, supervisors, administrators, the courts, other governmental agencies, reporters, and private individuals. Further, the efficiency of a department is directly related to the quality of its reports and reporting procedures.

Return to the example of the officer who was called to the scene of a hit-and-run accident. This report would be used to continue the investigation of the offense. If the offender was apprehended, the report would be used by the prosecuting attorneys in preparing the case, by the police officer when testifying in court, by the judge in determining the facts of the case, and by a jury if a trial resulted. In fact: "Faced with a well-documented police report, defendants are more apt to cop a plea than go to trial, in hopes of a more lenient sentence. Indeed, it's not unfair to say that plea bargaining is often a trial by police report" (Scoville, 2000, p.37).

The report might also be used by the department in determining where dangerous intersections exist and in making future plans. Additionally, an officer's supervisor could use the report to evaluate the performance of the investigating officer. If the officer did not conduct a thorough investigation, her lack of thoroughness would show in the report.

➢ Application

Which of the following are legitimate uses of a report of an initial homicide investigation?

______ 1. Preserve essential facts of the case.

______ 2. Provide a basis for continuing the investigation.

______ 3. Supply information to other officers who become involved in the case.

______ 4. Refresh a witness's memory as to what he or she said occurred.

______ 5. Coordinate activities of the department's investigation.

______ 6. Compile statistics on homicides in a given city.

______ 7. Evaluate how well a case was handled.

______ 8. Refresh the investigating officer's memory during the trial.

______ 9. Provide information to insurance investigators.

■ ■ ■ ■ ■ ■ ■ ■ ■ ■ ■ ■ ■ ■ ■ ■

You should have checked all of the uses of reports—each is legitimate.

AUDIENCE—WHO READS THE REPORT?

Based on the uses of reports, you can readily see that your reports will be read by many different people: other officers, your supervisor, lawyers, judges and citizens. You are the on-site observer and recorder of facts related to a specific case that will later be needed by many other people:

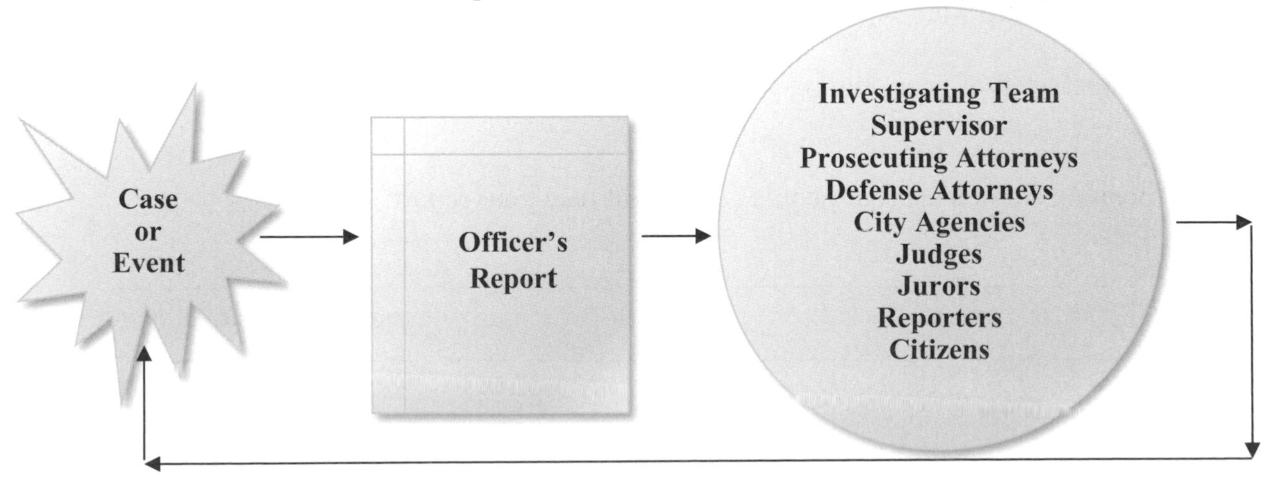

Most of your readers will have at least a high school education. Therefore, you do *not* need to simplify your report. But you *do* need to remember that you are writing to and for people who were not at the scene. Consequently, you must communicate clearly to your readers so they can relive it—tell them *what* happened, *when*, and *how*.

The report content is discussed in detail in the next chapter. For now, the important thing to remember is that your report will be read by many people for many difference reasons.

Reports are read and used by:

- **other officers.**
- **supervisors.**
- **attorneys and judges.**
- **jurors.**
- **city officials.**
- **reporters.**
- **citizens.**

➢ Application

When you think about your audience, you can assume your reader will (check all that apply):

______ 1. have at least a high school education.

______ 2. know the facts of the report.

______ 3. have a specific reason for reading the report.

______ 4. know the abbreviations used in law enforcement.

______ 5. know whether your report is accurate.

______ 6. be interested in your opinion about the guilt of the subject.

Name the positions of at least four people who might read your report:

7. ______________________ 9. ______________________

8. ______________________ 10. ______________________

■ ■ ■ ■ ■ ■ ■ ■ ■ ■ ■ ■ ■ ■ ■ ■

You should have checked 1 and 3. You *can* assume your reader will have at least a high school education and a specific reason for reading the report. You *cannot* assume that the reader will know the facts of the report, the abbreviations used in law enforcement, whether your report is accurate, or that the reader will be interested in your opinion about the guilt of the suspect.

For 7-10, check your answers against the list on p.6.

BEING READER FRIENDLY

Effective police reports are *readable*. They allow the reader to concentrate on what took place rather than on figuring out what the report writer is saying.

Reader-friendly writing avoids police jargon and abbreviations and communicates in plain, simple language. It is written as it would be spoken, and it considers its audience. Reader-friendly reports avoid referring the reader "above."

➢ Application

Read the paragraph below. Then answer the questions that follow it.

> Whereas, party of the first part, hereinafter "Mary," heretofore had an allegedly little party of the second part, accordingly "lamb," its fleece thereunto appertaining as white as snow; wherein, pursuant to everywhere thereof that said party of the first part would endeavor to exit, the aforementioned lamb, **arguendo**, was virtually sure forthwith to, at this point in time, go.
>
> — Mother Goose, J.D.
> (Lynn Ludlow, *Legalese*)

1. What is the paragraph a reader-*un*friendly version of? ______________________________

2. How did you feel as you read it? ____

   ____

3. With what profession do you associate this type of language? ______________________

4. Why do some people write like this? ____

   ____

▪▪▪▪▪▪▪▪▪▪▪▪▪▪▪▪▪

1. "Mary Had a Little Lamb"
2. Probably annoyed, perhaps confused, maybe amused. You would not want your readers to experience any of these feelings.
3. The legal profession—and some individuals in law enforcement.
4. They probably think it is impressive. But the purpose of writing is to *express*, not to impress.

Unfortunately, some reports do not consider the reader (the audience). For example, how would you, as reader, react to the following opening sentence from a report?

> D.U.I. at approx. 1816 on above stated date, above named def. observed driving nb in above stated manner by officers of BPD.

The sentence is very hard to follow, isn't it? What's wrong?

The sentence requires constant reference to information recorded at the beginning of the report. It does not tell the reader what happened. Reader-friendly reports avoid use of "the above." What happens when a reader comes across this phrase? Usually one of two things. The reader stops reading the report and goes "above" to look for the information, often losing their train of thought—and their place. Or the reader does not look "above," but then misses important information. If it's important enough to mention in the narrative, it should be repeated. If the writer of the report were thinking of the reader, the opening statement would read:

> Driving Under the Influence. At approximately 1816 hrs. on Feb. 12, 20--, I saw the driver, Charles Smith, weaving his vehicle from one side of the highway to the other.

This account is readable. It considers the reader.

Writing reader-friendly reports does not mean that your writing will end up sounding like: "Dick sees Jane." It does mean rewriting a sentence such as the following: "It should be noted that a male white juvenile subject, identified as subject Dick, in fact visually observes a female white juvenile subject, identified as subject Jane" (Rutledge, 2000, p.169). Rutledge says he'd prefer "Dick sees Jane" any day. So would most readers. And that's who reports are written for.

Finally, as Moore (2004, p.266) cautions, not only is police jargon difficult to read, such bureaucratic language may also give the impression the writer has something to hide: "Police who want to convey honesty and openness should first speak in a language that doesn't have to be run through a translator to be understood."

COMMON PROBLEMS WITH MANY POLICE REPORTS

Some officers think using police jargon, bureaucratic language, and big words makes their reports—and by extension, themselves—sound more credible. Unfortunately, this often has the opposite effect and can actually undermine the value of the officer's work.

Among the common problems in police reports are:

- **confusing or unclear sentences.**
- **conclusions and assumptions.**
- **extreme wordiness and overuse of police jargon and abbreviations.**
- **missing or incomplete information.**
- **misspelled words and grammatical/mechanical errors.**
- **referring to "above" information.**

➢ Application

Read the following report and identify the obvious problems.

> On the above date at or about approximatly 2200 hours this reporting officer responded to the above referenced location in reguards to a victum report that person or persons unknown had shot a bebe witch busted her window. She wants the alleged perpetrator of said shooting to be caught and must pay for fixing it. The window. This seems only fair.

Problems: ____

____

____

____

____

____

____

____

■ ■ ■ ■ ■ ■ ■ ■ ■ ■ ■ ■ ■ ■ ■ ■

Among the problems you should have seen are referring the reader "above" (on the above date), misspelled words (approximatly, reguards, victum, witch), jargon (this reporting officer, above referenced location, person or persons unknown, alleged perpetrator, said shooting) and unclear sentences. Also, the opinion, "This seems only fair," is inappropriate.

IMPORTANCE OF WELL-WRITTEN REPORTS

Given the many uses of reports and the number of individuals who rely on them, the importance of reports is obvious. What may not be so apparent is the need for *well-written* reports:

> Quite literally, life and death decisions hinge on facts as they are laid out in a police report. . . . Report writing is central to the successful prosecution of criminals, and that is important work. Sometimes cases are not filed because police reports are inadequate. A study conducted by the Coro Foundation at the request of the City of San Francisco . . found that police report writing was so poor that "effective criminal prosecution . . . is at risk," noting that the approximately 55,000 felony arrests each year resulted in just 2,000 prosecutions (Sievert, 2004, p.35).

Rutledge (pp.169-170) gives an extensive list of the benefits of reports written in straightforward, factual plain English, including less time spent writing reports, less typing time, less copying time and expense, less filing space and expense, less reading time by investigators and supervisors, less confusion as to what the report says, fewer rewrites, more complaints approved, more pleas, higher sentences on negotiated pleas, fewer trials, less court time for officers, and more convictions.

Well-written reports can save the department time and expense and result in better police work and more convictions.

Sievert (p.35) cites the trial lawyer's adage: "If you can't try the facts of the case, try the officer who reported the facts." Too often, poorly written reports cast doubt on the officer's credibility and, thus, play into the hands of criminal defendants and their lawyers: "Police reports which are hastily constructed and contain blatant errors contribute to the portrayal of officers as unskilled and inept. Juries and even District Attorneys equate sloppy police writing with sloppy thinking and careless investigative methods" (p.35).

Well-written reports reflect positively on your education, your competence, and your professionalism.

In addition, well-written reports can protect both the officer and the officer's department from lawsuits. As Molden (1996, p.13) emphasizes: "The more complex our society [becomes], the more litigious and demanding the criminal justice system, the greater will be the need for detailed, accurate and complete reporting by officers." According to Nowicki (1999, p.48), well-written reports can help keep excessive force litigation at bay: "Thorough, accurate reports can be a strong defense if your conduct with a subject is ever called into question."

Well-written reports can reduce legal liability for both the officer and the officer's department.

➢ Application

Read the following report and be prepared to give your reaction to it.

> At 0338 on 07-23-20-- a call was recieved from 6001 dover st who had information that a vahical had recked overhead door of undergd. gar. in apt. Upon our squad cars' arrivel it was told above named suspict was still in gar. Complanant (who is mgr of apt) said he was obviusly drunk. gar door was observed by myself to be off the track and bended up. And fiberglas broken in from being hit. Suspict said he had just come down to wash car and it hadn't been out of gar all day. Vehical was observed to have broken radio antena so it is the opinion of myself that he probably done it. Recked the door. Besides that top of right deck of right side passenger side shown damige like as if paint had been gouged by a metel thin what had exerted presher on it and gouged it. Suspict said he didnt no nothin about it. Mgr said he was lieing so he was red his rites and arrested by myself for damige to property.

1. Are the facts of the case clear to you? ______________________________
2. Are any opinions included in the report? ______________________________
3. What do you think of the officer who wrote it? ______________________________
4. What would the officer's supervisor probably think? ______________________________
5. How useful would this report be in court should the case go to trial? ______________________________

   ____

■ ■ ■ ■ ■ ■ ■ ■ ■ ■ ■ ■ ■ ■ ■ ■ ■ ■

Although answers will vary to these questions, the general reaction will no doubt be the same—negative. This poorly written report omits several important facts; includes opinions and conclusions of the reporting officer; presents a confused picture of what occurred; contains numerous errors in spelling, punctuation, and sentence structure; and leaves a poor impression of the officer who wrote it. It would be useless in a trial.

The writer of the preceding report may, in fact, be an excellent observer and investigator; unfortunately, this report does not show it. A reader of this report might conclude that the officer is either uneducated, ignorant, or careless. The reaction to the way in which the report is written might well carry over to a general negative feeling about the writer of the report. Such mistakes in writing might also indicate mistakes in observation. Whether these mistakes are the result of ignorance or carelessness, the effect is the same—the reader concludes that the writer of the report is not competent.

In contrast, a well-written report will reflect positively on the writer. It will give the reader confidence in the reporter's education, competence, and professionalism. Further, the well-written report will be useful to all who read it. In the next chapter, you will see how this same information would look in a well-written report.

The rest of this text will teach you how to write effective reports—how to avoid the errors found in the sample report.

Can you now list at least three reasons why your reports should be well written?

1. ______________________________

2. ______________________________

3. ______________________________

■ ■ ■ ■ ■ ■ ■ ■ ■ ■ ■ ■ ■ ■ ■ ■

Check your answers by reviewing the information on pp.10-11.

SUMMARY

A report is a permanent written record which communicates important facts to be used in the future. An administrative report deals with the routine functioning of the department or agency, whereas an operational report deals with the activities of law enforcement officers.

Reports are used to examine the past, keep other police officers informed, continue investigations, prepare court cases, provide the courts with relevant facts, coordinate law enforcement activities, plan for future law enforcement services, and evaluate law enforcement officers' performance.

Reports are read and used by other officers, supervisors, attorneys and judges, jurors, city officials, reporters, and citizens. Reader-friendly writing avoids police jargon and abbreviations and communicates in plain, simple language. It is written as it would be spoken, and it considers its audience. Reader-friendly reports avoid referring the reader "above."

Among the common problems in police reports are confusing or unclear sentences, conclusions and assumptions, extreme wordiness and overuse of police jargon and abbreviations, missing or incomplete information, misspelled words, grammatical/mechanical errors, and referring to "above" information.

Well-written reports can save the department time and expense and result in better police work and more convictions. Well-written reports reflect positively on your education, your competence, and your professionalism. Well-written reports can reduce legal liability for both the officer and the officer's department.

You may wish to review this chapter before taking the self-test on p.210.

REFERENCES

Molden, J. (1996, February). Basic report writing: Helping trainees learn to write crime reports. *Law and Order*, 13-14.

Moore, C. (2004, December). Plain English. *Law Enforcement Technology*, 266.

Nowicki, E. (1999, November). Report writing: Keep excessive force litigation at bay. *Police*, 48-51.

Rutledge, D. (2000). *The new police report manual* (2nd ed.). Incline Village, NV: Copperhouse Publishing Company.

Scoville, D. (2000, March). The dreaded report: We must do it, so why not get it write? *Police*, 36-38.

Sievert, G. (2004, Fourth Quarter). The essence of quality: Writing successful reports. *The Law Enforcement Trainer*, 35-39.

Chapter Two

CHARACTERISTICS OF A WELL-WRITTEN REPORT: CONTENT

Do you know:

- Which is more important: content or form?
- What are four characteristics of effective content?
- How to differentiate among facts, inferences and opinions?
- How to avoid conclusionary language?
- What questions an effective report answers?
- What crucial information must be included in a criminal offense report and why?

Key terms: conclusionary language, connotative, content, denotative, elements of the crime, fact, form, inference, objective, opinion, slanting

A WELL-WRITTEN REPORT: CONTENT VS. FORM

The effective report writer attends to two general areas: **content**, or what is said, and **form**, or how it is written.

Content and form are equally important.

A report that includes all the essential information and is well organized but is full of spelling errors and grammatical goofs is as bad as one which is error free but which omits essential facts or contains misinformation or conclusionary language. Effective writers pay attention to both content and form. This chapter focuses on the content of police reports. Chapter Three deals with the form or how the report is written.

The content of a well-written report is:

- **factual.**
- **accurate.**
- **objective.**
- **complete.**

FACTUAL

The basic purpose of any police operational report is to record the facts. A *fact* is a statement that can be proven. (It may be proven false, but it is still classified as a factual statement.) You will look at the truthfulness or accuracy of facts in a few pages, but first you need to clearly distinguish between three basic types of statements.

Fact: A statement which can be proven.
For example: The man has a bulge in his black leather jacket pocket.

Inference: A conclusion based on reasoning.
For example: The man is probably carrying a gun.

Opinion: A personal belief.
For example: Black leather jackets are cool.

You can discuss and debate facts and inferences logically and reasonably and come to some agreement on them. Opinions, however, reflect personal beliefs on which there is seldom agreement. For example, how do you resolve the differences between two people who are arguing over whether pie tastes better than cake? You can't. It's simply a matter of personal preference.

A well-written report is factual. It does *not* contain opinions.

Inferences (conclusions) can prove valuable in a report, provided they are based on sufficient facts. For example, if you wanted to verify the statement, "The driver of the car was drunk," you would need to supply several facts to support your inference, one such fact being that the driver had a blood alcohol content of over .08. Other facts might include your observations, such as the driver's slurred speech; red, watery eyes; and the strong odor of an alcoholic beverage.

An inference is not really true or false; it is sound or unsound (believable or not believable). The only way to make an inference sound (believable) is to provide facts to support it. One way to ensure that your inference is clearly an inference, instead of a fact, would be to use the word *apparently* (e.g., "The driver is apparently drunk.").

➢ Application

Read the following statements and label each as fact (F), inference (I), or opinion (O).

______ 1. The car was going 20 miles per hour and was weaving back and forth across the center line of the road.

______ 2. The car went off on the shoulder twice.

______ 3. The car hit a tree and stopped.

______ 4. The driver of the car was drunk.

______ 5. The driver of the car was dead.

______ 6. The crash killed the driver.

______ 7. The man had a heart attack before the accident.

______ 8. Drunken drivers deserve to be killed in accidents.

■ ■ ■ ■ ■ ■ ■ ■ ■ ■ ■ ■ ■ ■ ■ ■

1, 2, 3, and 5 are facts–the speed of the car, the descriptions of its movement, and the death of the driver are observable, provable statements.

4, 6, and 7 are inferences. Maybe the driver was drunk, or maybe he was having a heart attack. Either condition could explain the movement of the car. The man may have died from a heart attack rather than from the crash—more facts would be needed to make the inference sound.

8 is an opinion. How could you prove that drunken drivers deserve to be killed in accidents?

Clearly the police officer who reports seeing a car traveling 20 miles per hour, weaving back and forth across the center line, going off the shoulder twice, and running into a tree is on safer grounds than the officer who reports observing a drunken driver. If the man were treated as a drunk when in reality he was suffering a heart attack, the officer could be in serious trouble.

Stick to the facts. Make inferences only when sufficient facts are presented, and then clearly label the inferences.

➢ Application

Read the following excerpt and underline any inferences you find.

> On January 4, 20--, at 0356 I was checking downtown business doors on foot and found the rear door on the east side of the Alibi Bar damaged and the window in the door smashed out, probably by a hammer. The glass and plexiglass louvers over the storm windows were pulled out and lying on the sidewalk. Officer Andrews assisted me in getting into and searching the building. Neither he nor I could climb through the broken window without first removing the glass that was left, and then we could barely get in, so a small man or woman must have been involved. Once inside we found everything in order except for the cash drawer, which was open.

■ ■ ■ ■ ■ ■ ■ ■ ■ ■ ■ ■ ■ ■ ■

You should have underlined: probably a hammer, so a small man or woman must have been involved, and everything in order. All are inferences. There is no proof the window was broken by a hammer. A child might have been involved, or someone might have used a key and then broken the glass as a phony clue. The officer could not know that "everything was in order" without checking with the owner or manager.

Inferences are also referred to as **conclusionary language**.

Avoid conclusionary language in police reports.

Rutledge (2000, pp.110-111) describes how conclusionary language can pose difficulties for officers and prosecutors (Reprinted by permission of Copperhouse Publishing Company):

> I once got into a drunk driving trial where, according to the arresting officers, the defendant had "repeatedly refused" to take a chemical test. The defendant was named Sanchez, and at the trial he insisted, through a court interpreter, that he neither spoke nor understood any English. His defense that he couldn't possibly refuse an English-language request when he couldn't even understand it sold well with the jury, especially after the officer had to admit that he didn't recall exactly how or in what specific words the defendant had "refused" a test. The cop couldn't live with his conclusionary report. Neither could I. The defendant lived with it very comfortably, and he owed his acquittal directly to the same officer who had arrested him. Ironic?
>
> We would have been much better off if the cop had never used the conclusionary word "refused," but had instead married the defendant to his own words! The report could have helped the prosecution, instead of the defense, if it had been written like this:
>
>> After I explained the need to take a chemical test, SANCHEZ said, in Spanish-accented English, "Screw you, cop . . . I ain't taking no test, man. Why don't you take it yourself?" I told him he had to take a test or his license would be suspended. He said, "I don't need no license to drive man, . . . I know lots of people drive without a license. You ain't scared me man, and I ain't taking no stupid test . . . I'll beat this thing, too."
>
> See the difference? Not a single conclusion or interpretation. The reader gets to "hear" the same things the writer heard. The officer could have lived with something like that—the defendant couldn't. The same thing goes for these conclusionary interpretations:
>
> - He denied any involvement in the crime.
> - She consented to a search of the trunk.
> - Both waived their rights per Miranda.
> - He admitted breaking into the car.
> - He confessed to four more burglaries.

Be especially careful with statements about a person's state of mind or abilities. To say someone is "nervous" is an inference or conclusion. *Describe* the person's actions on which you based that inference. To say someone "could not walk a straight line" is also an inference. Perhaps they could, but simply did not feel like it. The *fact* is that the person "*did not* walk a straight line." Better yet, describe how the person did walk.

Another phrase to watch for is "The check was signed by John Doe." Unless you *saw* John Doe sign the check, that is an inference or conclusion. The fact is "The check was signed John Doe." One little word can change the entire meaning—and accuracy—of your report.

Problems also arise in the use of psychological terms such as *paranoid* or *psychotic* rather than describing the actual behavior and allowing the reader or qualified person to make the conclusion. Table 2-1 illustrates conclusionary language and what should replace it in effective police reports.

TABLE 2-1 Conclusionary Language and Substitutes

You can't live with these	. . . so use these, instead	You can't live with these	. . . so use these, instead
indicated refused admitted confessed denied consented identified waived profanity threatening obscene evasive unresponsive deceptive	a verbatim or approximate quotation of what was said	angry upset nervous excited happy unhappy intentional accidental attempted heard saw knew thought	when you're attributing these to someone else, identify the source of your conclusions
assaulted attacked accosted confrontation escalated struggle ensued resisted battered intimidated bullied forced	a factual account of who did what	matching the description suspicious furtive strange abnormal typical uncooperative belligerent combative obnoxious abusive exigent	the reasons for your belief that these apply

Source: Adapted from *The New Police Report Manual*, Devallis Rutledge, 2000, pp.135-136. Reprinted with permission of Copperhouse Publishing Company, Incline Village, Nevada.

➢ Application

Check the statements that are conclusionary and, therefore, should *not* be used in a police report.

_____ 1. The suspect threatened me.

_____ 2. The suspect spit on me.

_____ 3. The victim was overwrought.

_____ 4. The victim was hysterical.

_____ 5. The victim was crying and screaming, "Help me! Help me!"

_____ 6. As I approached the suspect, he saw me and took off running.

_____ 7. The witness said that she saw clearly what had happened.

■ ■ ■ ■ ■ ■ ■ ■ ■ ■ ■ ■ ■ ■ ■ ■ ■

1, 3, 4, and 6 are conclusionary. What is threatening? What is overwrought or hysterical? How do you *know* the suspect "saw" you? It would be more factual to write "He turned his head in my direction and then took off running."

ACCURATE

To be useful, facts must be accurate. An inaccurately recorded license number may result in losing a witness or suspect. Inaccurate measurement or recording of the distance of skid marks may lead to wrong conclusions.

An effective report accurately records the correct time and date; correct names of all persons involved; correct phone numbers and addresses; and exact descriptions of the crime scene, property, vehicles, and suspects involved. Have people spell their names. Repeat spellings and numbers for verification. Recheck measurements. Be sure of the accuracy of your facts.

A well-written report is accurate; it is specific.

You must have the case facts correct. If your report says four men were involved in a robbery and, in reality, three men and a woman were involved, your report would be inaccurate. If you are unsure of the sex of the individuals involved in an incident, you should identify them as "suspects" or "persons." If your facts come from a witness' statement rather than from your own observation, say so in your report.

To be accurate, you must be specific. For example, it is better to say, "The car was traveling in excess of 90 m.p.h." than to say, "The car was traveling fast." It is more accurate to describe a suspect as "approximately 6′ 6″ " than to describe him as "tall." Vague, imprecise words have no place in police reports. The following words and phrases should *not* be used because they are not specific:

a few
many
several
frequently
often
contact (how? call on the phone, write a letter, see in person, use ESP?)

➢ Application

Check the more accurate statement in each pair.

1. ______ a. The man had several beers.

   ______ b. The man had six Miller Genuine Drafts.

2. ______ a. The suspect was between 150 and 160 pounds.

   ______ b. The suspect was of medium build.

3. ______ a. The old car was driven by a young woman.

   ______ b. The 1972 green Ford was driven by a woman in her twenties.

4. Which of the following might result from inaccuracies in a police report?

   ______ a. The investigating team might be misled.

   ______ b. The reporting officer's competence might be questioned by his or her supervisor.

   ______ c. The reporting officer's competence might be questioned by the defense attorney.

   ______ d. Other facts of the report might also be questioned.

   ______ e. The prosecutor might be embarrassed by issuing a complaint based on inaccurate facts.

■ ■ ■ ■ ■ ■ ■ ■ ■ ■ ■ ■ ■ ■ ■ ■

1.b, 2.a, 3.b — these are the more accurate statements because they are more specific. *All* of the consequences (a-e) listed in 4 might result from inaccuracies in a police report.

Details of a report should be both factual and accurate.

➢ Application

Read the following excerpt from a police report and be prepared to evaluate it. Use the following criteria—Is the report: ☐ factual?
☐ accurate?

On 1-14-20-- at about 2000 hrs., an unidentified suspect and a friend began shopping at the Boutique Shop at 470 College Drive in Lansing. The suspect picked out two purchases, brought them to the sales clerk, Daniel Adams, and asked to charge them. Adams accepted a charge card from the suspect and entered it into their computer. The purchase was approved. He returned the card to the suspect and gave her the merchandise. The suspect then left the sales counter area and, within minutes, picked out a leather coat she wanted to purchase. She appeared unconcerned about the price. Adams asked her if it would be a charge again, and she replied, "Yes." Because of the large amount of the purchase, Adams asked for additional identification. The suspect said she would go out to the car and get more identification. She never returned.

The charge card, number 16-167-22, was in the name of Denise Parker. I retained it for evidence.

On the next day, 1-16-20--, I met with Ms. Parker at her house. She said that the charge card was missing from the cardcase that she kept in her billfold in her purse. She also said that none of her other cards were missing, so apparently somebody had removed the card and replaced the cardcase in her purse. She recalled that the only time she did not have her purse in her possession was a week before when she had her hair done at the Ultimate Beauty College, 6078 Drew Avenue. She had left her purse on the floor by the purses of the two students who were working on her hair. At one point, she was taken into a different area of the building where her hair was washed, and during the rest of the hour her chair was turned so her back was to the three purses. During this time, she recalled, the two students had been going into their own purses. They seemed nervous and appeared to be in a big hurry to leave the school. The description of the two students matched the descriptions of the two suspects at the Boutique.

➢ Evaluation

Evaluate the report by answering the following questions. For any negative response, give at least one example to support your evaluation.

1. Is the report factual? ______________________________

2. Is the report accurate? ______________________________

■ ■ ■ ■ ■ ■ ■ ■ ■ ■ ■ ■ ■ ■ ■

1. The report is generally factual. The inferences which are included are made by the victim of the crime, not by the reporting officer.
2. The report is *not* completely accurate. It states that the incident occurred on 1-14-20-- and that the officer contacted the owner of the credit card on the next day, 1-16-20--. One of the two dates is inaccurate.

OBJECTIVE

You have seen that reports must be factual. It is possible, however, to include only factual statements in a report and still not be objective. **Objective** means nonopinionated, fair, and impartial. Lack of objectivity can result from poor word choice and omission of facts.

A well-written report is objective, meaning it is nonopinionated, fair, and impartial.

Objectivity is attained by keeping to the facts, using words with nonemotional overtones, and including both sides of the account. You have already looked at the importance of sticking to the facts and leaving out personal opinions. The next means of achieving objectivity is through the words used. Consider the following:

> The man cried.
> The man wept.
> The man blubbered.

The first sentence is objective; the second makes a reader feel positive toward the man; the third makes a reader feel negative towards him.

Although you want to be specific, you must also be aware of the effect of the words you use. Words that have little emotional effect, e.g., *cried*, are called **denotative** words. The denotative meaning of a word is its *objective* meaning. In contrast, words that have an emotional effect are called **connotative** words, e.g., *wept*, *blubbered*. The connotative meaning of a word is its positive or negative overtones.

In the following group of sentences, which statement is clearly negative?

> Bill is a cop.
> Bill is a pig.
> Bill is a police officer.

"Pig" has negative connotations; it reflects the opinion of the person using it.

➢ Application

In the following series of words, circle the words that should *not* be used in reports because of their connotative meanings.

1. steal, rip off, take
2. shag, chase, pursue
3. angry, mad, ticked off
4. lady, woman, broad
5. ex-con, suspect, defendant
6. snitch, informant, reliable source

■ ■ ■ ■ ■ ■ ■ ■ ■ ■ ■ ■ ■ ■ ■ ■

1. rip off, 2. shag, 3. ticked off, 4. broad, 5. ex-con, 6. snitch. All of these terms have negative connotations for most readers.

Slanting is including only one side of a story or only facts that tend to prove or support the officer's theory, which can also make a report nonobjective. A good report includes both sides of an incident when possible. Even when facts tend to go against your theory about what happened, you are obligated to include them. Omitting important facts is *not* objective.

Compare the following three descriptions of a .45-caliber handgun:

1. The government model .45-caliber automatic handgun is versatile, with a wide range of ammunition available for any use. When properly cared for, it is completely dependable and proclaimed by many to be the finest weapon ever designed.

2. The government model .45-caliber automatic handgun has loose action and kicks so hard when fired you think your arm will break. It is so heavy that by the end of the day it feels as if it weighs a ton.

3. The government model .45-caliber automatic handgun is a gas-operated semiautomatic weapon that fires .45-caliber ammunition and weighs from 140 grams to 220 grams. Its capabilities range from soft nose to armor piercing. The weapon incorporates a clip magazine with a seven-shot capacity.

➢ Application

1. Which description is objective? ____________________

2. Which description is slanted in favor of the gun? ____________________

3. Which description is slanted against the gun? ____________________

4. Which description is appropriate for the type of report expected in police work? __________

   Why? ____________________

■ ■ ■ ■ ■ ■ ■ ■ ■ ■ ■ ■ ■ ■ ■ ■

1. Description 3 is objective—all facts about the gun are included.
2. Description l is slanted in favor of the gun—only positive facts are given.
3. Description 2 is slanted against the gun—only negative facts are given.
4. The objective description (3) is the only description appropriate for the type of reports written in police work because it includes the relevant facts. It does not include only one side—it is not slanted.

You can assure objectivity in your reports by avoiding words with emotional overtones and including all relevant facts.

➢ Application

Read the following excerpt from a police report and be prepared to evaluate it. Use the following criteria—Is the report:

- ☐ factual?
- ☐ accurate?
- ☐ objective?

Counterfeit-Altered U.S. Money

Evidence: One $1.00 bill Ser. #10602445A with $5.00 ends taped on.

On 2-14-20-- at approximately 1500 hrs. the complainant, Roy Roberts (1111 Third Ave.; DOB: 9-19-59; 555-9876) purchased gas and one quart of oil from the Economy Gas Station at 1616 East 59th St., Delmont, Michigan. The bill came to $5.00, and the complainant gave the pump jockey (Dan Foster, 227 Pine Ave.; DOB: 4-22-55; 555-2145) a $20.00 bill and received three $5.00 bills in change. The complainant stated that as he left the station he noticed that one of the $5.00 bills had another bill stuck to it, and upon further checking he found that the ends of a $5.00 bill had been taped onto a $1.00 bill. The complainant and his passenger (Bo Staman, 3144 Upton Ave.; DOB: 5-27-58; 569-9390) returned to the gas station and demanded to be given another $5.00 bill. The pump jockey refused and called the police, who routed the call to me.

When I arrived, the complainant told his story. The pump jockey stated that he had not given him that bill and had never seen it before. With the complainant's permission, I searched him, his passenger and his vehicle for another $5.00 bill which would have been in their possession to enable them to switch the bills around. I did not find any other than the two others given as change. I checked the bills in the gas station register and those on the pump jockey's person, but did not find any other bills. The only other employee present at the gas station at the time of the incident was a grease monkey. I also checked him and did not find any $5.00 bills nor altered money. Both the pump jockey and the grease monkey denied any knowledge of the funny money.

I confiscated the altered money. The pump jockey refused to pay the complainant the $5.00, so I told the complainant that his only recourse was to file in conciliation court[1].

It is my opinion that the pump jockey could have received the altered bill without noticing the altering and then given it back in change. But the bill was altered in such a sloppy and poor manner that it would have taken a very stupid person not to catch it.

➢ Evaluation

Evaluate the report by answering the following questions. For any negative response, give at least one example to support your evaluation.

1. Is the report factual? ____

2. Is the report accurate? ____

[1] Some states refer to conciliation court as small claims court.

3. Is the report objective? ____

■ ■ ■ ■ ■ ■ ■ ■ ■ ■ ■ ■ ■ ■ ■ ■

1. The report is basically factual. However, an inference (cited as an opinion) is made at the end.
2. The report is accurate.
3. The report is *not* objective. The writer uses several subjective words, e.g., *pump jockey* rather than *attendant*, *demanded* rather than *asked*, *grease monkey* rather than *mechanic*, *sloppy and poor manner* rather than describing how the alteration had been made, and *funny money* rather than *altered money*.

COMPLETE

Information kept in the reporting officer's head is of no value to anyone else involved in the case. An effective report contains answers to at least six basic questions:

Who?	When?
What?	How?
Where?	Why?

All applicable blanks at the top of the report form should be filled in. Some agencies require a slash mark, the abbreviation N.A. (not applicable), or the abbreviation UNK (unknown) to be placed in any box which does not contain information.

All *relevant* details should be included in the narrative portion of the report. Clearly, you cannot record everything; you must be selective. For example, in a report of a robbery, you *would* need a complete description of the stolen property and a physical description of the robber. You would *not* need physical descriptions of the victim or the witnesses, but you would want to record their names, addresses, and phone numbers, should you need to contact them again.

A well-written report is complete.
It answers the questions Who? What? Where? When? How? Why?

Each type of crime requires different information, but you will frequently need certain general information. For many reports you will need to record answers to questions such as:

WHO: are suspects? accomplices? A complete description would include:

sex
race/coloring
age
height
weight
hair: color, style, condition
eyes: color, size, glasses
nose: size, shape
ears: close to head or protruding

distinctive features: birthmarks, scars, beards, etc.
clothing
voice: high or low, accent
other distinctive characteristics, such as walk

were the victims?
was talked to?
were witnesses? saw or heard something of importance?
discovered the crime?
reported the incident? made the complaint?
investigated the incident? worked on the case?
marked and received the evidence?
was notified?
had a motive?

WHAT: type of crime was committed?
was the amount of damage or value of property involved?
happened? (Narrative of the actions of suspects, victims, and witnesses; combines information included under "How.")
weapons, vehicles, and/or tools were used? (Also under "How.")
evidence was found?
preventive measures (safes, locks, alarms, etc.) had been taken?
knowledge, skill, or strength was needed to commit the crime?
was said?
did the police officers do?
further information is needed?
further action is needed?

WHERE: did the incident happen?
was evidence found? stored?
do victims, witnesses, and suspects live?
do suspects frequent most often?
were suspects arrested?

WHEN: did the incident happen?
was it discovered?
was it reported?
did the police arrive on the scene?
were suspects arrested?
will the case be heard in court?

HOW: was the crime discovered?
does this relate to other crimes?
did the incident/crime occur?
was evidence found?
was information obtained?

WHY: was the crime committed? Was there intent? consent? motive?
was certain property stolen?
was a particular time selected?

The *who*, *what*, *when*, and *where* questions should be answered by factual statements. The *how* and *why* statements may require inferences on your part. When this is the case, clearly label the statements as inferences ("*it might be inferred that . . .*"). This is especially true when answering the question of motive. To avoid slanting the report, record all possible motives reported to you, no matter how implausible they may seem at the time.

➢ Application

Check the category of facts most relevant to the specific offense listed.

_____ 1. Regarding driving under the influence, it is most relevant to include a description of

a. the car b. the driver c. the driver's actions

_____ 2. Regarding shoplifting, the most relevant information is a description of

a. the store b. the stolen property c. the victim

_____ 3. Regarding assault by an unknown assailant, the most relevant information is a description of

a. the victim b. the assailant c. witnesses to the attack

Imagine you are interviewing the victim of an armed robbery. List at least three questions you should ask about each of the following:

4. WHAT?

a. ____

b. ____

c. ____

5. WHEN?

 a. ______________________________

 b. ______________________________

 c. ______________________________

6. WHERE?

 a. ______________________________

 b. ______________________________

 c. ______________________________

7. WHO?

 a. ______________________________

 b. ______________________________

 c. ______________________________

8. HOW?

 a. ______________________________

 b. ______________________________

 c. ______________________________

■ ■ ■ ■ ■ ■ ■ ■ ■ ■ ■ ■ ■ ■ ■ ■ ■

1.c, 2.b, 3.b. For 4-8, check your answers by referring to pp.25-27. Your answers may differ in wording, but the general idea of the question should be included.

A report should give as full an account as possible.

A Reminder: Recall from Chapter One that to be complete, a report should contain all essential information in the narrative. It should not refer the reader "above" for needed information if it is to be complete—and reader friendly.

➢ Application

Read the following excerpt from a police report and be prepared to evaluate it. Use the following criteria—Is the report:
- ☐ factual?
- ☐ accurate?
- ☐ objective?
- ☐ complete?

Auto Theft Arrest

On the above date, at approximately 1610 hrs., I was dispatched to a motor vehicle accident at #15 Circle West in Trenton. When I arrived I found the above-listed vehicle with extensive damage to the right side. The vehicle was running, and the driver's door was standing open. A paper boy at the scene said that he had heard the car coming, saw it leave the road and then come at him, hitting the stones and lawn in front of #15 Circle West. He saw two teenage boys leave the car and run east. He described the boys as wearing red jackets, jeans, and tennis shoes. One was taller than the other.

I immediately drove around Circle West to Circle East after giving the dispatcher the license number of the vehicle and asking that the owner be contacted to determine if the vehicle was stolen. I noticed two boys answering the description of the suspects walking across Division Avenue, going north. As I drove toward the boys, they ran behind the houses on Circle East. I gave chase, caught up with one boy, tackled him, handcuffed him, placed him under arrest for auto theft, and advised him of his rights. He denied any knowledge of the incident. I then returned to the scene of the accident, but the paper boy had left.

➢ Evaluation

Evaluate the report by answering the following questions. For any negative response, give at least one example to support your evaluation.

1. Is the report factual? ____________________
2. Is the report accurate? ____________________
3. Is the report objective? ____________________
4. Is the report complete? ____________________

■ ■ ■ ■ ■ ■ ■ ■ ■ ■ ■ ■ ■ ■ ■ ■

1. Yes. There are no inferences or opinions.
2. Yes. As far as the reader can determine, the report is accurate.
3. Yes. The report is objective; there is no slanting nor use of connotative words.
4. No. Not only does it begin with "the above," but the report is like an unfinished novel. The reader does not know what happened to the other suspect nor if the only witness (the paper boy) was ever found and identified. It is uncertain if the car was even stolen—the boys may have had permission to use it and panicked when they had the accident. A premature arrest based on an incomplete investigation could result in a false arrest lawsuit.

ELEMENTS OF THE CRIME

An act is not considered a crime unless it violates specific conditions set forth by law. These conditions, known as the **elements of the crime**, must exist and be proven to exist for an act to be called a specific kind of crime. Thus, to be complete, a criminal report *must* include this crucial content. A criminal report that does not address each element of the crime will negatively impact the chances of a case successfully progressing through the criminal court process.

The elements of the crime are conditions that must exist and be proven to exist for an act to be called a specific kind of crime. Successful prosecution of a criminal case requires each element to exist and be documented by the reporting officer.

The offenses covered in this section include murder, rape, robbery, burglary, larceny or theft, arson, and assault.

It is not the intent of this section to cover the elements of each specific criminal offense for every state; each state's laws vary considerably. However, a common thread exists, and that thread is common law—the basis of our system of laws and for the wording of many states' statutes. Thus, the elements for the offenses listed in this section will be outlined in general terms or in terms consistent with common law. You may wish to add those variables which apply to your jurisdiction at the end of each "Elements" subsection. Space is provided for this.

Each offense subsection contains two parts:

1. Elements of the offense.
2. Phrases or sentences to write in your narrative to enhance the report's effectiveness.

NOTE: Be especially careful not to interpret the elements listed in the following pages as the exact wording of the laws which apply to your own jurisdiction. Refer to your own state's penal code for that wording. Space is provided for your notes at the end of each "Elements" subsection.

Murder

Murder is defined as the killing of one person by another with malice aforethought (i.e., deliberate, willful, and with preformed intent).

❖ Elements

Generally speaking, the following elements need to be proved:

A. *First Degree Murder*
1. Deliberate, willful, and with preformed intent
2. Lying in wait, or
3. In the commission of an inherently dangerous felony, such as arson, rape, robbery, sodomy, burglary, or mayhem

Notes: ______________________________

____

____

B. *Second Degree Murder*
1. All other murders

Notes: ______________________________

____

____

C. *Voluntary Manslaughter*
1. Intentional homicide (killing)
2. Created in the "heat of passion"

Notes: ______________________________

____

____

D. *Involuntary Manslaughter*
1. Unintentional homicide (killing)
2. During an unlawful act less than a felony, or
3. During a lawful act committed in an unlawful manner

Notes: ______________________________

____

____

❖ **Phrases or Sentences to Write in Your Report:**

- At (time) on (date) I was dispatched to....
- Upon arrival at (time) I saw....
- A (white/black/Hispanic/etc.) male lying....
- I checked....
- I saw his pupils were fixed and dilated....
- I radioed Dispatch for....(medical assistance/supervisor, etc.)....
- I examined the wound/injury....
- I closed off/secured the area....
- I searched for (weapon)....
- I talked to....(RP/witness/neighbor, etc.)
- It appeared....
- I located and collected (items of evidence)....
- I ensured....
- I carefully....
- I thoroughly (what you did) by....
- I saw....
- I photographed....
- I (or ID Tech Jones, etc.) videotaped/recorded....
- I prepared a log of....
- Describe the scene/position of the body/location of evidence.
- Witness John Smith told me the following: (Start new paragraph describing what he told you.)

Rape

Rape is defined as the unlawful carnal knowledge (sexual intercourse) of a person by force and against their will.

❖ **Elements**

Generally speaking, the following elements need to be proved:

1. Unlawful — by a person other than a spouse (Note: Spousal rape in many states is covered by a separate statute.)
2. Penetration, however slight
3. By force
4. Against the will (without consent)
5. A person cannot consent when they are:
    a. Below the age of consent
    b. Unconscious
    c. Asleep
    d. Intoxicated
    e. Insane or mentally disabled

Notes: ____

____

____

❖ **Phrases or Sentences to Write in Your Report:**

- At (time) on (date) I was dispatched to....
- Upon arrival at (time) I talked to the victim, (victim's name), in the presence of (support person). (Victim) told me the following:
- I transported (victim's name) to:
- Dr. (name) examined (victim).....
- I located and collected (items of evidence).....
- I thoroughly searched....
- I ensured....
- I saw....
- I (or ID Tech Jones, etc.) photographed/videotaped (scene/victim/vehicle/suspect, etc.)....
- I carefully....
- I interviewed (suspect's name), first reading him his Miranda Rights. He waived his rights by.... (explain what he said to waive his rights if the waiver was not recorded). He told me the following:

Robbery

Robbery is defined as the felonious taking of the personal property from the person of another against his will by the means of force or fear.

❖ **Elements**

Generally speaking, the following elements need to be proved:

1. Felonious (with unlawful intent)
2. Taking
3. Personal Property
4. From the person (or immediate presence)
5. Against his will (without permission)
6. By force or fear

Notes: ____

____

____

❖ **Phrases or Sentences to Write in Your Report:**

- At (time) on (date) I was dispatched to....
- Upon arrival at (time), I talked to the victim, (victim's name), who told me the following:
- I radioed suspect and vehicle descriptions to Dispatch for a Be-On-the-Lookout (BOLO) alert to other units.
- I (or ID Tech Jones, etc.) searched, photographed, videotaped, etc.....
- I talked to Witness (Witness' name), who told me the following:
- I (or ID Tech Jones, etc.) located and collected (items of evidence)....
- I interviewed (suspect's name), first reading him his Miranda Rights. He waived his rights by.... (explain what he said to waive his rights if the waiver was not recorded). He told me the following:

Burglary

Burglary is defined as the breaking and entry of the dwelling house of another in the nighttime with the intent to commit a crime therein. (Note: "in the nighttime" may not apply in your state.)

❖ **Elements**

Generally speaking, the following elements need to be proved:

1. Breaking (use of even the slightest force to enter)
2. Entry (the slightest intrusion of any part of the body or device as an extension)
3. Dwelling house (habitable building, whether occupied or not, and any extension thereof)
4. Of another
5. In the nighttime (may not apply in your state)
6. With *intent* to commit a crime (such as larceny, rape, arson, etc.) therein

Notes: ____

____

____

❖ **Phrases or Sentences to Write in Your Report:**

- On (date) at about (time), I was dispatched to (address) regarding the report of a burglary.
- Upon arrival, I talked to the (reporting party/victim), (name), who told me the following:
- I searched....
- I photographed....
- I dusted (object) for latent fingerprints, but found none (or, and lifted)....
- It appeared that the point of entry/exit was....
- I talked to (name), (a witness/neighbor, etc.), who told me the following:
- I checked the neighborhood for....

Larceny or Theft

Larceny or theft is defined as the felonious taking by trespass of the personal property of another with the intent to permanently deprive that person of the property.

❖ **Elements**

Generally speaking, the following elements need to be proved:

1. Felonious (unlawful intent—not mistake or accident)
2. Taking
3. Trespass (without consent)
4. Of another (from the possession, i.e., care and control)
5. With intent to permanently deprive

Notes: ____

____

____

❖ **Phrases or Sentences to Write in Your Report:**

- On (date) at about (time), I was dispatched to (address/location) regarding the report of a theft.
- Upon arrival, I talked to the (reporting party/victim), (name), who told me the following:
- I dusted (object) for latent fingerprints, but found none (or, and lifted)....
- I searched for....
- I photographed....
- I talked to Witness (name), who told me the following:

Arson

Arson is defined as the willful and malicious burning of the dwelling of another. (In most states, arson now extends to the property and lands of another.)

❖ **Elements**

Generally speaking, the following elements need to be proved:

1. Willful and malicious (intentionally, or with wanton and willful disregard of the risk, and with a bad or evil purpose)
2. Burning
3. Dwelling (occupied, even though not at home)
4. Of another

Notes: ____

____

____

❖ **Phrases or Sentences to Write in Your Report:**

- On (date) at about (time), I was dispatched to (address) to investigate the report of an arson (or fire).
- Upon arrival at about (time), I saw....
- I cordoned off....
- I assigned....
- I notified....
- I (or ID Tech Jones, etc.) photographed/videotaped/ searched, etc.)....
- I talked to....
- It appeared....
- I (or ID Tech Jones, etc.) located and collected (items of evidence)....
- I prepared a log of....
- I (or ID Tech Jones, etc.) diagrammed....
- Witness John Smith told me the following: (Start new paragraph describing what he told you).

Assault

In most jurisdictions, assault is defined as an unlawful attempt, coupled with the present ability, to commit a violent injury upon the person of another. However, the degrees and forms of assault vary widely from state to state. For example, assault can vary in degree from "simple assault" or "assault and battery" (the completed act) to "assault with a deadly weapon" or "assault with great bodily injury." It can vary in form from simple assault of another to spousal abuse, child abuse, or elder abuse.

For the purposes of demonstration, only the simplest degree and form of assault will be discussed in this section.

❖ **Elements**

Generally speaking, the following elements need to be proved:

1. Unlawful attempt
2. Coupled with present ability to
3. Do violent injury to another person

Notes: ____

____

____

❖ **Phrases or Sentences to Write in Your Report:**

- On (date) at about (time), I was dispatched to (location) regarding the report of a (type of assault).
- Upon arrival at about (time), I talked to the victim, (name), who told me the following:
- I photographed the victim/obtained a medical release, etc.....
- I searched....
- I located and collected (items of evidence)....
- I photographed....
- I talked to Witness (name), who told me the following:
- I interviewed (suspect's name), first reading him his Miranda Rights. He waived his rights by....(explain what he said to waive his rights if the waiver was not recorded). He told me the following:

A NOTE ABOUT ARREST REPORTS

To arrest a person, you must have probable cause (reasonable cause to believe) that a crime occurred (all elements of the crime must exist) and that the person you are arresting is the one who committed it. After the arrest, you must explain in writing what you did—factually, accurately, objectively, and completely. You must document all observations made, information collected, and actions taken. Recall the Who? What? Where? When? Why? And How? questions presented in this chapter. A good report seeks to answer these matters of content.

Your arrest report must clearly show the reader, step-by-step, how you came to form your belief, what actions you took, and that you did not violate the arrested person's constitutional rights in the process. The authority of police to arrest someone—to restrict or ultimately remove their freedom in society—is a profound power, not to be taken lightly, and one that is closely monitored by the criminal justice system. A properly written arrest report will clearly show the reader that you acted in a reasonable and prudent manner throughout the process—a process that will be closely scrutinized at every level. Arrest reports are discussed again in Chapter Four.

SUMMARY

Content and form are equally important. The content of a well-written report is factual, accurate, objective, and complete.

A well-written report is *factual*. It does *not* contain opinions. Avoid conclusionary language in police reports. A well-written report is *accurate*; it is specific. Details of a report should be both factual and accurate. A well-written report is *objective*, meaning it is nonopinionated, fair, and impartial. You can assure objectivity in your reports by avoiding words with emotional overtones and including all relevant facts. A well-written report is *complete*. It answers the questions Who? What? Where? When? How? Why? A report should give as full an account as possible.

A complete criminal report addresses the elements of the crime, conditions that must exist and be proven to exist for an act to be called a specific kind of crime. Successful prosecution of a criminal case requires each element to exist and be documented by the reporting officer.

You may wish to review the chapter before taking the self-test on p.212.

REFERENCE

Rutledge, D. (2000). *The new police report manual* (2nd ed.). Incline Village, NV: Copperhouse Publishing Company.

Chapter Three

CHARACTERISTICS OF A WELL-WRITTEN REPORT: FORM

Do you know:

- What makes a report well written?
- How to distinguish between well-written and poorly written statements?
- How to evaluate a report by set criteria?

Key terms: concise, mechanically correct, mechanics

A WELL-WRITTEN REPORT: FORM

You looked at a poorly written report on p.11 and probably reacted very negatively to it. This is *not* the type of impression you want to leave on others.

➢ Application

Reread the report on p.11 and compare it with this one.

> At 0338 on February 23, 20--, I was dispatched to the apartment building at 6001 Dover St. to investigate a reported vandalism. Upon arrival I talked to the manager, who told me the suspect had driven his vehicle into the overhead door of the apartment's underground garage and had damaged the door. The suspect, who was still in the garage, had apparently been drinking. I examined the fiberglass garage door and saw it was off the track, bent up, and broken in. I saw red paint transfers on the broken section of the door.
>
> In the garage I talked to the suspect, who said he had just come down to wash his car, which hadn't been out of the garage all day. I saw that the suspect's red vehicle had a broken antenna and that the right deck of the passenger side had been gouged. The suspect denied any knowledge of the damage either to his car or the garage door.
>
> The manager insisted that the suspect was lying. The suspect then struck the manager and called him a "damn liar." The manager attempted to retreat, but the suspect kept after him, hitting him three times before I could restrain him. I placed the suspect under arrest for assault. Other charges are pending further investigation.

Generally, what differences did you notice between this report and the account of the same incident presented on p.11?

■ ■ ■ ■ ■ ■ ■ ■ ■ ■ ■ ■ ■ ■ ■

You should have noticed several differences between the well-written report on p.39 and the poorly written report on p.11. The most obvious differences are in spelling and punctuation. However, the well-written report also makes use of paragraphs, avoid opinions, and is less wordy. In form, a well-written report has at least six characteristics.

The form of a well-written report is:

- **concise.**
- **clear.**
- **mechanically correct.**
- **written in standard English.**
- **legible.**

It should also be on time.

It takes knowledge and practice to write well. You can't expect instant results. This chapter concentrates on recognizing well-written sentences, on telling "good" writing from "bad," effective from ineffective. In the rest of this text, you'll work on how you can achieve these same characteristics of good writing in your own reports.

CONCISE

In your efforts to be complete, as discussed in Chapter Two, you must use good judgment. You cannot possibly include everything. What you *do* include should be as **concise** as possible; no one wants to read a wordy report. Length does *not* mean quality. Some reports can be written in half a page; others may require 10 pages. No exact length can be specified, but your report will be effective if it includes all relevant information in as few words as possible. This does *not* mean, however, that you can leave out important details or such words as *a, an*, and *the.*

A well-written report is concise.

Basically, you can reduce wordiness two ways: (1) leave out unnecessary information and (2) use as few words as possible to record the necessary facts. Later in this text you'll practice the skill of writing concisely. For now, however, concentrate on recognizing wordy reports. For example, you should be able to tell that the phrase "blue in color" is wordy. Blue is a color, so you need record only the word *blue* in your description. A phrase such as "information which is of a confidential nature" should be recognized as a wordy way of saying "confidential information."

➢ Application

Read each of the following sentences. Underline any instances of wordiness. If you can, write a less wordy way of saying the same thing. If the sentence needs no change, write OK.

(*Because* or *Since*) (*Cautiously*)
Example: In view of the fact that the suspect was armed, the officer approached him with caution.

1. The officer made a note of the fact that the clock was square in shape.

2. The 6′ 3″ blonde male wore a tattered navy blue raincoat and carried a black umbrella.

3. It is the opinion of the victim that the thief called prior to the robbery for the purpose of determining if anyone was at home.

4. The 18-year-old girl wrote a check in the amount of $13.58, despite the fact that she had no checking account.

5. The victim's theory in reference to the crime comes into conflict with the facts of the present case currently under investigation.

6. The officer observed the suspect walk out of the store and made contact with him outside.

■ ■ ■ ■ ■ ■ ■ ■ ■ ■ ■ ■ ■ ■ ■

Your answers may differ slightly from those given below.

	Wordy	Concise
1.	made a note of the fact that square in shape	noted square
2.	— none; OK as is —	
3.	It is the opinion of the victim prior to for the purpose of determining	The victim believes before to determine
4.	in the amount of despite the fact that	for although
5.	in reference to comes into conflict present case currently	about or regarding conflicts case currently
6.	observed made contact with	saw contacted (it is even better to say *how* contact was made, e.g., talked to)

Being brief is not necessarily the same as being concise. Compare the following:

Brief:	He drove a car.
Concise:	He drove a 1988 blue Ford.
Wordy:	He drove a car which was a 1988 Ford and was blue in color.

Conciseness means you make every word count without leaving out important facts.

➢ Application

Read the following arrest report and be prepared to evaluate it. Use the following criteria—Is the report:

- ☐ factual? — Content
- ☐ accurate? — Content
- ☐ objective? — Content
- ☐ complete? — Content
- ☐ concise? — Form

For any negative response, be prepared to give at least one example of why you feel the report does not meet the criteria.

Citizen's Arrest Report - Theft*

Description: 1 pr. pants size 14 style #9607 Dept. 444 Lavender, Value $26.00
1 pr. pants size 12 style #9607 Dept. 444 Pink, Value $26.00

On this date, February 26, 20--, on or about approximately 1550 hrs., I, Susan Stokes, who am employed by the DD Department Store as a store detective, while on the second level of the DD Department Store with Carol Jones, who is also employed by DD as a store detective, did observe a male and a female in the corner of the women's department, which is located on the second floor also. The male was wearing sunglasses and looked familiar to me, although I could not place his name immediately at the time. I positioned myself in a manner so that I could see what the man and woman were doing in the corner and did observe a lavender pair of pants come off the rack and then a pink pair of pants come off the rack also. While they stood so that they were shielding one another, the male, who was later to be identified as Bernard Filson, no permanent address, DOB: 6-3-76, did roll up the lavender and the pink pants together and did conceal them in the inside of the bag while the female, who was later to be identified as Dawn Margaret Palmquist, 510 Sheridan No., DOB: 5-11-75, did hold the bag for him to put the pants into. They then together left the women's department and did walk towards the exit. I motioned to Carol at this time and together we went after the man and the woman and after identifying ourselves to them, we placed them under arrest for shoplifting. We then escorted them both down to our security office. The bag they concealed the pants in was a black and white plastic bag with horror pictures on it, and there was another identical appearing bag inside the first bag. The male suspect, Mr. Filson, verbally admitted to his part in the theft, but he would not sign a statement admitting to that fact. The female suspect, Miss Palmquist, would not sign a statement admitting to her part in the theft either. Police were called on or about approximately 1630 hrs.

* Note that a different format is used in this report. You will see different types of report formats throughout this text.

➢ Evaluation

Evaluate the report by answering the following questions. For any negative response, give at least one example to support your evaluation.

1. Is the report factual? ______________________________
2. Is the report accurate? ______________________________
3. Is the report objective? ______________________________
4. Is the report complete? ______________________________
5. Is the report concise? ______________________________

■ ■ ■ ■ ■ ■ ■ ■ ■ ■ ■ ■ ■ ■ ■

1. Yes, 2. Yes, 3. Yes, 4. Yes, 5. No. Instances of wordiness include *on this date*, *on or about*, *approximately*, *did observe*, *who was later to be identified*, etc.

CLEAR

A police report should have only one interpretation. Two people should be able to read the report and come up with the same picture. For example, "The man was tall" is open to interpretation, but the statement, "The man is 6′ 11″ " is not.

A well-written report is clear.

You can make your writing clear in several ways. You'll work on improving this skill later in the text, but for now, concentrate on telling when a statement is or is *not* clear.

- Use specific, concrete facts and details.

  Compare the following statements and determine which is clearer.

  1. The car sped away and turned the corner.
  2. The blue 1996 Cadillac Fleetwood pulled away from the curb, accelerated to approximately 65 m.p.h., and then turned off First Street onto Cleveland Avenue.

  The second statement is clearer because it contains concrete facts and details.

- Keep descriptive words and phrases as close as possible to the words they describe.

  Compare the following statements and determine which is clearer.

  1. He replaced the gun into the holster which he had just fired.
  2. He replaced the gun, which he had just fired, into the holster.

  The second statement is clearer because the phrase "which he had just fired" is placed close to the word it modifies (*gun*).

- Use diagrams and sketches when a description is complex.

  This is especially true in reports of accidents, homicides, and burglaries. The diagrams do not have to be artistic masterpieces. They should, however, be in approximate proportion and should help the reader follow the narrative portion of the report.

- Do not use uncommon abbreviations.

  Some abbreviations (Mr., Dr., Ave., St., Feb., Aug., NY, CA) are so commonly used they require no explanation. Other abbreviations, however, are commonly used only in law enforcement. Do not use these in your reports, since not all readers will understand them.

  Confusion can occur if two people have different interpretations of an abbreviation. For example, to most people, S.O.B. has a negative meaning. But for people in the health field, it means "short of breath." Use only abbreviations common to everyone.

- Use short sentences, well organized into short paragraphs.

  Short sentences are easier to read. Likewise, paragraphs should be relatively short, usually five to ten sentences. Each question answered in the report should have its own paragraph. The report should be organized logically, most commonly beginning with *when* and *where* and then telling *who* and *what*. The *what* should be in chronological order—that is, going from beginning to end without skipping back and forth. Chapter Four addresses how to structure the narrative.

➢ Application

Read each of the following statements. Indicate how each could be made clearer. Use the following letters to indicate your choices.

a. Add specific facts and details.
b. Place descriptive words closer to words they modify.
c. Add a sketch or diagram.
d. Eliminate uncommon abbreviations.
e. Shorten the sentence.

_____ 1. After opening the car door, the engine was started.

_____ 2. The body was in the far corner of the room about 10′ from the door and 5′ from the window. It was facing the west wall. The chair in the other corner was overturned.

_____ 3. The police officers drove past a church on a hill with a white steeple.

_____ 4. The suspects had driven off in an old car.

_____ 5. They drove nb on Stinson Avenue to the MPD.

_____ 6. After they left, the man, who was really a woman in disguise, ran around the corner and was out of view for a few minutes, but I followed and was able to catch up to the man before he could get into his car, a 1990 red Camry, and I questioned him at length about his disguise and his actions in the store from where the phone call was made.

______ 7. The thief stole many things.

______ 8. Officer Blake told Officer Jorgenson that he was invited to a party after work.

■ ■ ■ ■ ■ ■ ■ ■ ■ ■ ■ ■ ■ ■ ■

1.b (the engine did not open the car door), 2.c, 3.b (the hill did not have the white steeple), 4.a, 5.d, 6.e, 7.a, 8.b (who was invited to the party—Officer Blake or Officer Jorgenson?)

➤ Application

Read the following police report and be prepared to evaluate it. Use the following criteria—Is the report:

- ☐ factual?
- ☐ accurate?
- ☐ objective?
- ☐ complete?

} Content

- ☐ concise?
- ☐ clear?

} Form

For any negative response, be prepared to give at least one example to support your evaluation.

CHILD NEGLECT

On 9-23-20-- at 1248 hrs. I was dispatched to the above location in response to a child neglect call. The call was received by the dispatcher. Arriving at this location, the complainant, Mrs. Brownston, met me and gave me the following information regarding the case. Several minutes prior to my arrival Mrs. Brownston was at work at the above location in the capacity of a caretaker for the Colony Apartments, 5913 Reading Road. At this particular time in question, two young children appeared at the door requesting to come in to the office area. Mrs. Brownston recognized these children as occupants from 6113 Reading Road, Apt. #1D. She further related that this was not the first time these children had come to the office area of the apartment complex in search of shelter. The children told Mrs. Brownston and me that their mother had left their apartment this morning with a man and had told them to go to a friend's home or the office if she didn't come home by dinner. The children didn't know where their mother could be reached. I then asked the children when they had last eaten and was told that they had not eaten since yesterday. At this time I instructed Mrs. Brownston and another tenant (Sherri S. Strong, 5913 Reading Road, Apt. #13, Tel #555-6738) to accompany me and the children to their apartment to confirm the fact that the children's mother was, in fact, not at home. The children's apartment is located on the ground level, with entry to the apt. via sliding glass patio doors. This patio area is within an 8 ft. high fenced area with a gate. From this area, and looking into the apartment, it appeared as though a fight or other incident had occurred as clothing and debris were scattered everywhere. One of the sliding glass doors was partially open. At this time I knocked on the door and called out and identified myself as a police officer. Receiving no answer, the door was opened. Because of the disarray of the apartment, and fearing possible foul play, I entered the apartment via the glass door, again identifying myself and my presence within the apartment. Again I received no response from within. In checking the entire apartment, every room was found to be the same as the living room—a terrible mess. At this time, because of the unhealthy condition of the apartment and because the children's mother could not be reached, the children were put into protective custody and transported to the EPD to arrange for custody.

➢ Evaluation

Evaluate the report by answering the following questions. For any negative response, give at least one example to support your evaluation.

1. Is the report factual? ____________________

2. Is the report accurate? ____________________

3. Is the report objective? ____________________

4. Is the report complete? ____________________

5. Is the report concise? ____________________

6. Is the report clear? ____________________

■ ■ ■ ■ ■ ■ ■ ■ ■ ■ ■ ■ ■ ■ ■

1. Not entirely. The report is factual, except for the inference that a fight or incident had occurred.
2. Yes. The report appears to be accurate.
3. Yes. The report is objective.
4. No. The report lacks important details, such as the children's names, ages, and the mother's name. It also uses "the above" rather than supplying the information.
5. No. The report is extremely wordy—*prior to* (before); *at this particular time in question* (just before 1248); *appeared at the door requesting to come into the office area* (asked to enter the office); *further related that* (said); *to confirm the fact that the children's mother was, in fact* (to confirm that the mother was); *called out and identified myself* (identified myself); and *at this time* (then). Also, repetition of the address is not necessary.
6. No. Descriptive words and phrases are misplaced—*arriving at this location, the complainant* (the complainant did not arrive, the officer did); *to their apartment* (whose apartment—the caretaker's, the tenant's, or the children's?); *receiving no answer, the door* (the door did not fail to receive an answer). Specific details are omitted—what does "terrible mess" mean? What is an "unhealthy condition"? The abbreviation "EPD" might be meaningless to some readers of the report. Further, the report is not organized into paragraphs to aid the reader.

MECHANICALLY CORRECT

If you were to *hear* the words, "Your chances of being promoted are good if you can write effective reports," you would probably feel differently than if you were to *read* the same words written like this: "Yur chanses of bein promottid are gud if you kin write efectiv riports." The **mechanics** involved in translating ideas and spoken words into written words *are* important. This includes spelling, capitalization, and punctuation.

Look back at the report on p.11. One reason you react negatively to this report is that it is not **mechanically correct**—it does not follow the rules for spelling, capitalization, and punctuation. When you translate your ideas into words, you should follow the rules for correct writing.

A well-written report is mechanically correct—it follows the rules for spelling, capitalization, and punctuation.

Much of this text concentrates on developing skill in spelling, capitalization, and punctuation. For now, however, concentrate on telling when a statement does or does *not* follow the rules.

➢ Application

Which of the following judgments might you make about a person who wrote the sentence "Yur chanses of bein promottid are gud if you kin write efectiv riports"?

______ 1. The writer is careless.

______ 2. The writer is uneducated.

______ 3. The writer is stupid.

■ ■ ■ ■ ■ ■ ■ ■ ■ ■ ■ ■ ■ ■ ■

You probably checked all three. Perhaps none of these judgments is true, but they are normal reactions to seeing a sentence containing mechanical errors. The writer of such a sentence is *not* necessarily careless, uneducated, or stupid—he or she simply has not learned and followed the rules.

A mechanically incorrect report leaves a poor impression of its writer.

➢ Application

Reread the report on p.11 and find at least 10 examples of incorrect spelling, capitalization or punctuation.

1. ______________________ 6. ______________________

2. ______________________ 7. ______________________

3. ______________________ 8. ______________________

4. ______________________ 9. ______________________

5. ______________________ 10. ______________________

■ ■ ■ ■ ■ ■ ■ ■ ■ ■ ■ ■ ■ ■ ■

At 0338 on 02-23-20-- a call was recieved from 6001 dover st who had information that a vahical had recked overhead door of undergd. gar. in apt. Upon our squad cars' arrivel it was told above named suspict was still in gar. Complanant (who is mgr of apt) said he was obviusly drunk. gar door was observed by myself to be off the track and bended up. And fiberglas broken in from being hit. Suspict said he had just come down to wash car and it hadn't been out of gar all day. Vehical was observed to have broken radio antena so it is the opinion of myself that he probably done it. Recked the door. Besides that top of right deck of right side passenger side shown damige like as if paint had been gouged by a metel thin what had exerted presher on it and gouged it. Suspict said he didnt no nothin about it. Mgr said he was lieing so he was red his rites and arrested by myself for damige to property.

STANDARD ENGLISH

People often disagree about what standard English is, and the standards between spoken and written English differ. For example, if you were to *say*, "I'm gonna go walkin' in the mornin'," it would probably sound all right. People often drop the g when they speak. In writing, however, this is not acceptable.

Just as there are rules for spelling, capitalization, and punctuation, there are rules for *what* words are used *when*. For example, it is standard to say "he doesn't" rather than "he don't"; "I don't have any" rather than "I ain't got none"; "he and I are partners" rather than "him and me are partners."

A well-written report is written in standard English.

Your experience with English will often tell you what is standard and what is not—especially if you have been raised in surroundings in which standard English is used. If you speak standard English, you will probably also write in standard English. But that is not always true. Later chapters discuss how to identify and use standard English. For now, see if you can identify some of the nonstandard expressions that follow.

➢ Application

Check the statements that are *not* in standard English. Underline the nonstandard word(s), and write the standard way of saying it above the underlined words. If it is in standard English, write OK.

_____ 1. Bob and I answered the call.

_____ 2. It weren't the first time him and me worked together.

_____ 3. It probably won't be the last time either.

_____ 4. I like working with Bob because he ain't bossy.

______ 5. Bossy people isn't easy to work with.

______ 6. The call was about a accident.

______ 7. Two cars, they run head on into each other.

______ 8. When we got there, the crowd was unbelievable.

______ 9. It don't seem like people use their heads in time of a emergency.

______ 10. When we seen what was happening, we got that-there crowd dispersed.

■ ■ ■ ■ ■ ■ ■ ■ ■ ■ ■ ■ ■ ■ ■

1. OK
2. weren't (wasn't); him and me (he and I)
3. OK
4. ain't (isn't)
5. isn't (aren't)
6. a (an)
7. they (leave out the comma and the word they); run (ran)
8. OK
9. don't (doesn't); a (an, or can be omitted)
10. seen (saw); that-there (that)

A report in nonstandard English leaves a poor impression of its writer.

➢ Application

Reread the report on p.11. List at least four examples of nonstandard English.

1. ______________________ 3. ______________________

2. ______________________ 4. ______________________

■ ■ ■ ■ ■ ■ ■ ■ ■ ■ ■ ■ ■ ■ ■

At 0338 on 02-23-20-- a call was recieved from 6001 dover st who had information that a vahical had recked overhead door of undergd. gar. in apt. Upon our squad cars' arrivel it was told above named suspict was still in gar. Complanant (who is mgr of apt) said he was obviusly drunk. gar door was observed by myself to be off the track and bended up. And fiberglas broken in from being hit. Suspict said he had just come down to wash car and it hadn't been out of gar all day. Vehical was observed to have broken radio antena so it is the opinion of myself that he probably done it. Recked the door. Besides that top of right deck of right side passenger side shown damige like as if paint had been gouged by a metel thin what had exerted presher on it and gouged it. Suspict said he didnt no nothin about it. Mgr said he was lieing so he was red his rites and arrested by myself for damige to property.

LEGIBLE and ON TIME

It does little good to learn to write well if no one can read it or if the report is turned in after it was needed.

A well-written report is legible. It must also be on time.

Ideally, reports would be typed. Often, however, this is not practical, and sometimes a poorly typed report is as difficult to read as an illegible one. If you do not type your reports, and if you know that you have poor handwriting, you may want to print your reports. Granted, this is slower than cursive, but a report that cannot be read is of little use to anyone.

➢ Application

Read the following statement.

[illegible]

Check the statements below that describe how you felt as you read the statement.

_____ 1. The writer is careless.

_____ 2. I don't know what the writer is saying.

_____ 3. I resent spending my time trying to figure out what this says.

_____ 4. The heck with it; I can't understand this.

Check the statements below which might be true of how you would feel if you needed another officer's report on an incident which occurred three days ago and was not yet available.

_____ 5. That officer is really inefficient.

_____ 6. That officer is making my job harder for me.

_____ 7. If that officer is so slow in doing reports, s/he's probably slow in fulfilling other duties.

_____ 8. That officer is irresponsible.

You may have checked all eight statements. When a report is illegible or late, it causes others to respond negatively to the individual responsible for the report.

SUMMARY

The form of a well-written report is concise, clear, mechanically correct, written in standard English, legible, and on time.

A well-written report is *concise.* Conciseness means you make every word count without leaving out important facts. A well-written report is *clear.* A well-written report is *mechanically correct*—that is, it follows the rules for spelling, capitalization, and punctuation. A mechanically incorrect report leaves a poor impression of its writer. A well-written report is written *in standard English.* A report in nonstandard English leaves a poor impression of its writer. A well-written report is *legible.* It must also be *on time.*

You may wish to review the chapter before taking the self-test on p.214.

Chapter Four

STEPS IN REPORT WRITING

Do you know:

- What steps to take in report writing?
- What procedures to use in obtaining information?
- How to take notes?
- How to organize notes?
- How to structure the narrative?
- How to refer to people in a report?
- Whether to include in a report the questions asked during interviews or interrogations?
- Which tense to use throughout a police report?
- How to evaluate a report?

Key terms: chronological, edit, narrative, proofread, tense (verb)

THE FIVE BASIC STEPS

Your report is the link between what happened in a specific case and what others know about it. You might visualize it like this:

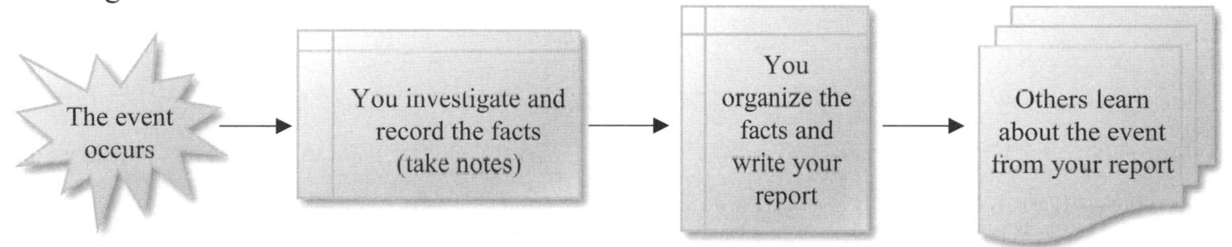

Your report must accurately reflect the facts of a case, so readers of the report know what happened. It will also help you recall the facts of the case, should it go to court. According to *Canons of Police Ethics*, Article 10:

> The law enforcement officer shall be concerned equally in the prosecution of the wrongdoer and the defense of the innocent. He shall ascertain what constitutes evidence and shall present such evidence impartially and without malice. In so doing, he will ignore social, political, and all other distinctions among the persons involved, strengthening the tradition of the reliability and integrity of an officer's word.
>
> The law enforcement officer shall take special pains to increase his perception and skill of observation, mindful that in many situations his is the sole impartial testimony to the facts of a case.

These facts cannot remain in the officer's head; they must be permanently recorded in a report.

> **The five basic steps in writing a report are:**
>
> 1. **Gather the facts: investigate, interview, interrogate.**
> 2. **Record the facts immediately: take notes.**
> 3. **Organize the facts.**
> 4. **Write the report.**
> 5. **Evaluate the report: edit and proofread; revise if necessary.**

All of these steps relate to the characteristics of a well-written report discussed in Chapters Two and Three. The first two steps—gathering the facts and recording them—assure that your report is factual, accurate, objective, and complete. The third step—organizing the facts—helps assure that your report is clear and concise. The fifth step—evaluation—helps assure that your report is mechanically correct, written in standard English, and legible. Evaluation will also help to assure that your report has other characteristics of a well-written report.

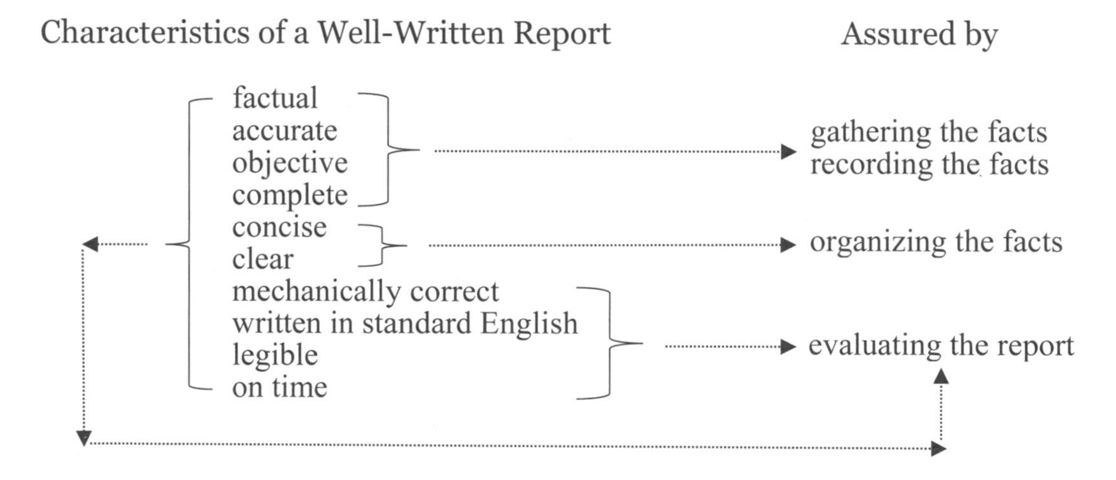

➢ Application

List the five steps in writing a report.

1. G ______________________________

2. R ______________________________

3. O ______________________________

4. W ______________________________

5. E ______________________________

1. Gather the facts; 2. Record the facts (take notes); 3. Organize the facts; 4 Write the report; 5. Evaluate the report (edit and proofread); revise if necessary

Notice the beginning letters of the first four steps spell the word *grow*; this may help you remember the steps and their order.

GATHERING THE FACTS—INVESTIGATING, INTERVIEWING, INTERROGATING

Investigative skills are much too complex to cover in-depth in this text. These skills are developed over time and through varied experiences. Appendix A contains general investigation checklists and tips for the major criminal offenses of murder, rape, robbery, burglary, larceny or theft, arson, and assault. These checklists outline activities and actions you will need to document in your report, and will assist you in collecting vital information for various offenses.

In this chapter you will briefly review some basic principles for gathering information for a police report and learn ways to make this step in report writing more efficient for you.

Recall that a report is a written record communicating relevant facts to be retained for future use. The first four characteristics of a well-written report—factual, accurate, objective, complete—focus on what you include in your report—that is, the content of the report. You've already looked at the information you should include (Chapter Two). Now look at how to get this information.

To gather information, observe and listen.

Start to gather information as soon as you know the subject of the report and its purpose. This text is limited to incident reports, although police officers write other kinds of reports as well.

Much of what you know about a case will come from asking questions and listening to the answers. Several simple procedures can make an interview with a witness, a victim, or a suspect more productive.

Prepare for each interview in advance if time allows. Know what questions you need to have answered.

Obtain your information as *soon after* the incident as possible. A delay may result in the subjects not remembering important details.

Be considerate of the subject's feelings. If someone has just been robbed, or seen an assault, or been attacked, the individual may be understandably upset and emotional. Allow them time to calm down before you ask too many questions. Remember: when emotions increase, memory decreases.

Be friendly. Try to establish rapport with the subject before asking questions. Use the person's name; look at the person as you ask questions; respond to the answers.

Use a private setting if possible. Eliminate as many distractions as you can so the subject can devote full attention to the questions you ask.

Eliminate physical barriers. Talking across a desk or counter, or through a car window, does not encourage conversation.

Sit rather than stand. This will make the subject more comfortable and probably more willing to engage in conversation.

Encourage conversation. Keep the subject talking by:

- Keeping your own talking to a minimum.
- Using open-ended questions such as, "Tell me what you saw."
- Avoiding questions that call for only a "yes" or "no" answer.
- Allowing long pauses. Pauses in the conversation should not be uncomfortable. Subjects need time to think and organize their thoughts. Give subjects all the time needed.

Ask simple questions. Do not use law enforcement terminology when you ask your questions. Keep your language simple and direct.

Ask one question at a time. Allow the subject to answer one question completely before going to the next question.

Listen to what is said and how it is said.

Watch for indications of tension, nervousness, surprise, embarrassment, anger, fear, or guilt.

Establish the reliability of the subject by asking some questions to which you already know the answers.

Be objective and controlled. Recognize that many people are reluctant to give information to the police. Among the several reasons for this reluctance are fear or hatred of authority, fear of reprisal, lack of memory, or unwillingness to become involved. Keep control of yourself and your situation. Do not antagonize the subject, use profanity or obscenity, lose your temper, or use physical force. Remain calm, objective, and professional.

➢ Application

Imagine you are interviewing the victim of an armed robbery that just occurred. List three factors to consider as you interview the victim.

1. ____

2. ____

3. ____

Check the statement in each pair that would be more effective during an interview.

4. _____ a. Did you see the suspect?

   _____ b. What did you see?

5. _____ a. How many shots were fired?

   _____ b. What happened after the suspect pulled his gun?

6. _____ a. This is your second armed robbery. Were there any similarities between the two robberies?

   _____ b. This is your second armed robbery. Were there any similarities in the modus operandi?

Which of the following should be avoided during the interview? Check all that apply.

_____ 7. the long pause

_____ 8. "yes-no" questions

_____ 9. open-ended questions

_____ 10. police terminology

■ ■

For 1-3, you might give several answers. Check your answers by reviewing the material on pp.55-56.

4. b is more effective—it is open-ended; a would require only a "yes" or "no" answer.
5. b is more effective—it is open-ended; a would require only a simple number in the answer.
6. a is more effective—it avoids the use of police terminology (*modus operandi*).

"Yes-no" questions (8) and police terminology (10) should be avoided during an interview. You should use the long pause (7) and open-ended questions (9).

TAKING NOTES

Notes are a permanent aid to your memory. Good notes aid in investigating a case, in writing the report, and in testifying in court.

Record all relevant information legibly, in ink, in a notebook.
Felt-tip or ballpoint pens are acceptable.

➢ Application

Several procedures should be followed in taking field notes. Common sense provides the reasons behind these procedures. Give one valid reason for each procedure in the space provided.

1. Use a notebook—not scraps of paper.

   Reason: ______________________________

2. Use ink.

   Reason: ______________________________

3. Write legibly.

   Reason: ______________________________

4. Identify the notes with your name, the date, and the case number.

   Reason: ______________________________

5. Record all relevant facts as you get them.

   Reason: ______________________________

6. Check spelling, numbers, and dates as you record them.

   Reason: ______________________________

7. Use freehand sketches if the situation calls for it.

   Reason: ______________________________

8. Omit words such as *a*, *an*, and *the*; use common abbreviations, but do not devise your own shorthand.

   Reason: ______________________________

■■■■■■■■■■■■■■■■■

1. Scraps of paper can easily be lost. Use a notebook which is easy to carry around (3-3/4″ x 6-3/4″ is a good size). A loose-leaf notebook is best because it is easy to organize, you can remove and add pages, and it looks more professional in court. Keep it full of blank paper and well organized. You

may want to use index tabs to separate sections: offense reports, follow-up, arrests, wanted and missing persons, stolen cars, and so on. Remove the notes when they've served their purpose and file them by case number. (Some officers destroy their notes after writing the report.)

2. This is a permanent record. Therefore, you should use ink rather than pencil, which can easily be changed. Also, pencil can become blurred and smudged. It is a good idea to have at least two pens with you in case one runs out of ink during an investigation.
3. Other people may rely on your notes in investigating the case. And you don't want to waste time later on trying to figure out what you've written.
4. You may work on several different cases in any one day. It is important to identify what notes belong to what case. Do this on each page of notes.
5. Don't wait until later to write down information. You may forget some important details. Obviously you won't write down everything that is said, but you should write down anything which might be important. A good rule of thumb is: "When in doubt, write it down."
6. Accuracy requires that you verify all spelling, numbers, and dates as they are recorded. This can be done simply by repeating them aloud as you write them and getting verification from the subject.
7. Sketches can help clarify a scene or situation. They can also aid your memory as you write the report.
8. To take notes rapidly, it is necessary to omit some words and to use abbreviations. You should not devise your own shorthand, however, since others may also use your notes.

Good notes have many of the same characteristics of good reports.
Good notes are clear, complete, concise, accurate, and objective.
Good notes are a prerequisite for a good report.

➢ Application

List at least five procedures to be followed in taking notes.

1. ______________________________

2. ______________________________

3. ______________________________

4. ______________________________

5. ______________________________

■ ■ ■ ■ ■ ■ ■ ■ ■ ■ ■ ■ ■ ■ ■

You may have given any five of the following:

- Use a notebook—not scraps of paper.
- Use ink.
- Write legibly.
- Identify the notes with your name, the date, and the case number.
- Check spelling, numbers, and dates as you record them.
- Use freehand sketches if the situation calls for it.
- Omit words such as *a*, *an*, and *the*, and use common abbreviations.

Good notes include all relevant facts.

➢ Application

Read the following paragraph. Then record the relevant facts as you would if you had obtained the information during an interview with a witness.

> The victim—Sally Sacks, 1101 Pine Drive—reported that on 1-5-20-- at about 1610 hrs. she was driving her 1999 Ford Escort southbound on Wooddale Avenue approaching W. 58th Street. She became aware of the suspect auto tailgating her vehicle and slowed her car. She then resumed her speed; as she did so, the suspect auto attempted to pass her on the left, but dropped behind her again. The victim then came to a stop at W. 58th Street and proceeded to turn to the right (westbound on W. 58th). As she turned, the suspect followed around the corner, coming around her left side, overtaking her, and passing her. As he did so, he cut in on her and their vehicles collided (her left front to his right side). The suspect drove on, and she accelerated and got the license number, California 1AGC752.

Make your notes in the space that follows.

____

____

____

____

____

____

■ ■ ■ ■ ■ ■ ■ ■ ■ ■ ■ ■ ■ ■ ■

Sample notes:

> Victim: on 1-5-20-- approx. 1610 hrs. she was driving '99 Ford Escort s.bound on Wooddale Ave. approaching W. 58th St. She noted car tailgating her and slowed, then resumed speed. So did car behind. It tried to pass on left side but dropped behind. Victim stopped at W. 58th St. and turned right (w.bound 58th). Other car followed, came around left side, overtook her, passed, and cut in. Vehicles collided—her left front to his right side. Car drove on. She sped up and got license #, CA 1AGC752.

ORGANIZING YOUR INFORMATION

Organization is critical to an effective report. If a report skips from one idea to another, repeats or goes back and forth in time, it will not present a clear picture of what happened. (And it will leave a negative impression on the reader.)

Organize your information.
Report it in chronologically arranged paragraphs.

Two aids in organizing your information are to (1) organize your field notebook and (2) make an outline or report plan.

Organize your field notebook. One aid to a well-organized report is a well-organized notebook, with well-organized notes. Establish a set pattern of gathering information, whether it is information obtained through observation or through asking questions. You may want to have in the front of your notebook a list of questions to ask and then try to ask the questions in this order.

In addition to aiding organization, covering a list of questions or a checklist can save time, money, and cases simply because, if you complete an interview without having covered and recorded all relevant facts, you have lost what may be the only opportunity to gather critical information. You may also want to have separate sections for each type of information: offense/arrest notes, follow-up notes, vacations/empty houses, etc. You should also start a new page for each case or incident.

Make an outline or report plan. Plan before you write. Ideally, you should make a rough outline of your report showing the main ideas to be included. As Lewis (1999, p.136) explains: "Writing is slower than thinking. You will leave out thoughts as your mind races ahead of your pen. Outline important points so thoughts will not be left out." If this is too time-consuming, you might try going through your notes with a pencil, numbering each item in the order it is to be used.

➢ Application

Number the following items to show the order in which they should appear in a report.

______ a. Gatto says he was walking back to his apartment with his mail.

______ b. Dispatched at 2315 hrs., 6-18-20--.

______ c. Thiel saw Gatto with mail and got angry.

______ d. Suspect: Kris Thiel, resident manager, 1688 High Street, Apt. 1.

______ e. I told Gatto to phone District Attorney's Office.

______ f. Assault victim: Jorge Gatto, 1688 High Street, Apt. 5.

______ g. Thiel checked mailbox; his check was not there.

______ h. Thiel hit Gatto in stomach with closed fist.

______ i. Thiel says he has been having problems with stolen retirement checks.

______ j. I told Gatto that Thiel denied hitting him; Gatto insisted on filing a complaint.

______ k. Thiel walked up to Gatto and accused him of stealing check.

______ l. Thiel accused Gatto of stealing check but didn't hit him.

■ ■ ■ ■ ■ ■ ■ ■ ■ ■ ■ ■ ■ ■ ■

a. 4, b .1, c. 9, d. 3, e. 12, f. 2, g. 8, h. 6, i. 7, j. 11, k. 5, l. 10

Using the order given, your report might look something like this:

> At 2315 hours I was dispatched to 1688 High Street, Apt. 5 to investigate a reported assault. On arrival I met with the victim, Jorge Gatto.
>
> Gatto told me he had been assaulted by the resident manager, Kris Thiel, who lived in Apt. 1. Gatto told me that he was walking back to his apartment with his mail when Kris Thiel walked up to him from behind, accused him of stealing Thiel's retirement check, and hit him in the stomach with a closed fist. No one else saw the incident.
>
> I then talked to the suspect, Kris Thiel, who told me that he had been having problems with someone stealing his monthly retirement checks. When he looked into his mailbox today, his check was not there. He saw Gatto walking down the hallway with mail in his hand, and he thought Gatto had taken his check. He got angry and accused Gatto of stealing his check, but did not hit Gatto.

> After talking to Thiel, I explain to Gatto that Thiel denied hitting him. Gatto insisted on filing a complaint; therefore, I told him I would submit a copy of my report to the District Attorney's Office, and I recommended that he phone for an appointment to discuss the matter with a Deputy District Attorney.

Three other aids in organizing information are to use (1) paragraphs, (2) chronological order, and (3) a set pattern for the opening sentence.

Use paragraphs to aid the reader. A paragraph corresponds to a heading in the outline of your report. Each paragraph should focus the reader's attention on a specific aspect of the report. Paragraphs should usually be short (100 words or less). Notice in the preceding report that each paragraph deals with one specific aspect of the incident, and each paragraph is short.

Use chronological order. Since most reports contain information about a sequence of events, the most logical pattern of organization is **chronological**—that is, going in time from the beginning to the end. Notice that chronological order is used in the preceding report. The report begins with the complaint and then relates the incidents involved.

Establish a format for your introductory sentence. You may want to have a set pattern for the opening sentence of your reports. Getting started on a report may be easier if you simply begin with the time, date, and complaint or incident and how you became involved. For example:

> At about 2315 hours on 4-7-20--, I was dispatched to 2378 Pine Street to investigate a burglary.
>
> On 4-7-20-- at about 2315 hours, I was dispatched to 2378 Pine Street to investigate a burglary.

➢ Application

As a brief review, list two steps that aid in writing well-organized reports:

1. ____

2. ____

Now list three steps you can take to help organize your information:

3. ____

4. ____

5. ____

▪▪▪▪▪▪▪▪▪▪▪▪▪▪▪▪

1. Organize your field notebook and notes.
2. Make an outline or report plan.
3. Use paragraphs.
4. Use chronological order.
5. Establish a format for your introductory sentence.

STRUCTURING THE NARRATIVE

The law enforcement **narrative** is essentially a technical report structured in chronological order describing a sequence of investigative events. Those events are:

1. You, the reporting officer, receive information by either viewing something or by being told something, e.g., by examining a crime scene or by interviewing a victim or witness.
2. You act on the information you receive, e.g., by collecting evidence, by talking to other witnesses, etc.
3. Your actions cause you to receive additional information, e.g., new witnesses to talk to, other areas to search, etc.
4. You act on the new information you receive.

This process continues until you have exhausted all leads, completed the investigation, or turned the case over to another entity, such as the detective division.

The narrative should first set the stage. Give the date, time, how you came to be involved, and the type of incident. For example:

> On 9-7-20-- at about 0750 hours, I was dispatched to the Downtown Marina regarding the report of a felony theft. Upon arrival at 0800 hours, I talked to the victim, Norman Smith.

The next paragraph of the narrative should explain what information you received. For example:

> Smith said he arrived at the Downtown Marina at about 0730 hours to work on his boat. When he went to his walled boat dock, he discovered the dock's door was open and his boat and motor were missing. He did not go inside the dock but immediately phoned the police. He had locked the door the night before at about 1930 hours when he left the dock. The boat and motor were in the dock at that time. He had no idea how the boat and motor were taken. (See Property Loss Section for full description of the missing items.)

The following paragraph should explain what you did about the information you received. For example:

> I checked the open door and saw that the lock appeared to be broken and that the knob had marks on it. The marks appeared similar in pattern to pipe wrench jaws. I searched the area and located a 14-inch pipe wrench on the dock behind the door. I saw no other items of evidence.

The narrative should then explain what you did about the new information you received. For example:

> I collected the door knob and pipe wrench as physical evidence. I photographed the scene. I radioed a description of the boat and motor to dispatch for entry into the NCIC computer system. I checked the area for witnesses but found none. I booked the collected items and negatives into the evidence section (refer to the evidence sheet for details).

The final paragraph of the narrative should explain the disposition of your investigation. For example:

> Case referred to the detective division for follow-up.

The completed narrative should look like this:

> On 9-7-20-- at about 0750 hours, I was dispatched to the Downtown Marina regarding the report of a felony theft. Upon arrival at 0800 hours, I talked to the victim, Norman Smith.
>
> Smith said he arrived at the Downtown Marina at about 0730 hours to work on his boat. When he went to his walled boat dock, he discovered the dock's door was open and his boat and motor were missing. He did not go inside the dock but immediately phoned the police. He had locked the door the night before at about 1930 hours when he left the dock. The boat and motor were in the dock at that time. He had no idea how the boat and motor were taken. (See Property Loss Section for full description of the missing items.)
>
> I checked the open door and saw that the lock appeared to be broken and that the knob had marks on it. The marks appeared similar in pattern to pipe wrench jaws. I searched the area and located a 14-inch pipe wrench on the dock behind the door. I saw no other items of evidence.
>
> I collected the door knob and pipe wrench as physical evidence. I photographed the scene. I radioed a description of the boat and motor to dispatch for entry into the NCIC computer system. I checked the area for witnesses but found none. I booked the collected items and negatives into the evidence section (refer to the evidence sheet for details).
>
> Case referred to the detective division for follow-up.

- **The opening paragraph of a police report states the time, date, type of incident, and how you became involved.**
- **The next paragraph contains what you were told by the victim(s) or witness(es). For each person talked to, use a separate paragraph.**
- **Next record what you did based on the information you received.**
- **The final paragraph states the disposition of the case.**

Describing the Offense

The opening sentence of the report should include the correct description of the offense. For example, you might be dispatched to a robbery that turns out to be a burglary. To explain why they responded as they did, some officers include the incorrect information received from dispatch like this: "On 04-08-20-- at 1230 hours I responded to a burglary (dispatched as a robbery)."

The sections of each state's penal code have titles that describe the offense. The title should be similar to (if not the same as) the descriptive wording in the penal code, for example:

OFFENSE		TITLE
Doing damage to property	is	Malicious Mischief[1]
Willful and malicious burning	is	Arson
Breaking and entering	is	Burglary[2]

Many of your reports will describe incidents–that is, activities or circumstances that should be reported, but which are not crimes, arrests, or crime-related. Incidents include such things as:

Abandoned vehicle	Found property	Neighborhood dispute
Animal bite	Lost person	Occupational accident, e.g., explosion
Firearms accident	Mental case	Suicide

Each law enforcement department has its own list of titles; therefore, check with your department to learn which titles to use in your reports.

Complete forms accurately. Forms force you to record the details of an incident or case. Complete all relevant blanks. Use "n/a" if a blank is not applicable. Use "unk." if the information called for is not known.

Remember that most of the people who read the report will know nothing of the crime, the initial investigation, or the arrest, other than what the report tells them.

Keep your writing straightforward and simple. Usually you should write as you would talk. Avoid legal terminology, technical words, and "bookish" words. The best general rule is to use short, simple words, sentences, and paragraphs.

---

[1] Some states refer to *Malicious Mischief* as *Vandalism*.

[2] Some states' penal codes title *Burglary* as *Breaking and Entering*.

➢ Application

Check the appropriate title in each pair.

1. _____ a. Loony
   _____ b. Mental Case
2. _____ a. Window Breaking
   _____ b. Malicious Mischief (or Vandalism)
3. _____ a. Drunk Driving
   _____ b. Driving Under the Influence
4. _____ a. Suicide
   _____ b. Shot Self in Head
5. _____ a. Abandoned Vehicle
   _____ b. Auto Left on Roadside

■ ■ ■ ■ ■ ■ ■ ■ ■ ■ ■ ■ ■ ■ ■ ■

1.b, 2.b, 3.b, 4.a, 5.a

The Importance of Structuring the Narrative to Build a Case

As first mentioned in Chapter 2, the authority of police to arrest people is an awesome power, one that requires an officer to diligently explain, in writing, the events preceding an arrest, as well as all actions taken while executing the arrest. More than one case has been thrown out because the arrest report failed to adequately explain how the officer developed the probable cause necessary to make the arrest.

Appendix B illustrates, step-by-step, how an arrest report should be structured so as to demonstrate the arresting officer acted lawfully.

USING NAMES AND COURTESY TITLES

The first time a person is named, give the full name, for example, Jerry J. Adams. After that, use only the last name unless more than one person with the same last name is included in the report. If two or more individuals having the same last name are included in the report, use their first initial and last name, e.g., J. Adams.

In a paragraph containing what a person has told you, give the person's name in the first sentence. After that, use a pronoun (*he* or *she*). Do *not* keep repeating the person's name.

Do not use courtesy titles (Mr., Mrs., Ms., Dr., etc.) unless there is a specific reason. If you use a courtesy title for one individual in the report, use them for all individuals. Be especially careful if using the courtesy title, *Dr.* Most people think of a physician when this title is used. It is better to say Mary Johnson, MD, or Jack Halone, PhD. It *is* acceptable to use a rank designation if another officer is referred to in your report, e.g., Sgt. McKinley arrived on the scene.

When using names and courtesy titles in a report, remember the following:

- **Use a person's full name the first time; after that, use only the last name unless more than one person with the same last name is included in the report.**
- **If two or more individuals having the same last name are included in the report, use their first initial and last name.**
- **Do not keep repeating the person's name; use pronouns.**
- **Do not use courtesy titles unless there is a specific reason.**

➢ Application

Look at the report on p.65 (the complete narrative) and answer the following questions.

1. How is the victim named in the first paragraph? ____________________

2. How is the victim named in the first sentence of the second paragraph? ____________

3. How is the victim named in the remaining sentences in the second paragraph? ________

4. Are any courtesy titles used in this report? ____________________

■ ■ ■ ■ ■ ■ ■ ■ ■ ■ ■ ■ ■ ■ ■

1. Norman Smith
2. Smith
3. he
4. no

OMITTING QUESTIONS

Incident reports should tell a story. They should not be a question/answer dialog. For example, do not include in your report, "I asked the victim what happened" or "I asked her what was missing." Including the questions asked not only makes the report wordy, it also disrupts the flow of the story a person has told you.

Do *not* include in your report the questions asked to victims, witnesses, or suspects.

➢ Application

Read the following paragraph and cross out the questions that should not be included in the report. Also make any changes in the use of names and courtesy titles.

> I asked Ms. Sally Anderson what happened. Sally said that someone had broken into her backyard and destroyed her flower gardens. I asked Sally how extensive the damage was. Ms. Anderson told me it would cost her hundreds of dollars and hours of time to repair the damage. I then asked Ms. Sally Anderson if she had any idea who might have done this. Sally responded that she had no idea who could have done it. I asked Sally Anderson if she knew of any similar damage to other homes in the neighborhood. Sally responded no.

In the space below, write the paragraph as it should have been written.

____

____

____

____

____

■■■■■■■■■■■■■■■■

Your rewrite might look something like the following:

> Sally Anderson said someone had broken into her backyard and destroyed her flower gardens. She said it would cost hundreds of dollars and hours of time to repair the damage. She had no idea who could have done it and knew of no similar incidents in her neighborhood.

Compare the length of the two paragraphs. Also notice how much easier it is to follow the rewrite. The story is told simply and clearly.

USING PAST TENSE

A police report is a record of things that are over—they have already happened. English uses verb **tense** to show time. Verbs may be in the present (I see), past (I saw), or future (I will see).

Stay in the past tense throughout a police report.

If you write <u>John Olson lives at 123 Main Street</u>, and if the case should go to court several months later, the defense attorney is very likely to ask: "Does John Olson still live there?" You probably won't know and will have to respond: "I don't know." For every instance of present tense, the same question may be asked.

➢ Application

Check the statements that should *not* be used in police reports because they use the present tense.

_____ 1. Smith works at Target.

_____ 2. McKenzie's phone number is (612) 555-8888.

_____ 3. Preston is unemployed.

_____ 4. The victim wishes to press charges.

_____ 5. A television set and stereo were missing.

■ ■ ■ ■ ■ ■ ■ ■ ■ ■ ■ ■ ■ ■ ■ ■ ■

You should have checked all except #5. 1-4 could have changed since the report was written.

A WORD ON COMPUTERS

Computer-assisted report entry is becoming popular in many departments, and it does make report writing easier and more efficient. However, as Cox (1994, p.8) cautions: "In many departments, writing skill is diminished due to overconfidence in technological hardware. However data may be disseminated, the facts are selected by humans, input [by humans], and retrieved by humans. Machines can't put in what isn't there, or take out what should not be."

EVALUATING YOUR REPORT

Two procedures are used in evaluating your writing: editing and proofreading.

When you **edit**, you look at the content of the report. Is it based on facts? Is the reasoning sound? Is the information specific? Do the facts need interpretation? Is it non-opinionated, fair, and impartial? Has too much or too little information been included? Are the sources of information the best available? Is it organized chronologically? In short, you are making sure your report is:

- factual.
- accurate.
- objective.
- complete.
- chronological.

When you **proofread**, you look at the form of the report. Have you been concise and clear? Have you used correct spelling, capitalization, and punctuation? Have you used standard written English? In short, you are making sure your report is:

- concise.
- clear.
- mechanically correct.
- written in standard English.

Edit and proofread your reports.

Both editing and proofreading are necessary for a careful evaluation of your report. It might have excellent content, but if the form is sloppy or incorrect, your report will be ineffective. Likewise, it may have excellent form, but it is of little value if the content is insufficient. Form and content are integrally related. One affects the other.

➢ Application

Indicate which procedure would be involved in the following revisions in a report. Use "E" to indicate editing; use "P" to indicate proofreading.

_____ 1. Correcting a spelling error.

_____ 2. Adding an important detail.

______ 3. Moving a modifier closer to the word it modifies.

______ 4. Changing a capital letter to a small letter.

______ 5. Eliminating a conclusionary statement.

______ 6. Changing a period to a semicolon.

■ ■ ■ ■ ■ ■ ■ ■ ■ ■ ■ ■ ■ ■ ■ ■ ■

1.P, 2.E, 3.E, 4.P, 5.E, 6.P

Note: Always edit *first*. There is little point in checking the spelling or punctuation of a sentence that you may omit or change entirely. *After* you have edited your report and are certain that it clearly states all important details, proofread for errors in spelling, capitalization, and punctuation.

As you proofread, you may find it helpful to use some standard proofreading marks such as:

Mark	Meaning	Example
ℊ	Delete	This woord
^	Add	This wrd
∾	Transpose	This wrod
stet	Leave as was	This word stet
/	Make lower case	This worD
≡	Make upper case (caps)	this word
___	*Italics* for typeset text; underline for typewritten text	Italics for typeset
~~	Make **bold**	Make bold
#	Add space	Thisword #
⁐	Close up space	Thi s word
¶	Paragraph here	This word. ¶
	Bring up	This word
	Move here	This word

In Chapters Two and Three you practiced evaluating reports by answering these questions:

- Is the report *factual*?
- Is the report *accurate*?
- Is the report *objective*?
- Is the report *complete*?
- Is the report *chronological*?
- Is the report *concise*?
- Is the report *clear*?
- Is the report *mechanically correct*?
- Is the report *written in standard English*?

These same questions should be asked of each report you write. You should already be able to evaluate your own reports for the first four characteristics. The rest of this text will concentrate on conciseness, clarity, and mechanical correctness.

Before turning to these characteristics, a few suggestions about evaluation are in order. First, as you reread your reports, switch your viewpoint to that of the reader. Put yourself in the reader's shoes. Would the reader know what you are saying? Reading the report aloud may help you get a better feel for how it sounds. Also, since it is difficult to criticize your own writing, have another officer or associate read and evaluate the report. Ask if they understand what happened; if so, you probably have an effective report.

APPEARANCES COUNT

As previously stated, your report reflects on your competence and your professionalism. Take pride not only in the content and form of your reports but also in their physical appearance. Use wide margins and plenty of white space. Skip a line between paragraphs. Use good quality paper. Remember how many people may be reading your reports.

SUMMARY

The five basic steps in writing a report are gathering the facts (investigate, interview, interrogate), recording the facts immediately (take notes), organizing the facts, writing the report and evaluating the report (edit and proofread; revise if necessary).

To gather information, observe and listen. Record all relevant information legibly, in ink, in a notebook. Felt-tip or ball-point pens are acceptable. Good notes have many of the same characteristics of good reports. Good notes are clear, complete, concise, accurate and objective. Good notes are a prerequisite for a good report. Good notes include all relevant facts.

Organize your information. Report it in chronologically arranged paragraphs. The opening paragraph of a police report states the time, date, type of incident and how you became involved. The next paragraph contains what you were told by the victim(s) or witness(es). For each person talked to, use a separate paragraph. Next record what you did based on the information you received. The final paragraph states the disposition of the case.

When using names and courtesy titles in a report, remember to use a person's full name the first time; after that, use only the last name unless more than one person with the same last name is included in the report. If two or more individuals having the same last name are included in the report, use their first initial and last name. Do not keep repeating the person's name; use pronouns. Also, do not use courtesy titles unless there is a specific reason.

Do *not* include in your report the questions asked to victims, witnesses or suspects. Remember to stay in the past tense throughout a police report. Finally, edit and proofread your reports.

You may wish to review this chapter before taking the self-test on p.217.

REFERENCES

Cox, C. R. (1994, December 15). But will they be able to write a report? *Law Enforcement News*, 8, 10.

Lewis, S. (1999, July). Writing tips for adult learners. *Law and Order*, *47*(7), 135-136.

Chapter Five

PRINCIPLES OF CLEAR WRITING

Do you know:

- When to use the first person?
- When to use the active voice?
- Where to place your modifiers?
- How to make your pronouns clear?
- How to make your sentences parallel?

Key terms: active (voice), dangling modifier, first person, modifiers, parallelism, passive (voice), pronoun, squinting modifier, subject, third person, verb

You are already familiar with many of the principles involved in clear writing. It's now time to look at these principles closely and to practice using them in writing clearly. In this chapter you will learn to write clearly by avoiding those elements listed on the right below, using instead those elements listed on the left.

Clarity results from:	*Lack of clarity results from:*
First person	Third person
Active voice	Passive voice
Correct modification	Incorrect modification
Proper pronoun reference	Faulty pronoun reference
Use of parallelism	Lack of parallelism

Each of these elements is explained in this chapter. You will be given examples of clear and unclear writing; you will identify clear and unclear writing; you will correct unclear sentences; and, finally, you will practice writing clear sentences of your own.

FIRST PERSON

Using the **first person** means you refer to yourself as "*I*." For example, "*I* handcuffed the suspect." Traditionally, many police officers have not been so direct, instead using the **third person**, "*this officer*." For example, "*This officer* handcuffed the suspect." First person writing is recommended for law enforcement reports because it is more direct, clearer, and less wordy.

Use the first person to refer to yourself.

➢ Identification

Identify each statement below as first person (F) or third person (T).

_____ 1. The investigating officer responded to the scene.

_____ 2. This reporting officer chased the suspect down the alley.

_____ 3. I caught him before he could escape.

_____ 4. This officer pulled his gun and fired.

■ ■ ■ ■ ■ ■ ■ ■ ■ ■ ■ ■ ■ ■ ■

1.T, 2.T, 3.F, 4.T

➢ Improvement

Improve the following sentences by changing them from third person to first person.

1. This officer was promoted.

   ____

2. This responding officer tended to the victim's injuries.

   ____

3. This reporting officer served the subpoena.

   ____

4. The undersigned officer then secured the crime scene.

   ____

■ ■ ■ ■ ■ ■ ■ ■ ■ ■ ■ ■ ■ ■ ■

1. I was promoted.
2. I tended to the victim's injuries.
3. I served the subpoena.
4. I then secured the crime scene.

ACTIVE VOICE

A sentence may be either active or passive. This is an easy distinction to make if you think about what the words *active* and *passive* mean. (Forget about the term *voice*; it is a technical grammatical term you do not need to understand to write well.)

To determine if a sentence is active or passive, follow these steps:

First, find the **subject** (tells *who*) and the **verb** (tells *what was done*) of a sentence.

For example: Sentence 1: The man shot the woman.

	subject	verb
	who	*did what*

Sentence 2: The woman was shot by the man.

	subject	verb
	who	*did what*

Then ask, "What was done and did the subject of the sentence do it?"

In Sentence 1: Yes, the man did the shooting.
In Sentence 2: No, the woman did *not* do the shooting.

Notice that in Sentence 2, the woman did *not* act; she was *acted upon*. She was *passive*.

If the subject performs the action, the sentence is *active*.
If the subject does *not* perform the action, the sentence is *passive*.

In the sentence, "The gun was fired by the fugitive," what was done? Firing. Did the gun *do* the firing? No. Therefore, this sentence is passive. The subject of the sentence, the gun, did *not* perform the action. Written in active voice, the sentence would read, "The fugitive fired the gun."

➢ Application

Compare the following two sentences:

Sentence 1: The child was beaten by the mother.
Sentence 2: The mother beat the child.

Determine which is active and which is passive by completing these steps:

1. Find the subject and the verb of each sentence.

   Sentence 1: subject: ______________________ verb: ______________________

   Sentence 2: subject: ______________________ verb: ______________________

2. Determine if the subject performed the action.

   Sentence 1: ____

   Sentence 2: ____

3. Identify each sentence as either active or passive.

   Sentence 1: ______________________

   Sentence 2: ______________________

■ ■ ■ ■ ■ ■ ■ ■ ■ ■ ■ ■ ■ ■ ■

1. Sentence 1: The subject is the child; the verb is was beaten.
   Sentence 2: The subject is the mother; the verb is beat.
2. Sentence 1: The subject (child) did not do the beating (the child received the beating).
   Sentence 2: The subject (mother) did perform the action of beating.
3. Sentence 1: Passive.
   Sentence 2: Active.

One reason for using the active voice will be clear if you count the words in the following sentences.

Active:	The man shot the woman.	(5)
Passive:	The woman was shot by the man.	(7)
Active:	The mother beat the child.	(5)
Passive:	The child was beaten by the mother.	(7)
Active:	The speeding car struck the wall.	(6)
Passive:	The wall was struck by the speeding car.	(8)

Active:	John won the first three rounds.	(6)
Passive:	The first three rounds were won by John.	(8)

Notice that the active sentences are shorter and less wordy. They are also more forceful and direct. In short, they are clearer.

Use the active voice.

➢ Identification

Identify each sentence as either active (A) or passive (P).

______ 1. The large pizza was eaten by the patrolman.

______ 2. The patrolman ate the large pizza.

______ 3. At this time, because the children's mother could not be reached, the children were put into protective custody and transported to the police station.

______ 4. The garage door was observed to be off the track and bent up.

______ 5. The officer found the murder weapon in a culvert.

■ ■ ■ ■ ■ ■ ■ ■ ■ ■ ■ ■ ■ ■ ■ ■

1.P, 2.A, 3.P, 4.P, 5.A

Statements are usually clearer in the active voice.

➢ Improvement

Improve the following sentences by changing them from passive to active. If the sentence is already active, leave it and write OK.

1. The suspect was arrested by Officer Donnelly. ______________________________

   ____

2. On Friday, 9-13-20--, a fire was discovered at the above location by the manager of the store.

   ____

3. Jay Anderson was interviewed at the school in the presence of his father by Officer Jorgenson.

   ____

4. The victim's body was discovered in the living room area by firefighters. ______________

   ____

5. The medical examiner took pictures of the victim and removed his body. ______________

   ____

6. Southern Security notified this department at 2016 hours that a bomb had gone off in a locker.

   ____

7. The man was described by the caretaker's wife, Mrs. Seifert, as a white male, approximately 35 years old, 6′ 2″, 175 pounds, with black hair.

   ____

   ____

■ ■ ■ ■ ■ ■ ■ ■ ■ ■ ■ ■ ■ ■ ■ ■ ■

1. Officer Donnelly arrested the suspect.
2. On Friday, 9-13-20--, the manager of the store discovered a fire at the above location.
3. Officer Jorgenson interviewed Jay Anderson at the school in the presence of his father.
4. Firefighters discovered the victim's body in the living room.
5. OK
6. OK
7. The caretaker's wife, Mrs. Seifert, described the man as a white male, approximately 35 years old, 6′ 2″, 175 pounds, with black hair.

Although most sentences should be in the active voice, a *passive* sentence is acceptable in the following situations:

1. If the doer of the action is unknown, unimportant, or obvious.

   Example: The gun had been fired three times.
   ⇒ We don't know who fired it. This is better than "Someone had fired the gun three times."

Example: The boy has been suspended six times.
⇒ Who suspended him is not important.

Example: Felix Umburger was paroled in April.
⇒ *Who* is obviously the parole board.

2. When you want to call special attention to the receiver of the action rather than the doer.

Example: Officer Morris was promoted after the examination.
⇒ Not only is it unimportant who promoted him, you want to call attention to Officer Morris.

3. When it would be unfair or embarrassing to be mentioned by name.

Example: The wrong film was sent.
⇒ Better than: Sergeant Fairchild sent the wrong film.

Example: Insufficient evidence was gathered at the crime scene.
⇒ Better than: Detective Hanks gathered insufficient evidence at the crime scene.

➢ Practice

Read the following sentences. Determine if each is active (A) or passive (P) and if it should be changed. If it should be changed, make the change in the space provided. If it should not be changed, simply write OK.

_____ 1. I was informed by the manager that they have a security system. ____________________

____

_____ 2. The complainant was advised by me to be cautious, but not to let the matter interfere with his activities. ____

____

_____ 3. The suspect was released on bail last Thursday. ____________________________

____

_____ 4. At 2140 hours on 02/21/20--, the defendant was placed under arrest by me for furnishing liquor to a minor. ____

____

_____ 5. The defendant was then driven to the precinct by myself and the store nurse.

____

■ ■ ■ ■ ■ ■ ■ ■ ■ ■ ■ ■ ■ ■ ■

1. P Should be active: The manager informed me that they have a security system.
2. P Should be active: I advised the complainant to be cautious, but not to let the matter interfere with his activities.
3. P OK as it is; who released him is not important.
4. P Should be active: At 2140 hours on 02/21/20--, I placed the defendant under arrest for furnishing liquor to a minor.
5. P Should be active: The store nurse and I then drove the defendant to the precinct.

The active voice is preferable,
unless there is a specific reason to use the passive voice.

➢ Application

Use the following facts to write an opening paragraph in a vandalism report. You will need to supply such information as how the vandalism was reported and what actions were taken.

WHO:	Subject(s): Unknown. Victim: Tim M. Jones, 6707 10th St., Pompano Beach, FL 33062.
WHAT:	Damage of private property; specifically, cutting the vinyl top of Jones' 1996 Pontiac Sunbird and scratching the painted finish.
WHEN:	Between 2330 hrs., July 3, 20--, and 1930 hrs., July 4, 20--.
WHERE:	The parking lot adjacent to 6707 10th St., Pompano Beach, FL 33062.
HOW NOTIFIED:	Call from victim at 1935 hours, July 4, 20--.
HOW:	With an unidentified sharp object.
WHY:	Unknown.

Write your report on your own paper. Be sure to use the active voice most of the time.

■ ■ ■ ■ ■ ■ ■ ■ ■ ■ ■ ■ ■ ■ ■

Check your report by this criterion:

⇒ Is each sentence in the active voice unless there is a specific reason for using the passive voice? ______ Yes ______ No

The following sample report gives you an idea of how this report might have been written.

Vandalism

On July 4, 20--, at 1935 hours, I received a phone call from Tim M. Jones, 6707 10th St., Pompano Beach, FL 33062, regarding damage to his car.

Jones reported that he had driven his 1996 Pontiac Sunbird home from a downtown bar about 2330 hrs., July 3, 20--, and parked it in the parking lot adjacent to his home. When he went out to the parking lot at about 1930 hrs., July 4, 20--, he discovered that the top had been cut and that the exterior painted finish had been scratched in five places. He had no idea who might have done the damage. There were no witnesses to the vandalism.

I advised Mr. Jones to contact his insurance agent.

Note that all sentences are active except the one containing the information that the top had been cut and the finish scratched. This sentence is passive because the doer of the action is unknown. The passive voice is preferred to a sentence such as, "He discovered that person or persons unknown (or someone) had cut the top and scratched the finish."

MODIFICATION

The importance of including details has already been discussed in Chapter Two. How you add these details is critical to clear writing.

Many details can be stated as **modifiers**—words that describe other words. For example, in the phrase, "the new, blue uniform," the words *new* and *blue* modify the word *uniform*. In the phrase "the only suspect," the word *only* modifies the word *suspect*. In the sentence, "The police officer who fired the shot was accurate," the phrase *who fired the shot* modifies the word *police officer*.

➢ Application

Underline the modifiers in the following sentences.

1. He was only late once, but he was quickly fired.

2. The angry suspect refused to answer.

3. The squad car with the emergency equipment was unavailable.

4. The robbery was committed by someone who knew what he was doing.

5. He placed the evidence in an envelope.

■ ■ ■ ■ ■ ■ ■ ■ ■ ■ ■ ■ ■ ■ ■ ■ ■

1. only, once, quickly
2. angry
3. squad, with the emergency equipment
4. who knew what he was doing
5. in an envelope

Misplaced Modifiers

Clear writing demands that modifiers *not* be separated from the words they modify. This is especially true of the words *almost*, *just*, *merely*, *nearly*, and *only*.

Place modifiers as close as possible to the words they modify.

Examples:

Wrong:	He gave the gun to his partner <u>that he had bought for his friend</u>.
Right:	He gave the gun <u>that he had bought for his friend</u> to his partner.
Reason:	He did not buy his *partner* for a friend; he bought the *gun*.
Wrong:	She could see the men who robbed her <u>through her window</u>.
Right:	She could see <u>through her window</u> the men who robbed her.
Reason:	The men did not *rob her* through her window; she *saw* them through her window.
Wrong:	By skipping lunch, Joe had <u>nearly</u> lost ten pounds.
Right:	By skipping lunch, Joe had lost <u>nearly</u> ten pounds.
Wrong:	He <u>only</u> shot one victim.
Right:	He shot <u>only</u> one victim.

➢ Identification

Underline the modifiers in each sentence and identify whether the modification is correct (C) or incorrect (I). If incorrectly modified, rewrite the sentence correctly in the space underneath.

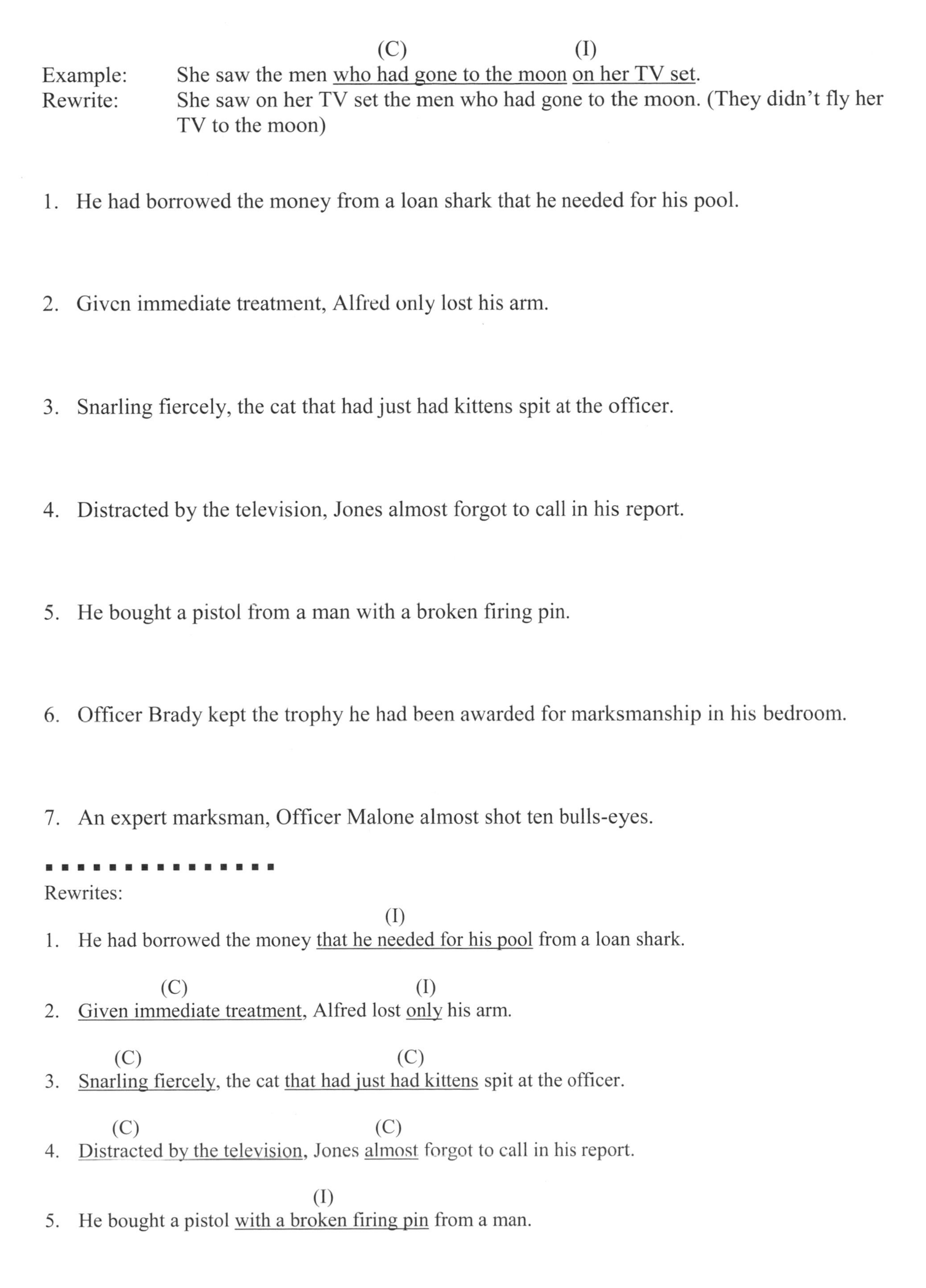

(C) (I)
Example: She saw the men who had gone to the moon on her TV set.
Rewrite: She saw on her TV set the men who had gone to the moon. (They didn't fly her TV to the moon)

1. He had borrowed the money from a loan shark that he needed for his pool.

2. Given immediate treatment, Alfred only lost his arm.

3. Snarling fiercely, the cat that had just had kittens spit at the officer.

4. Distracted by the television, Jones almost forgot to call in his report.

5. He bought a pistol from a man with a broken firing pin.

6. Officer Brady kept the trophy he had been awarded for marksmanship in his bedroom.

7. An expert marksman, Officer Malone almost shot ten bulls-eyes.

■ ■ ■ ■ ■ ■ ■ ■ ■ ■ ■ ■ ■ ■ ■ ■

Rewrites:

(I)
1. He had borrowed the money that he needed for his pool from a loan shark.

(C) (I)
2. Given immediate treatment, Alfred lost only his arm.

(C) (C)
3. Snarling fiercely, the cat that had just had kittens spit at the officer.

(C) (C)
4. Distracted by the television, Jones almost forgot to call in his report.

(I)
5. He bought a pistol with a broken firing pin from a man.

6. Officer Brady kept in his bedroom (I) the trophy he had been awarded for marksmanship (C).

7. An expert marksman (C), Officer Malone shot almost (I) ten bulls-eyes.

Note that in 1 and 5, the phrases from a loan shark and from a man will be in the correct position when the misplaced modifiers are moved.

Misplaced modifiers may confuse the reader.

➢ Improvement

For each of the following sentences, underline any misplaced modifiers and rewrite the sentence using correct modification.

Example: He cleared his throat and addressed the victim, choosing his words well.
Rewrite(s): He cleared his throat and, choosing his words well, addressed the victim.
or Choosing his words well, he cleared his throat and addressed the victim.

1. The officer ordered the man to stop several times.

2. The police reached the conclusion that DeChaine killed her because her driver's license was found in his home.

3. Here are some suggestions for handling obscene phone calls from the police department.

4. The robber was a 5′ 10″ man, with a heavy mustache weighing 155-160 pounds.

5. We then took the keg back to the station which was three-fourths empty.

6. The suitcase was found on the hallway floor partially opened.

7. I saw two males in the back seat holding beer cans who appeared to be juveniles.

8. Having forgotten to take her pills, his wife had gotten nearly pregnant.

9. Without asking to be repaid, the sergeant nearly loaned us all the money we needed.

10. The search turned up a black man's wallet.

■ ■ ■ ■ ■ ■ ■ ■ ■ ■ ■ ■ ■ ■ ■ ■

Rewrites:

1. Several times the officer ordered the man to stop.
2. Because her driver's license was found in his home, the police reached the conclusion that DeChaine killed her.
3. Here are some suggestions from the police department for handling obscene phone calls.
4. The robber was a 5′ 10″ man, weighing 155-160 pounds, with a heavy mustache.
5. We then took the keg, which was three-fourths empty, back to the station.
6. The partially opened suitcase was found on the hallway floor. *or* The suitcase was found partially opened on the hallway floor.
7. I saw two males who appeared to be juveniles holding beer cans in the back seat.
8. Having forgotten to take her pills, his wife had nearly gotten pregnant.
9. Without asking to be repaid, the sergeant loaned us nearly all the money we needed.
10. The search turned up a man's black wallet.

Squinting Modifiers

In a **squinting modifier**, a word or phrase could modify both the word it follows and the word it precedes. As a result, you can have two possible meanings for the sentence.

Modifiers should clearly modify only one word or phrase.

Examples:

Wrong: The rains that the crops had needed badly damaged the roads.
Right: The rains that the crops had badly needed damaged the roads.

Wrong: He decided at that instant to fire his gun.
Right: At that instant he decided to fire his gun.

➢ Identification

Underline any squinting modifiers and place a check mark above the two words or phrases they might modify. Then rewrite the sentence to be clear.

✓ ✓

Example: The man who watched her steadily sipped his drink.
Reason: The man may have been *watching* steadily or *sipping* steadily
Rewrite: The man who steadily watched her sipped his drink. *or* The man who watched her sipped his drink steadily.

1. The bullet that had pierced his chest deeply worried the doctor.

2. The officer had planned without the victim's statement to arrest the suspect.

3. The witness he had questioned awkwardly began to leave.

■ ■ ■ ■ ■ ■ ■ ■ ■ ■ ■ ■ ■ ■ ■

✓ ✓

1. The bullet that had pierced his chest deeply worried the doctor.
Rewrites: The bullet that had deeply pierced his chest worried the doctor. *or* The bullet that had pierced his chest worried the doctor deeply.

✓ ✓

2. The officer had planned without the victim's statement to arrest the suspect.
Rewrites: The officer had, without the victim's statement, planned to arrest the suspect. *or* The officer had planned to arrest the suspect without the victim's statement.

✓ ✓

3. The witness he had questioned awkwardly began to leave.
Rewrites: The witness he had awkwardly questioned began to leave. *or* The witness he had questioned began to leave awkwardly.

Placement of the modifier can determine the meaning of a sentence.

➢ Improvement

Improve the following sentences by correcting any squinting modifiers. Underline the modifier, place a check mark above the words it could possibly modify, and rewrite the sentence to be clear. If it correct as is, write OK.

1. The woman Mark was dating secretly wanted to get married.

2. The brakes that he applied badly marked the road.

3. The door that he opened quickly closed.

4. He looked sadly at the damaged car.

5. He had planned with his accomplice to rob the liquor store.

■ ■ ■ ■ ■ ■ ■ ■ ■ ■ ■ ■ ■ ■ ■

1. The woman Mark was ✓dating <u>secretly</u> ✓wanted to get married.
   Rewrites: The woman Mark was secretly dating wanted to get married. *or* The woman Mark was dating wanted to get married secretly. *or* Secretly, the woman Mark was dating wanted to get married.

2. The brakes that he ✓applied <u>badly</u> ✓marked the road.
   Rewrites: The brakes that he badly applied marked the road. *or* The brakes that he applied marked the road badly.
3. The door that he ✓opened <u>quickly</u> ✓closed.
   Rewrites: The door that he quickly opened closed. *or* The door that he opened closed quickly.

4. OK
5. He had ✓planned <u>with his accomplice</u> ✓to rob the liquor store.
   Rewrites: He had, without his accomplice, planned to rob the liquor store. (he did the planning alone) *or* He had planned to rob the liquor store without his accomplice. (he was going to rob alone)

Dangling Modifiers

A **dangling modifier** is a group of words that does not refer clearly and logically to any word in the sentence.

> **Place modifiers so they refer clearly and directly to a word or phrase in the sentence.**

Examples:

Wrong:	Upon arrival, the complainant told me what happened. (The complainant did not arrive.)
Right:	Upon my arrival, the complainant told me what happened.
Wrong:	By following directions, mistakes were avoided.
Right:	By following directions, the officers avoided mistakes.

➢ Identification

Underline the modifiers in the following sentences and place a check above the word(s) being modified. If the modifier does *not* have a word for which you can place a check, or if the checked word is the *wrong* word to be modified, place a "D" (for dangling) above the modifier.

D ✓

Example: By keeping to the back roads, the police were avoided. (The police did not keep to the back roads.)

1. Completely exhausted, the man collapsed to the floor.
2. Although only standing there innocently, the police arrested him.
3. To remove the evidence of his crime, his wife's body was burned.
4. Before arresting him, the suspect should have been told of his rights.

■ ■ ■ ■ ■ ■ ■ ■ ■ ■ ■ ■ ■ ■ ■

✓

1. Completely exhausted, the man collapsed to the floor. (OK as written)

D ✓ ✓

2. Although only standing there innocently, the police arrested him. (Who is standing there—the police or him?)

D ✓

3. To remove the evidence of his crime, his wife's body was burned. (Rewrite: His wife's body was burned to remove the evidence of his crime. *Or* better yet, if you know "he" did the burning: He burned his wife's body to remove the evidence of his crime.)

D ✓

4. Before arresting him, the suspect should have been told of his rights. (Rewrite: The suspect should have been told of his rights before he was arrested.)

Dangling modifiers are puzzling to the reader.

➢ Improvement

Rewrite any sentences that contain dangling modifiers. If no changes are needed, write OK.

1. When completely plastered, volunteers will paint the property room.

   ____

2. Seeing nothing there of interest, the stakeout was abandoned.

   ____

3. Submit the report with the required supplements attached to your sergeant.

   ____

4. Miami police killed a man with a machete.

   ____

5. By opening the car door, the heat became more bearable.

   ____

6. After entering the store, the telephone rang.

   ____

7. Three cars were reported stolen by the Concord police yesterday.

   ____

8. Walking up the hill, two paths were found.

   ____

9. Kissing his wife good-bye, the house was quickly left by the lieutenant.

   ____

10. To ensure arresting the correct person, you should obtain a complete description.

____

■ ■ ■ ■ ■ ■ ■ ■ ■ ■ ■ ■ ■ ■ ■ ■

1. Volunteers will paint the property room when it is completely plastered.
2. Seeing nothing there of interest, we abandoned the stakeout.
3. Submit to your sergeant the report with the required supplements attached.
4. Miami police killed a man who had a machete.
5. When we opened the car door, the heat became more bearable. *or* By opening the car door, we made the heat more bearable.
6. After we entered the store, the telephone rang.
7. The Concord police reported three cars stolen yesterday.
8. We found two paths as we walked up the hill. *or* Walking up the hill, we found two paths.
9. Kissing his wife good-bye, the lieutenant quickly left the house.
10. OK

Correct modification can do much to make your writing clear.
When you edit your reports, pay careful attention to your modifiers.
Be certain they are as close as possible to the word(s) they modify.

➢ Application

Write a short (two or three paragraph) report describing the stop of an apparently drunken driver. You will need to supply all the details. Try to use as many modifying words and phrases as possible. (Use your own paper to write this report.)

■ ■ ■ ■ ■ ■ ■ ■ ■ ■ ■ ■ ■ ■ ■ ■

Check your report:

⇒ Are all sentences in the active voice (unless there is a specific reason for using the passive voice)? _____ Yes _____ No

⇒ Are all modifiers correctly placed? _____ Yes _____ No

⇒ Does your report meet the criteria for an effective report? (see p.46) _____ Yes _____ No

PRONOUN REFERENCE

A **pronoun** is a word used in place of a noun. For example:

Noun	*Pronoun*
Hank	he
Karen	she
Officers Malone and Schultz	they
the house	it

If you were to read the sentence, "He was late," you would have no idea who *he* referred to. The sentence would not be clear. Always be sure that a pronoun refers to a specific noun.

Pronouns should clearly refer to only one person or object.

Examples:

Wrong: When I nod my head, you hit it.
Right: When I nod my head, you hit the anvil.

Wrong: I saw Joe talking to Fred today, and he looked angry. (*Who* looked angry–Joe or Fred?)
Right: I saw Joe talking to Fred today, and Joe looked angry.

➢ Identification

Underline the pronouns in the following sentences. Place a check above the noun referred to by the pronoun. If there is no noun referred to, or if two nouns could be referred to by the same pronoun, place a question mark (?) above the pronoun.

Example: My sister (✓) called Joyce (✓) before she (?) left the office. (*Who* left the office? My sister or Joyce?)

1. Alfred told Marty that he would soon be a police officer.

2. After taking the key from the purse, the robber threw it in the river.

3. Having heard much about the movie, I wanted to see it.

4. Angered by the hostile language, Mark told Al he would have to leave.

5. The vice-president told the detective that he had almost no reason to suspect the migrant workers.

■ ■ ■ ■ ■ ■ ■ ■ ■ ■ ■ ■ ■ ■ ■ ■

1. Alfred ✓ told Marty ✓ that he ? would soon be a police officer.

2. After taking the key ✓ from the purse ✓, the robber threw it ? in the river.

3. Having heard much about the movie ✓, I wanted to see it.

4. Angered by the hostile language, Mark ✓ told Al ✓ he ? would have to leave.

5. The vice-president ✓ told the detective ✓ that he ? had almost no reason to suspect the migrant workers.

An unclear pronoun reference leaves a question in the reader's mind.

➢ Improvement

Improve the following sentences by correcting any instances of faulty pronoun reference. You will need to decide to whom you want the pronoun to refer.

Example: Alfred told Marty that he would soon be a police officer.

Change to: Alfred told Marty, "I will soon be a police officer."
or: Alfred told Marty, "You will soon be a police officer."

1. Alberto tried a full-gainer off the ten-meter board. It is always dangerous.

____

2. Dr. Davis told his brother that he was in good health.

____

3. If the first chapter of the book bores me, I don't read it.

____

4. Sam told the policeman that he had made a mistake.

____

5. Paul told his brother that he would never understand true love.

____

6. Officer Peterson read the suspect the Miranda warning which he understood.

____

7. The suspect was seen by Jim Mays, the resident manager, while he was in the elevator.

____

■ ■ ■ ■ ■ ■ ■ ■ ■ ■ ■ ■ ■ ■ ■ ■

Here are possible revisions. Your sentences may be worded slightly differently.

1. Alberto tried a full-gainer, always dangerous, off the ten-meter board.
   Alberto tried a full-gainer off the always dangerous ten-meter board.
2. Dr. Davis told his brother, "I am in good health."
   Dr. Davis told his brother, "You are in good health."
3. If the first chapter of the book bores me, I skip that chapter.
   If the first chapter of a book bores me, I don't read the book.
4. Sam told the policeman, "I made a mistake."
   Sam told the policeman, "You made a mistake."
5. Paul told his brother, "I will never understand true love."
   Paul told his brother, "You will never understand true love."
6. Officer Peterson read the Miranda warning, which he understood, to the suspect.
   Officer Peterson read the suspect the Miranda warning, which the suspect understood.
7. While Jim Mays, the resident manager, was in the elevator, he saw the suspect.
   While the suspect was in the elevator, Jim Mays, the resident manager, saw him.

Do *not* overuse pronouns. It is acceptable to use proper names repeatedly to minimize confusion. For example:

> James Wright and Joe Flynn were stopped in front of 172 Main Street in Montgomery. Wright said that they had just left Wright's home and that Flynn was there all day with Wright and Wright's wife.

Even though this sentence uses *Wright* five times, it is clear in thought and is better than:

> James Wright and Joe Flynn were stopped in front of 172 Main Street in Montgomery. He said that they had just left his house and that he was there all day with him and his wife.

When in doubt, use the proper name, not a pronoun.

PARALLELISM

Parallel means equal or similar. Clear writing uses **parallelism**, that is, the same type of structure for similar parts of a sentence.

Word similar ideas in similar ways.

Examples:

Wrong:	Jim drew a deep breath and his eyes closed. (active/passive)
Right:	Jim drew a deep breath and closed his eyes. (active/active)
Wrong:	Officer White asked the witness' name, phone number, and where he lived.
Right:	Officer White asked the witness' name, phone number, and address.

You don't have to know how to name the different structures used in a sentence. You should be able to see (and hear, if you read the sentence aloud) when a sentence contains different structures.

➢ Identification

Place a ✓ beside any sentence which is not parallel and OK by those that are parallel.

_____ 1. A police officer should be neat and clean.

_____ 2. Jogging is better exercise than to swim.

_____ 3. The suspect was described as approximately 6′ 3″, light brown hair, wearing a long green coat.

_____ 4. Mrs. Dix described the suspect as a small, slight, effeminate, white male customer.

_____ 5. A citizen's arrest was made by the complainant, and I took custody of the defendant.

■ ■ ■ ■ ■ ■ ■ ■ ■ ■ ■ ■ ■ ■ ■ ■

1. OK, 2. ✓, 3. ✓, 4. OK, 5. ✓

The use of parallelism results in smoother sentences.

➢ Improvement

Rewrite any sentences that are not parallel. Otherwise, write OK.

1. As part of his daily exercise he alternates between running and walking.

 ____

2. The suspect barely tolerated his wife, largely ignored his children, and his job he neglected almost completely. ______________________________

 ____

3. Acting wisely is more difficult than to think wisely.

 ____

4. Police officers want respect and to be liked.

 ____

5. The victim was badly cut on the arm, had a fractured rib, and two teeth were knocked out.

 ____

6. Officer Holt pursued the suspect, commanded him to halt, and then the suspect was apprehended by him. ______________________________

 ____

7. Despite his grumbling, George found eating his words easier than to lose his job.

 ____

8. The department decided that to buy the equipment was probably cheaper than leasing it.

 ____

9. The policewoman was tall, with blond hair and a graceful manner. ____________________

____

10. The burglar was obviously experienced and had an intelligent mind. ____________________

____

■ ■ ■ ■ ■ ■ ■ ■ ■ ■ ■ ■ ■ ■ ■

Here are possible revisions. Your sentences may be worded slightly differently.

1. OK
2. The suspect barely tolerated his wife, largely ignored his children, and almost completely neglected his job.
3. Acting wisely is more difficult than thinking wisely. *or* To act wisely is more difficult than to think wisely.
4. Police officers want to be respected and liked. *or* Police officers want respect and friendship.
5. The victim had a bad cut on the arm, a fractured rib, and two knocked-out teeth.
6. Officer Holt pursued the suspect, commanded him to halt, and then apprehended him.
7. Despite his grumbling, George found eating his words easier than losing his job. *or* Despite his grumbling, George found that to eat his words was easier than to lose his job.
8. The department decided that buying the equipment was probably cheaper than leasing it. *or* The department decided that to buy the equipment was cheaper than to lease it.
9. The policewoman was tall, blond, and graceful. *or* The policewoman was a tall, graceful blond.
10. The burglar was obviously experienced and intelligent.

SUMMARY

Use the first person to refer to yourself. If the subject performs the action, the sentence is in the active voice. If the subject does *not* perform the action, the sentence is in the passive voice. Use the active voice. Statements are usually clearer in the active voice. The active voice is preferable, unless there is a specific reason to use the passive voice.

Place modifiers as close as possible to the words they modify. Misplaced modifiers may confuse the reader. Modifiers should clearly modify only one word or phrase. Placement of the modifier can determine the meaning of a sentence. Place modifiers so they refer clearly and directly to a word or phrase in the sentence. Dangling modifiers are puzzling to the reader. Correct modification can do much to make your writing clear. When you edit your reports, pay careful attention to your modifiers. Be certain they are as close as possible to the word(s) they modify.

Pronouns should clearly refer to only one person or object. An unclear pronoun reference leaves a question in the reader's mind. When in doubt, use the proper name, not a pronoun.

Word similar ideas in similar ways. The use of parallelism results in smoother sentences.

You may wish to review this chapter before completing the self-test on p.219.

Chapter Six

CHOOSING THE RIGHT WORDS

Do you know:

- What types of words are preferred in police reports?
- How to achieve the appropriate tone in a police report?
- What specific techniques can be used to reduce wordiness?
- How eliminating unnecessary words affects a report's effectiveness?

Key terms: redundant, tone

WORD CHOICE

The words used in a police report must be carefully selected. Some officers use lots of police jargon and big words, perhaps thinking that will impress the reader. That's a mistake. The writer's job is to convey information clearly. Rutledge (2000, p.64) reports on a survey where people were asked what the term *recrement* meant. The term had been used in a police report stating: "The officer used a recrement of force." Only 2 percent of those surveyed could correctly identify what was meant. Next they were given six alternatives to this term. The first, *supererogation*, was understood by 3 percent. The second, *superfluity*, by 10 percent. The third, *surplusage*, by 25 percent, even though it isn't really a word! The fourth, *overabundance*, was understood by 85 percent, and the fifth, *excess*, by 95 percent. What do you think was the alternative understood by 100 percent of those surveyed? *Too much*. That's plain English. If you want your reader to understand what you write, do *not* use legal, technical, unfamiliar, or slang words.

Use common words, but avoid slang.

Examples:

Wrong: He <u>inaugurated</u> the investigation.
Right: He <u>began</u> the investigation.

Wrong: <u>Said</u> informant <u>terminated</u> the discussion.
Right: <u>The</u> informant <u>ended</u> the discussion.

Wrong:	The witness was a total fox.	(slang)
Right:	The witness was an attractive woman.	

NOTE: Law enforcement officers tend to overuse the words *stated* and *advised* in their narratives. It is better to simply write *said* (e.g., The victim *said* he was robbed.)

➢ Practice

In the spaces provided, give a more common alternative for each word or group of words.

1. advised — 1. ____________________
2. approximately — 2. ____________________
3. ascertained — 3. ____________________
4. commenced — 4. ____________________
5. contacted — 5. ____________________
6. demonstrated — 6. ____________________
7. detected — 7. ____________________
8. endeavored — 8. ____________________
9. exited — 9. ____________________
10. indicated — 10. ____________________
11. informed — 11. ____________________
12. initiated — 12. ____________________
13. inquired — 13. ____________________
14. noted — 14. ____________________
15. notified — 15. ____________________
16. observed — 16. ____________________
17. proceeded — 17. ____________________
18. related — 18. ____________________

19. rendered assistance 19. ______________________

20. stated 20. ______________________

21. stationary mode 21. ______________________

22. transported 22. ______________________

23. utilized 23. ______________________

24. It is impossible for one adequately to assess the worth of a volume merely by examining the outer covering.

____

25. An individual who vacillates when there is need of action will find himself beyond the hope of future success.

____

■ ■ ■ ■ ■ ■ ■ ■ ■ ■ ■ ■ ■ ■ ■ ■

1. told; 2. about; 3. determined, found out; 4. started; 5. called; 6. showed; 7. smelled, felt, heard, saw; 8. tried; 9. left; 10. said, pointed, nodded; 11. told; 12. began, started; 13. asked; 14. saw, said; 15. told, wrote; 16. saw; 17. went, began; 18. told; 19. helped; 20. said; 21. stopped; 22. took; 23. used; 24. You can't judge a book by its cover; 25. He who hesitates is lost.

➢ Identification

Underline any words which should *not* commonly be used in report writing. If the sentence is correct, write OK.

1. He sent a check in lieu of cash.
2. The robber failed to ascertain the facts necessary to effectuate the crime.
3. His account of the crime was lousy, but he gave a swell description of the suspect.
4. The investigation will be held in abeyance pending further investigation.
5. Said information is herewith ordered to appear in court.

■ ■ ■ ■ ■ ■ ■ ■ ■ ■ ■ ■ ■ ■ ■ ■

1. in lieu of; 2. ascertain, effectuate; 3. lousy, swell; 4. in abeyance, pending; 5. said, herewith

Reports should be straightforward and factual, using common words.

➢ Improvement

Improve the following sentences by underlining any words that should *not* commonly be used in report writing and substituting common words. Sometimes the word can be left out and no replacement word added.

Example: The aforesaid case was closed last week. (no replacement word needed)

1. He used a club in lieu of a nightstick.
2. After obtaining said statement, the officer questioned the other party.
3. The investigation commenced with a careful search of said premises.
4. The suspect was letiginous and hirsute.
5. The arsonist blew in from Miami, caught a flick, torched the theater, and then split for Reno.
6. The victim expired prior to the arrival of the ambulance.
7. The corpus delicti was typical of the psychopath's modus operandi.
8. All police personnel functioning in the capacity of supervisors will indicate that they have had the opportunity to take due cognizance of said notice by transmitting signed acknowledgment of receipt of same.
9. I observed that, by the way the man was driving, he was smashed.

■ ■ ■ ■ ■ ■ ■ ■ ■ ■ ■ ■ ■ ■ ■ ■

1. He used a club instead of a nightstick.
2. After getting the statement, the officer questioned the other person.
3. The investigation began with a careful search of the premises.
4. The suspect had freckles and a beard.
5. The arsonist came from Miami, saw a movie, set fire to the theater, and then left for Reno.
6. The victim died before the ambulance arrived.
7. The facts surrounding the murder were typical of the psychopath's usual manner of operation.
8. All police supervisors should send a signed statement that they have received the notice.
9. I saw by the way the man was driving that he was intoxicated.

TONE

The **tone** of a report refers to how the writer relates to the reader, that is the "tone of voice" used to present information. Tone may be described as friendly, serious, distant, angry, bitter, sarcastic, argumentative, or objective.

Police reports should use a serious, objective tone.

Examples:

Inappropriate: He interviewed the broompusher.
Appropriate: He interviewed the custodian.

Inappropriate: The suspect began to sweat bullets.
Appropriate: The suspect began to perspire heavily.

➢ Practice

In the middle blank, give an appropriate alternative for the terms in the right and left columns.

	Positive/Formal	Neutral/Informal	Negative/Slang
1.	dine	____________________	chow down
2.	fortitude	____________________	guts
3.	man's best friend	____________________	mutt
4.	inebriated	____________________	soused
5.	pass on	____________________	croak
6.	residence	____________________	pad

■■■■■■■■■■■■■■■■■

1. eat, 2. courage, 3. dog, 4. intoxicated, 5. die, 6. house

➢ Identification

Underline the word or words in each sentence which are inappropriate for a police report.

1. The burglary victim blubbered as he looked around his empty living room.
2. The perpetrator of this computer crime must have been an egghead.
3. The only witness to the attack was the old maid who lived next door.
4. The driver of the truck was obviously plastered.
5. The woman was walking to her car when she got popped.

■ ■ ■ ■ ■ ■ ■ ■ ■ ■ ■ ■ ■ ■ ■ ■

1. blubbered, 2. egghead, 3. old maid, 4. plastered, 5. popped

➢ Improvement

Improve the following sentences by underlining the inappropriate word or words and replacing them with a more neutral/informal word.

1. The man ran down the alley and got into some wheels. ____________________
2. The suspect was accused of abusing and neglecting the rug rat. ____________________
3. The defendant has been in the slammer on three previous occasions. ____________________
4. The detective received the call from a snitch. ____________________
5. The woman reached into her purse and pulled out a piece. ____________________

■ ■ ■ ■ ■ ■ ■ ■ ■ ■ ■ ■ ■ ■ ■ ■

1. replace <u>some wheels</u> with *car* or *vehicle*
2. replace <u>rug rat</u> with *child*
3. replace <u>the slammer</u> with *jail*
4. replace <u>a snitch</u> with an *informant*
5. replace <u>piece</u> with *gun*

Note: Be especially careful of the word *claim*. If you write, “The victim claimed that the television cost $500,” it may sound as though you don’t believe the victim.

CONCISENESS

One characteristic of an effective report is that it is concise—all unnecessary words have been left out. By being concise, you can make your reports shorter and cut down reading time. Being concise does *not* mean leaving out important details. For example, look at the following wordy sentence:

> He gave chase to a car that was a green 1981 Cadillac, personalized license SHYSTER.

It would *not* be right to improve the sentence this way:

> He gave chase to a car.

It *would* be right to correct it like this:

> He chased a green, 1981 Cadillac, personalized license # SHYSTER.

The details about the car are important and should not be omitted. But the phrases "gave chase to" and "a car that was" are unnecessary.

In Chapter Three you looked at some ways to reduce wordiness. Now it's time to become very specific about writing concisely, since this is one of the greatest weaknesses of most reports, not just reports written by police officers.

One way to reduce wordiness is to eliminate **redundant** words and phrases, that is, words that repeat themselves.

Do not be redundant.

Examples:

Wordy: The car was green in color.
Concise: The car was green. (green is a color)

Wordy: He repeated each and every word.
Concise: He repeated each word. *or* He repeated every word.

➢ Practice

In the spaces to the right, give a more concise way of expressing the idea in the left column.

1. month of July 1. ______________________
2. important essentials 2. ______________________
3. brown in color 3. ______________________
4. basic fundamentals 4. ______________________
5. small in size 5. ______________________
6. state of California 6. ______________________
7. at a later date 7. ______________________

■ ■ ■ ■ ■ ■ ■ ■ ■ ■ ■ ■ ■ ■ ■ ■

1. July; 2. essentials (by definition, an essential is important); 3. brown; 4. basics, fundamentals (mean the same); 5. small; 6. California; 7. later

➢ Identification

Place a check by those sentences that contain redundant words or phrases. Write OK by those that don't.

________ 1. The suspect lived in the city of Miami.

________ 2. The victim worked nights and was gone when the fire broke out.

________ 3. If the lab destroys the samples, we'll have to sample over again.

________ 4. The suspicious package was square in shape and ticking loudly.

________ 5. The officer must first and foremost secure the scene of the crime.

________ 6. It is essential that you complete the entire form.

■ ■ ■ ■ ■ ■ ■ ■ ■ ■ ■ ■ ■ ■ ■ ■

1. ✓, 2. OK, 3. ✓, 4. ✓, 5. ✓, 6. OK

➢ Improvement

Underline any redundant words that should be removed to make each sentence more concise. If no changes are needed, write OK.

1. The detective was not sure the witness had spoken the actual truth.
2. The victim asked the question about the likelihood of testifying in court.
3. We assembled together a group of six women for the lineup.
4. The woman said she'd stop by at a time when her children were in school.
5. After stealing the man's wallet, the thief continued on up the street.
6. The gloves were exactly identical to the ones the killer had worn. The same identical shoes had also been worn.
7. The man had only ordered the magazine to receive the free gift.
8. The sergeant knew from past experience that crime was a problem in that neighborhood.
9. To write the report, I had to refer back to my notes and go over each and every detail.
10. The suspect's hair was short in length and red in color.

■ ■ ■ ■ ■ ■ ■ ■ ■ ■ ■ ■ ■ ■ ■

1. The detective was not sure the witness had spoken the actual truth.
2. The victim asked the question about the likelihood of testifying in court.
3. We assembled together a group of six women for the lineup.
4. The woman said she'd stop by at a time when her children were in school.
5. After stealing the man's wallet, the thief continued on up the street.
6. The gloves were exactly identical to the ones the killer had worn. The same* identical shoes had also been worn. (* you could also keep "same" and remove "identical"—use only one)
7. The man had only ordered the magazine to receive the free gift. (gifts *are* free)
8. The sergeant knew from past experience that crime was a problem in that neighborhood.
9. To write the report, I had to refer back to my notes and go over each* and every detail. (* you could also keep "each" and remove "every")
10. The suspect's hair was short in length and red in color.

You can also write *concisely* by:

1. Using the active voice.

   Wordy: The suspect was searched by the police officer.
   Concise: The police officer searched the suspect.

2. Using positive statements.

   Wordy: He was not very often on time.
   Concise: He was usually late.

3. Combining ideas into one sentence.

   Wordy: The suspect was tall. He was slender. He had a scar.
   Concise: The tall, slender suspect had a scar.

4. Avoiding frequent use of there is and there are.

   Wordy: There are many police officers risking their lives daily.
   Concise: Many police officers risk their lives daily.

5. Writing with verbs, not nouns.

   Wordy: The officer conducted an interview with Jack Jones.
   Concise: The officer interviewed Jack Jones.

6. Omitting all needless words.

   Wordy: He is a man who fears nothing.
   Concise: He fears nothing.

You don't need to remember these specific ways to reduce wordiness, but you *do* need to recognize and eliminate wordiness in your reports.

Make every word count.

Examples:

Wrong: The paint had been gouged by a metal object that had exerted pressure on it.
Right: A metal object had gouged the paint.

Wrong: Although he did not really want to, the witness told his version of the crime.
Right: Reluctantly, the witness told his version of the crime.

➢ Practice

In the spaces to the right, make each of the following phrases less wordy. You may want to think of a sentence using the phrase.

Example: on the occasion of (wordy) when (concise)

WORDY	CONCISE
1. in view of the fact that	1. ______________________
2. with reference to	2. ______________________
3. made a note of	3. ______________________
4. for the purpose of	4. ______________________
5. subsequent to	5. ______________________
6. along the lines of	6. ______________________
7. in case	7. ______________________
8. for the reason that	8. ______________________
9. comes into conflict with	9. ______________________
10. in the event that	10. ______________________
11. with respect to	11. ______________________
12. gives information to	12. ______________________
13. despite the fact that	13. ______________________
14. in the amount of	14. ______________________
15. in the nature of	15. ______________________
16. have need for	16. ______________________
17. is of the opinion	17. ______________________
18. had the feeling	18. ______________________
19. attempt to ascertain	19. ______________________

20. the perpetrator of the crime 20. ______________________________

21. observed 21. ______________________________

22. upon an individual basis 22. ______________________________

■ ■ ■ ■ ■ ■ ■ ■ ■ ■ ■ ■ ■ ■ ■ ■

1. since, because; 2. about; 3. noted; 4. for; 5. after; 6. like; 7. if; 8. because, since; 9. conflicts; 10. if; 11. about; 12. informs, tells; 13. although; 14. for; 15. like; 16. need; 17. believes, thinks; 18. felt; 19. determine; 20. the suspect; 21. saw; 22. individually

Eliminating unnecessary words makes your reports more effective.

➢ Identification

Underline any words that could be left out or replaced with something more concise. If no changes are needed, write OK.

1. Officer Gray took custody of two children ages six and eight years of age.
2. Dr. Hardy believes the detective could be of assistance in this matter.
3. Harold Hickory said that he has been in the State of Iowa for one month.
4. He also said that Jack Olson asked about the same identical clock that morning.
5. Officer Sorem ran on foot after the suspect.
6. He had seen a 1999 Honda Accord, green in color, parked next door.
7. Prior to this date and for a period of time of approximately six weeks, this department has been investigating a number of burglaries in this city.
8. The suspect then entered the vehicle and started it up.
9. I recognized his as being one Earl Robert O'Connor.
10. I looked into the suspect vehicle and saw from the outside of the car what appeared to be a fur piece that was light brown in color and appeared to be quite large in size.

■ ■ ■ ■ ■ ■ ■ ■ ■ ■ ■ ■ ■ ■ ■ ■

1. Officer Gray took custody of two children ages six and eight years <u>of age</u>.
2. Dr. Hardy believes the detective could <u>be of assistance</u> in this matter. (replace with the word *help*)

3. Harold Hickory said that he has been in the State of Iowa for one month.
4. He also said that Jack Olson asked about the same identical clock that morning. (omit one of these two words)
5. Officer Sorem ran on foot after the suspect.
6. He had seen a 1999 Honda Accord, green in color, parked next door. (move *green* to before *1999*)
7. Prior to this date and for a period of time of approximately six weeks, this department has been investigating a number of burglaries in this city. (replace *a number of* with *several*)
8. The suspect then entered the vehicle and started it up.
9. I recognized his as being one Earl Robert O'Connor.
10. I looked into the suspect vehicle and saw from the outside of the car what appeared to be a fur piece that was light brown in color and appeared to be quite large in size. (rewrite: *a large, light brown fur piece*)

In concise writing, every word counts.

➢ Improvement

Improve the following sentences by making every word count. Cross out all unnecessary words and phrases, insert any needed words, or rewrite the sentence if words need to be rearranged.

1. This report contains information that is of a confidential nature.
2. I opened the .410 shotgun to determine whether or not it was loaded.
3. I received a phone call from Mr. George Hattell who is the resident manager.
4. The gun was on the floor beside her body and her right arm, close to where the elbow bends.
5. The living room did not appear to have anything out of place. It was very neat.
6. There were no ice trays or alcoholic liquor bottles left out in the open.
7. We noticed that the temperature was very warm and that the thermometer registered at approximately 81-82 degrees.
8. We noticed that there was a lot of static electricity in the apartment.
9. There were two glasses, highball-type glasses, in the sink area of the kitchen.
10. The floor had a large amount of blood that appeared to be fairly dried or dry.
11. The glass that was on the vanity that contained possibly an alcoholic beverage was a highball glass and it had approximately ¾" of liquid in the bottom of the glass.

12. The seat of the toilet and the cover were in the down position.

13. The victim was lying in a position on her back.

14. The victim's father's name was Michael H. Reed. His address was Route #2, Silver Bay, California. His telephone number was 209-555-9999. Another possible telephone number for Mr. Reed was 209-555-9907 if he could not be reached at 209-555-9999.

■ ■ ■ ■ ■ ■ ■ ■ ■ ■ ■ ■ ■ ■ ■ ■

Rewrites:

1. This report contains confidential information.
2. I opened the .410 shotgun to determine if it was loaded.
3. I received a phone call from Mr. George Hattell, resident manager.
4. The gun was on the floor beside her right elbow.
5. The living room was orderly.
6. No ice trays or liquor bottles were in view.
7. The thermometer registered between 81 and 82 degrees.
8. We noticed much static electricity in the room.
9. Two highball-type glasses were in the kitchen's sink area.
10. The floor had a large amount of blood that appeared dry.
11. The highball glass on the vanity contained approximately ¾" of possibly alcoholic liquid.
12. The toilet seat and cover were down.
13. The victim was lying on her back.
14. The victim's father was Michael H. Reed, of Route #2, Silver Bay, CA, telephone number 209-555-9999 or 209-555-9907.

➢ Application

List seven ways to write more concisely.

1. ______________________________

2. ______________________________

3. ______________________________

4. ______________________________

5. ______________________________

6. ______________________________

7. ______________________________

■ ■ ■ ■ ■ ■ ■ ■ ■ ■ ■ ■ ■ ■ ■ ■

In any order:

1. Eliminate redundant words and phrases.
2. Use the active voice.
3. Use positive statements.
4. Combine ideas into one sentence.
5. Avoid frequent use of *there is* and *there are*.
6. Write with verbs, not nouns.
7. Omit all needless words.

Caution: Although you usually want to use words that are common, simple, and to the point, in some instances this is not necessarily the best alternative. Consider this advice: "An important part of training is how an officer explains himself in court. An ASR [aerosol spray] does not 'blind,' it temporarily closes the eyes by causing the capillaries of the eyes to dilate. An ASR does not 'choke,' it causes uncontrollable coughing by temporarily inflaming the mucous membranes of the throat. It does not cause 'pain,' it produces extreme discomfort" (Clede, 1992, p.58). See the point?

A Final Note: Work for a happy medium in choosing the words used in your reports. Include enough information, but not too much.

SUMMARY

Choosing the right words is a critical step in report writing. Use common words, but avoid slang. Reports should be straightforward and factual. Police reports should use a serious, objective tone. Do not be redundant. Eliminating unnecessary words makes your reports more effective. In concise writing, every word counts.

You may wish to review this chapter before completing the self-test on p.221.

REFERENCES

Clede, B. (1992, September). A bouquet of aerosol sprays. *Law and Order*, 57-58.

Rutledge, D. (2000). *The new police report manual* (2nd ed.). Incline Village, NV: Copperhouse Publishing Company.

Chapter Seven

GRAMMAR

Do you know:

- Which form of the pronoun to use?
- How to make your verb agree with your subject?
- When to use adjectives and adverbs?
- How to make your sentences negative?
- When to use articles?

Key terms: adjective, adverb, article, grammar

Grammar refers to the rules for how words change and combine to form sentences. You were introduced to grammar in Chapter Four in the discussion of *tense*. In English, our verbs change their form to indicate time: past, present, and future. For example:

Yesterday I wrote the report.	Past tense
Today I write the report.	Present tense
Tomorrow I will write the report.	Future tense

Most grammatical errors are like felonies—very serious. They can destroy the credibility of the writer. Because writing grammatically is so important, you may wish to read this chapter more than once to make certain you have mastered the concepts. This is especially true if you struggled with grammar previously.

The good news is that you are *not* going to have to diagram sentences or name parts of speech in this chapter. Fortunately, most police officers do *not* have major grammatical problems in their writing. Most of the problems are mechanical, e.g., spelling, capitalization, punctuation—problems that occur when you transfer ideas into written rather than spoken form.

A few kinds of grammatical errors *do* occur frequently in police reports. These include nonstandard use of:

- pronouns.
- subject and verb agreement.
- adjectives and adverbs.
- negation.
- articles.

You'll look at each category, beginning with the most troublesome and difficult (pronouns), and work through to the least troublesome and easiest (articles).

USE OF PRONOUNS

Recall, a pronoun is a word that takes the place of a noun. For example, instead of saying "Officer Jones," you could say "he." *He* is a pronoun. In English, pronouns change their form depending on how they are used in a sentence. Most of the changes cause little difficulty, but with a certain few you must be careful.

If the pronoun is the subject of the sentence, use:
I, we, you, he, she, it, they, who, whoever, whosoever.

If the pronoun is the object of the sentence, use:
me, us, you, him, her, it, them, whom, whomever, whomsoever.

If the pronoun is used to show possession, use:
my, mine, our, ours, your, yours, his, her, hers, its, their, theirs, whose, whosoever.

Examples:

Wrong:	Jim Lewis and me arrested the suspect.	
Right:	Jim Lewis and I arrested the suspect.	(subject)
Wrong:	He gave Jim and I a very rough time.	
Right:	He gave Jim and me a very rough time.	(object)
Wrong:	Us officers must stick together.	
Right:	We officers must stick together.	(subject)

Note: If you have difficulty deciding on the correct pronoun to use, read the sentence using just the pronoun you are having difficulty with, leaving out any potentially confusing words. For instance, in the first set of examples above, if you leave out "Jim Lewis and," you should be able to "hear" that "I arrested the suspect" is right and that "me arrested the suspect" is *not* right. Similarly, in the second set of examples, you should "hear" that "He gave me a very rough time" is right and that "He gave I a very rough time" is *not* right. Finally, in the third set of examples, "We must stick together" sounds right, whereas "Us must stick together" does *not* sound right. If in doubt, leave the confusing words out.

➢ Practice

Select the correct pronoun to be used in each instance.

1. The cards were sent to Tom and (she/her).
2. My partner and (I/me) have worked together for seven years.
3. It's (there's/theirs), not (your's/yours).
4. The two witnesses, Mr. Jones and (she/her), were there.
5. Between you and (I/me), I think we arrested the wrong person.
6. That problem is now entirely between you and (he/him).
7. Let's you and (I/me) run down this lead.
8. (Us/We) police officers must stand united on the issues.
9. The sergeants, Rogers, and (he/him) were given the report yesterday.

■ ■ ■ ■ ■ ■ ■ ■ ■ ■ ■ ■ ■ ■ ■

1. her—sent to her, not sent to she
2. I—I have worked, not me have worked
3. theirs, yours—possessive pronouns do not have apostrophes
4. she—she was there, not her was there
5. me
6. him
7. me—let us = let you + let me; not let I
8. We—We must stand, not Us must stand
9. he—he was given the report, not him was given the report

One frequent error occurs with the pronoun *myself*.

Use the pronoun *myself* only after having used the pronoun *I* or *me*.

Examples:

Wrong:	I entered the apartment and identified me.
Right:	I entered the apartment and identified myself.
Wrong:	Officer Hanson and myself returned to the department.
Right:	Officer Hanson and I returned to the department.

➢ Practice

Correct any pronoun errors in the following sentences. Sometimes you may need to change the word *myself* to either *I* or *me* to correct the sentence. If no changes are needed, write OK.

1. Officer Thomas Jorgenson and myself waited at the scene of the crime.
2. John and myself went to 1818 Thirteenth Avenue and knocked on the door.
3. He told both Officer Jorgenson and myself that we could not enter.
4. The suspect had been arrested twice before by myself and Detective Wills.
5. I myself had signed the first complaint.
6. When Officer Jorgenson and myself knocked again, there was no answer.
7. The entire episode was witnessed by myself and Detective Wills, who had been called to the scene.
8. Detective Wills told Officer Jorgenson and myself that we had to get a warrant.

■ ■ ■ ■ ■ ■ ■ ■ ■ ■ ■ ■ ■ ■ ■ ■

1. Officer Thomas Jorgenson and I waited at the scene of the crime.
2. John and I went to 1818 Thirteenth Avenue and knocked on the door.
3. He told both Officer Jorgenson and me that we could not enter.
4. The suspect had been arrested twice before by Detective Wills and me. (Put yourself last.)
5. OK
6. When Officer Jorgenson and I knocked again, there was no answer.
7. The entire episode was witnessed by Detective Wills and me, who had been called to the scene.
8. Detective Wills told Officer Jorgenson and me that we had to get a warrant.

Note: In sentences 4 and 7, you reverse the order of the pronoun *me* and *Detective Wills*, so that the phrase reads, “Detective Wills and me.” In general, nouns should be listed before pronouns.

Formal writing requires the use of *whom* rather than *who* any time it is the object of the sentence. Informal writing, however, tends to avoid the use of *whom* **unless** it comes directly after a preposition, e.g., *to*, *for*, *with*. We recommend this informal handling of *who* and *whom*.

Use the pronoun *whom* following prepositions.

Example:

Wrong: To who did the witness report?
Right: To whom did the witness report?

➢ Practice

Correct any errors in use of pronouns in the following sentences. If correct, write OK. (**Note**: Consider informal style correct in this exercise.)

1. With whom did you go?
2. Who did Sergeant Miller give the report to?
3. He is the suspect whom we arrested last week for a similar crime.
4. Who filed the report?
5. Is it the lieutenant whom rejected the report and the arrest?
6. No, it was the captain, whom we all know is very particular about such matters.
7. If it is rejected again, who is to blame?
8. I would like to know to who I should report next week.

▪▪▪▪▪▪▪▪▪▪▪▪▪▪▪▪▪▪

1. OK (*with* is a preposition)
2. OK
3. He is the suspect who we arrested last week for a similar crime.
4. OK
5. Is it the lieutenant who rejected the report and the arrest?
6. No, it was the captain, who we all know is very particular about such matters.
7. OK
8. I would like to know to whom I should report next week. (*to* is a preposition)

Use the pronoun *who* or *whom* to refer to people.
Do <u>not</u> use the pronoun *that*.

Examples:

Wrong: He is the man <u>that</u> I saw.
Right: He is the man <u>who</u> I saw.

Wrong: It is the captain <u>that</u> is responsible.
Right: It is the captain <u>who</u> is responsible.

➢ Practice

Correct any errors in pronouns in the following sentences. If correct, write OK.

1. He is a man that can be trusted.
2. Mr. Gerald was the only person that had gone into the washroom.
3. It was the clerk who had seen him enter.
4. But it was the manager that reported the incident.
5. The suspect referred to a girlfriend that had been with him that night.
6. The security chief reported that there was a male and female in the parking lot that were arguing.
7. The female had the car keys and some compact discs that belonged to the male.
8. It was I that had to investigate the incident.
9. I guess it's because I'm the only one that is currently dating.
10. Upon reaching the scene I discovered that this couple wasn't the only couple that was having a dispute.

■ ■ ■ ■ ■ ■ ■ ■ ■ ■ ■ ■ ■ ■ ■

1. He is a man <u>who</u> can be trusted.
2. Mr. Gerald was the only person <u>who</u> had gone into the washroom.
3. OK
4. But it was the manager <u>who</u> reported the incident.
5. The suspect referred to a girlfriend <u>who</u> had been with him that night.

6. The security chief reported that there was a male and female in the parking lot who were arguing.
7. OK
8. It was I who had to investigate the incident.
9. I guess it's because I'm the only one who is currently dating.
10. Upon reaching the scene I discovered that this couple wasn't the only couple who was having a dispute.

Pronoun Review

Before continuing, review the main trouble spots with pronouns.

- Use *I, we, you, he, she, it, they, who, whoever, whosoever* as **subjects**.
- Use *me, us, you, him, her, it, them, whom, whomever, whomsoever* as **objects**.
- Use *my, mine, our, ours, your, yours, his, her, hers, its, their, theirs, whose, whosoever* as **possessives**.
- Use the pronoun *myself* only after having used the pronoun *I* or *me*.
- Use the pronoun *whom* only after prepositions.
- Do not use the pronoun *that* to refer to people; use *who*.

➢ Practice

Correct any errors in pronouns in the following sentences.

1. On February 22, 20--, Officer Garcia and myself arrested a suspect that was loitering outside a liquor store.

2. Officer Garcia and me were suspicious of his actions, so us approached him.

3. There was another man that was standing near Officer Garcia and myself.

4. I asked whom he was, but he ignored my inquiry.

5. It was then that Officer Garcia and myself thought perhaps the first suspicious man and him were partners.

■ ■ ■ ■ ■ ■ ■ ■ ■ ■ ■ ■ ■ ■ ■ ■

1. On February 22, 20--, Officer Garcia and I arrested a suspect who was loitering outside a liquor store.
2. Officer Garcia and I were suspicious of his actions, so we approached him.
3. There was another man who was standing near Officer Garcia and me.
4. I asked who he was, but he ignored my inquiry.
5. It was then that Officer Garcia and I thought perhaps the first suspicious man and he were partners.

SUBJECT AND VERB AGREEMENT

English verbs change their endings, depending on the subject of the sentence. As with the pronouns, you should be able to "hear" when sentences are in standard English. For example, you know that <u>I run</u> sounds all right but that <u>he run</u> does not. If you are a native speaker of standard English, you can "hear" that <u>he run</u> should be <u>he runs</u>.

Rather than spending time learning rules about subject and verb agreement, concentrate on isolating the subject and verb of the sentence and listening to how they sound together.

➢ Practice

Match the verbs in the right column to the correct pronouns in the left column. (**Note**: If you can*not* match these verbs to the correct pronouns, refer to a grammar book under "Agreement" and work through some of the exercises provided.)

I _______	am
you _______	
he _______	are
we _______	
they _______	is

■ ■ ■ ■ ■ ■ ■ ■ ■ ■ ■ ■ ■ ■ ■ ■

I am	(It doesn't *sound* right to say "I are" or "I is.")
you are	(It doesn't *sound* right to say "you am" or "you is.")
he is	(It doesn't *sound* right to say "he am" or "he are.")
we are	(It doesn't *sound* right to say "we am" or "we is.")
they are	(It doesn't *sound* right to say "they am" or "they is.")

Subject and verb should agree.
Pick out the subject and verb of the sentence and say them together to determine if they agree.

Examples:

Wrong: <u>John</u>, together with Harry and Ted, <u>were</u> assigned the case.
Right: <u>John</u>, together with Harry and Ted, <u>was</u> assigned the case.

Wrong: There <u>is</u> to be <u>three contestants</u> in the shooting contest.
Right: There <u>are</u> to be <u>three contestants</u> in the shooting contest.

➢ Practice

Select the correct verb for each sentence. Underline subject and verb.

1. In our department there (is/are) nine detectives.

2. One of the major causes of such crimes (is/are) poverty.

3. Everyone, including the officers, (is/are) registering a complaint.

4. The captain, as well as his staff, (distrust/distrusts) the report.

5. There (is/are), according to my report, only two suspects in the case.

6. Police officers, like sergeants and lieutenants, (think/thinks) the case is important.

7. The two witnesses, not the police officer, (state/states) that the suspect was a small woman.

8. Each officer, unlike his superiors, (write/writes) many reports each week.

▪▪▪▪▪▪▪▪▪▪▪▪▪▪▪

1. In our department there <u>are</u> <u>nine detectives</u>.
2. <u>One</u> of the major causes of such crimes <u>is</u> poverty.
3. <u>Everyone</u>, including the officers, <u>is</u> registering a complaint.
4. <u>The captain</u>, as well as his staff, <u>distrusts</u> the report.
5. There <u>are</u>, according to my report, only <u>two suspects</u> in the case.
6. <u>Police officers</u>, like sergeants and lieutenants, <u>think</u> the case is important.
7. <u>The two witnesses</u>, not the police officer, <u>state</u> that the suspect was a small woman.
8. <u>Each officer</u>, unlike his superiors, <u>writes</u> many reports each week.

For singular subjects joined by *and*, use a plural verb.

For singular subjects joined by *or*, the verb agrees with the closer subject.

***One*, *everybody*, *someone*, and *each* take a singular verb.**

Periods of time, amounts of money, weights, and measures are usually singular. These are collective nouns—they refer to a single unit.

Examples:

Wrong:	Officer Jones and Officer Wong is going.
Right:	Officer Jones and Officer Wong are going. (They are going.)
Wrong:	The victim or the witnesses is lying.
Right:	The victim or the witnesses are lying. (Witnesses is the subject closer to the verb.)
Wrong:	Everyone, including the witnesses, are going.
Right:	Everyone, including the witnesses, is going.
Wrong:	Fifty dollars are a lot to pay for a parking fine.
Right:	Fifty dollars is a lot to pay for a parking fine.

➢ Practice

Select the correct verb to use in each sentence.

1. Ten miles (is/are) too far to walk.
2. Either the witness or the defendant (is/are) going to be believed.
3. Neither the witness nor the defendants (has/have) been called to the stand.
4. Both the defendant and the witness (is/are) in the courtroom.
5. Each of the police officers, as well as the supervisors and administrators, (was/were) at the protest meeting.

■ ■ ■ ■ ■ ■ ■ ■ ■ ■ ■ ■ ■ ■ ■ ■

The words in parentheses show you how you might rephrase the sentence so that you can "hear" if the verb agrees with the subject or not. Try to get into the habit of rephrasing sentences about which you are uncertain.

1. is (the distance is), 2. is (defendant is singular—the defendant is), 3. have (defendants is plural—the defendants are), 4. are (they are), 5. was (each one was)

ADJECTIVES AND ADVERBS

Adjectives and adverbs are modifiers, i.e.*, they add details or specifics to a phrase or sentence. An **adjective** is a word that modifies a noun, e.g.*, "The *new* gun misfired." An **adverb** is a word that modifies a verb, an adjective, or other adverb, e.g., "The officer *quickly* returned the gun." Notice that the adverb ends in *-ly*. This is usually the sign of an adverb. Sometimes -ly may be added to nouns to make them adjectives, e.g., *manly*. Most often, however, -ly is added to adjectives to make them adverbs, e.g., the adjective *bad* becomes the adverb *badly* when -ly is added.

* **Note**: *i.e.* means "that is;" *e.g.* means "for example." You will learn to use these abbreviations in your own writing later in the book.

Use adjectives to modify nouns. Use adverbs to modify all other words.
***Good* is an adjective; *well* is an adverb.**
***Real* is an adjective; *really* is an adverb.**

Examples:

Wrong:	He did a well job.	
Right:	He did a good job.	(adjective modifying the noun job)
Wrong:	He did the job good.	
Right:	He did the job well.	(adverb modifying the verb did)
Wrong:	The officer was real tired.	
Right:	The officer was really tired.	(adverb modifying the adjective tired)

If you are not sure whether a word is an adjective or an adverb, look it up in the dictionary. Adjectives are indicated by the abbreviation "adj." and adverbs by the abbreviation "adv."

Another problem with adjectives and adverbs can occur when a comparison is made, e.g., "Joe is *taller* than Jim, but Bill is the *tallest* of the three." Adding the ending *-er* to a word is the same as saying "more." Adding the ending *-est* to a word is the same as saying "most." Do *not* use both.

Do *not* use double comparatives.

Examples:

Wrong:	Frank is more quicker than Harry.
Right:	Frank is quicker than Harry.
Right:	Frank is more quick than Harry.
Wrong:	Of all the witnesses, she gave the most vividest description.
Right:	Of all the witnesses, she gave the most vivid description.
Right:	Of all the witnesses, she gave the vividest description.

Note: *-er* and *more* are used to compare two things; *-est* and *most* are used to compare three or more things.

➢ Practice

Correct any errors in the use of adjectives and adverbs in the following sentences. If correct, write OK.

1. The witness felt badly that he had not gotten the license number.

2. He had tried real hard to get it, but it was too dark and the car was moving too quick.

3. Nevertheless, the officer was real mad that the witness had not gotten the license number.

4. The witness did the most clearest job of describing the suspect.

5. He described him as real tall and slender with perfect tailored clothes.

6. I am sure glad he got such a good look at the suspect.

7. The man was also a real cooperative witness.

8. It would be well if all witnesses were so cooperative.

9. I am surely thankful that the case is finally solved.

10. I feel I did my job good.

■ ■ ■ ■ ■ ■ ■ ■ ■ ■ ■ ■ ■ ■ ■ ■ ■ ■

1. The witness felt bad that he had not gotten the license number.
2. He had tried really hard to get it, but it was too dark and the car was moving too quickly.
3. Nevertheless, the officer was really mad that the witness had not gotten the license number.
4. The witness did the clearest job of describing the suspect. (or most clear)
5. He described him as really tall and slender with perfectly tailored clothes.
6. I am surely glad he got such a good look at the suspect.
7. The man was also a really cooperative witness.

8. It would be good if all witnesses were so cooperative.
9. OK
10. I feel I did my job well.

Note: In sentences 2, 3, 5, and 7, you probably used the adjective *really*, but *very* would be a better choice. Do not use *real* as an adjective.

NEGATION

You've probably heard the expression, "Two negatives make a positive." This implies that if you say, "I don't have no apple," it means that you *do* have an apple. Actually, most people would understand what you meant if you said, "I don't have no apple," but they would also probably infer that you did not have a very good command of standard English.

Avoid double negatives.

The words *but, only, hardly*, and *scarcely* are negative. The words *no* and *never* are obviously negative.

Examples:

Wrong: I didn't have but one choice.
Right: I had but one choice.

Wrong: I couldn't hardly see the license.
Right: I could hardly see the license.

➢ Practice

Correct any instances of use of the double negative in the following sentences.

1. Upon approaching the intersection, the driver didn't make no complete stop.

2. The oncoming car couldn't hardly be blamed for hitting him.

3. He had no choice but to hit the other car or a pedestrian.

4. I don't hardly think he should have hit the pedestrian.

5. I couldn't hardly believe he was found guilty of reckless driving.

■ ■ ■ ■ ■ ■ ■ ■ ■ ■ ■ ■ ■ ■ ■ ■

1. Upon approaching the intersection, the driver didn't make a complete stop.
2. The oncoming car could hardly be blamed for hitting him.
3. OK
4. I don't think he should have hit the pedestrian. *or* I hardly think he should . . .
5. I could hardly believe he was found guilty of reckless driving.

USE OF ARTICLES

An **article** is a word used with a noun to make it more specific. English has three articles: *a, an*, and *the*. You learned earlier to leave out *a*, *an*, and *the* when taking notes. This is correct. However, when you write your report, do *not* leave these articles out. It makes reading the report difficult.

**Do not leave out *a*, *an*, or *the* in your reports.
Use *a* before words beginning with a consonant sound;
use *an* before words beginning with a vowel sound.**

The vowels in English are a, e, i, o, u, and sometimes y. All other letters are consonants. Remember, however, it is the *sound*, not the actual letter, that counts, e.g., *a* homicide, *an* hour.

Examples:

Wrong: Suspect seen driving red Taurus. (acceptable for notes)
Right: The suspect was seen driving a red Taurus.

Wrong: Complete list of items taken in burglary is attached.
Right: A complete list of items taken in the burglary is attached.

➤ Practice

Add articles where needed in the following sentences. If no additions are needed, write OK.

1. Victim said old stickers on front and rear doors were on home when she bought it.
2. Suspect was arrested for warrant held by Shasta County Sheriff's Office.
3. I arrived at approximately 1026 to find deceased slumped down in easy chair in upstairs den.
4. Deceased was apparently alone when she died.

5. Other department personnel at scene were Captain Newcomb and Sergeant Adams.

6. TV and light were on in den; kitchen light was on, as was desk light in living room.

■ ■ ■ ■ ■ ■ ■ ■ ■ ■ ■ ■ ■ ■ ■ ■ ■

1. The victim said the old stickers on the front and rear doors were on the home when she bought it.
2. The suspect was arrested for a warrant held by the Shasta County Sheriff's Office.
3. I arrived at approximately 1026 to find the deceased slumped down in an easy chair in the upstairs den.
4. The deceased was apparently alone when she died.
5. Other department personnel at the scene were Captain Newcomb and Sergeant Adams.
6. The TV and the* light were on in the den; the kitchen light was on, as was the desk light in the living room.
   (* the word the before light is optional)

SUMMARY

If the pronoun is the subject of the sentence, use *I, we, you, he, she, it, they, who*, *whoever, whosoever*. If the pronoun is the object of the sentence, use *me, us, you, him, her, it, them, whom*, *whomever, whomsoever*. If the pronoun is used to show possession, use *my, mine, our, ours, your, yours, his, her, hers, its, their, theirs, whose, whosoever*.

Use the pronoun *myself* only after having used the pronoun *I* or *me*. Use the pronoun *whom* following prepositions. Use the pronoun *who* or *whom* to refer to people. Do *not* use the pronoun *that* to refer to people.

Subject and verb should agree. Pick out the subject and verb of the sentence and say them together to determine if they agree. For singular subjects joined by *and*, use a plural verb. For singular subjects joined by *or*, make the verb agree with the closer subject. *One*, *everybody*, *someone*, and *each* take a singular verb. Periods of time, amounts of money, weights, and measures are usually singular. These are collective nouns—they refer to a single unit.

Use adjectives to modify nouns. Use adverbs to modify all other words. *Good* is an adjective; *well* is an adverb. *Real* is an adjective; *really* is an adverb.

Do *not* use double comparatives. Avoid double negatives.

Do not leave out *a*, *an*, or *the* in your reports. Use *a* before words beginning with a consonant sound; use *an* before words beginning with a vowel sound.

You may wish to review this chapter before taking the self-test on p.223.

Chapter Eight

SENTENCES THAT MAKE SENSE

Do you know:

- How to write in complete sentences?
- How to punctuate two sentences which are joined together?
- How to combine several ideas into one sentence?

Key terms: imperative, -ing word group, predicate, run-on sentence, sentence fragment, split predicate, subject, subsentence

The sentence is the basic unit of a report (or any piece of writing). A series of clear, effective, well-organized sentences can communicate your information about a specific case or incident to the reader. If you write in incomplete sentences (fragments), or if you run your sentences together, your reader may end up with a confused idea of what you are trying to communicate. (The reader may also have a negative impression of you.)

Learning to write effective sentences takes skill and practice. One of the best ways to improve your "sentence skill" is to read and to pay attention to how others construct sentences. There is a high correlation between the person who reads a lot and the person who writes well.

SENTENCES

Every complete sentence must have two parts:

1. You must *name* what you are talking about: the **subject**.
2. You must *tell* something about it: the **predicate**.

For example, read the following sentences and notice the subjects and predicates.

Subject (names)	**Predicate** (tells)
The gas station on the corner	just caught on fire.
The suspect	accused the victim of hitting him.
On 01-02-20--, I	received a call from George Axel.

You practiced identifying subjects and predicates in Chapter Five when you learned about active and passive voice. If you read only the subject part of the sentence, you'll see that it can't stand alone. If you read only the predicate part of the sentence, you'll see that it can't stand alone either. You need *both* parts.

Both subjects and predicates may include modifiers (descriptive phrases and words). For example, in the first sample sentence, the phrase on the corner is part of the subject; it modifies the gas station. In the second sample sentence, the phrase of hitting him is part of the predicate; it modifies accused the victim.

Write complete sentences. Include both a subject and a predicate.

Examples:

Wrong:	The gas station on the corner. Just caught fire.
Right:	The gas station on the corner just caught fire.
Wrong:	The suspect. Accused the victim of hitting him.
Right:	The suspect accused the victim of hitting him.

➢ Practice

Read the following groups of words as though they made up a report. Use the following letters to indicate whether each is a subject, a predicate, or both a subject and a predicate. Modifiers must be part of the subject or predicate.

S = Subject (names)
P = Predicate (tells)
SP = Subject and predicate (a complete sentence)

______ 1. On the above date and time.

______ 2. The defendant physically assaulted the victim.

______ 3. In their apartment at the above location.

______ 4. The victim and defendant were husband and wife.

______ 5. And had been married for three years.

______ 6. These two parties.

______ 7. Were involved in an argument.

______ 8. The defendant got the victim on the floor.

______ 9. And began choking her.

______ 10. The victim said she was unable to breath and feared for her life.

■ ■ ■ ■ ■ ■ ■ ■ ■ ■ ■ ■ ■ ■ ■ ■

1.S, 2.SP, 3.P, 4.SP, 5.P, 6.S, 7.P, 8.SP, 9.P, 10.SP

➢ Practice

Identify the subject and the predicate by drawing a single line under the subject and a double line under the predicate. Sometimes sentences are scrambled; the subject does not always come first.

Examples: Nobody saw the robber.
Dark was the night.

1. The victim was told to leave.

2. Bruise marks were noted about the victim's neck and throat.

3. Photos were taken by the investigating team.

4. Officer Hernandez transported the victim home.

5. She was advised to contact the city attorney.

6. "Stop," called the officer.

7. Down dropped the latch.

8. The man was finally arrested.

9. Around the corner sped the car.

10. Pop goes the weasel.

■ ■ ■ ■ ■ ■ ■ ■ ■ ■ ■ ■ ■ ■ ■ ■

1. The victim was told to leave.
2. Bruise marks were noted about the victim's neck and throat.
3. Photos were taken by the investigating team.
4. Officer Hernandez transported the victim home.
5. She was advised to contact the city attorney.

6. "Stop," called the officer.
7. Down dropped the latch.
8. The man was finally arrested.
9. Around the corner sped the car.
10. Pop goes the weasel.

In a question, the subject is usually found in the middle of the sentence. If you have difficulty finding the subject and predicate in questions, make the question into a sentence and then identify the subject and predicate, e.g., turn "Is this man guilty?" into "This man is guilty."

➢ Practice

Underline the subject with one line and the predicate with two lines.

1. Is that woman guilty?

2. Do you think so?

3. Who stole the car?

4. Will you arrest the man?

5. Did he have a search warrant?

■ ■ ■ ■ ■ ■ ■ ■ ■ ■ ■ ■ ■ ■ ■ ■ ■

1. Is that woman guilty?
2. Do you think so?
3. Who stole the car?
4. Will you arrest the man?
5. Did he have a search warrant?

The only time you can leave out the subject of a sentence is in a command—also called the **imperative**. For example, in the sentence "Close the window," it is all right to leave out the subject "You" since the listener understands that the speaker is addressing him or her. Compare "Close the window" with the following sentences:

> Am lonesome for home.
> Am having a good time.
> Will write soon.

These are *not* commands, so they are not all right. They must have a subject such as "I am lonesome for home," "I am having a good time," and "Bill will write soon."

➢ Practice

In the following sentences, the subjects are missing. If it is all right to leave out the subject, write OK. If it is wrong to omit the subject, put a ✓ in the blank.

_____ 1. Be careful.

_____ 2. Halt.

_____ 3. Will return your call in the morning.

_____ 4. Stop that man.

_____ 5. Am certain of the suspect's identity.

■ ■ ■ ■ ■ ■ ■ ■ ■ ■ ■ ■ ■ ■ ■ ■ ■

1.OK, 2.OK, 3. ✓, 4.OK, 5. ✓

SENTENCE FRAGMENTS

A **sentence fragment** is a group of words that does not have both a subject and a predicate. The only exception to this is commands, in which the subject may be left out because it is understood, e.g., "Stop."

Avoid sentence fragments.

Examples:

Wrong: The officer chased the suspect. <u>And caught him</u>.
Right: The officer chased the suspect <u>and caught him</u>.

Wrong: He got a ticket. <u>Speeding down the street</u>.
Right: He got a ticket <u>speeding down the street</u>.

Wrong: Knowing we could not detain them long. <u>We were through</u>.
Right: Knowing we could not detain them long, <u>we were through</u>.

The three most common kinds of sentence fragments are examined on the next few pages.

The first kind of sentence fragment is called a **split predicate**. Here the writer states the subject and half of the predicate. Then the last part of the predicate is put into a sentence of its own—a fragment. For example: "The officer chased the suspect. And caught him." There is only one subject for both sentences: "The officer." To correct this kind of mistake, you need to remove the period after the word *suspect* and change the capital *A* on *And* to a small *a*, like this:

> The officer chased the suspect and caught him.

Notice there is *no comma* before the word *and.*

➢ Practice

In the following sentences, eliminate any fragments by connecting them to the complete sentence.

1. The campers cut a clearing. And put up their tent.

2. The burglar unlocked the window. And climbed through.

3. He found several antiques. But no money.

4. He was able to open the outer entry door. And was able to crawl a short distance on the floor. But could not reach the victim's apartment.

5. The manager phoned the police dispatcher. And said the apartment was on fire.

■ ■ ■ ■ ■ ■ ■ ■ ■ ■ ■ ■ ■ ■ ■ ■

1. The campers cut a clearing and put up their tent.
2. The burglar unlocked the window and climbed through.
3. He found several antiques but no money.
4. He was able to open the outer entry door and was able to crawl a short distance on the floor but could not reach the victim's apartment.
5. The manager phoned the police dispatcher and said the apartment was on fire.

The second kind of fragment is known as an **-ing word group.** It cannot stand alone. For example, "speeding down the street" is a fragment; it must be attached to a sentence.

If the -ing word group is attached at the beginning of a sentence, put a comma after it: "Speeding down the street, he got a ticket." (If the -ing word group is very short, the comma is sometimes omitted.) If an -ing word group is attached at the end of a sentence, do *not* use a comma before it: "He got a ticket speeding down the street." It is important to watch where you put the -ing word groups. For example, in the sentence "He got a ticket speeding down the street," you have a *misplaced modifier* (-ing word group); the ticket was not speeding down the street. That sentence should have read, "He got a ticket *for* speeding down the street."

➢ Practice

Read the sentences below. Decide which sentence you want to attach the -ing word group to. Make the needed corrections.

1. The comedian gnawed at the bone. Barking like a dog. Everybody laughed.

   ____

2. He is on the phone. Calling the witness. Shall I interrupt him?

   ____

3. He noticed a large amount of smoke. Coming from the building. So he called the fire department.

   ____

4. The manager watched the suspect. Putting the necklace into her purse. The suspect looked around and started to leave.

   ____

5. Hearing the siren. The man pulled his car over. Failing to signal.

   ____

■ ■ ■ ■ ■ ■ ■ ■ ■ ■ ■ ■ ■ ■ ■ ■

1. Barking like a dog, the comedian gnawed at the bone. Everybody laughed. *or* The comedian, barking like a dog, gnawed at the bone. Everybody laughed.
2. He is on the phone calling the witness. Shall I interrupt him?
3. He noticed a large amount of smoke coming from the building. So he called the fire department. (You could also put a comma after building.)
4. The manager watched the suspect. Putting a necklace into her purse, the suspect looked around and started to leave. (The -ing word group could also be attached to the first sentence.)
5. Hearing the siren, the man pulled his car over, failing to signal.

The third type of fragment is known as a **subsentence**. A subsentence does have a subject and a predicate, but it still cannot stand alone. It *depends* on a main sentence for its meaning. Subsentences tell *what kind, why, which, when*, or *where.* For example, in the sentence, "I went home," you might want to tell when. You could add the subsentence "after it got dark." Then your sentence would read: "After it got dark, I went home," or "I went home after it got dark." Notice that you have a subsentence and a complete sentence. Both have a subject and a predicate:

> After it got dark, I went home.

Notice, also, that a word is left over in the subsentence: *after.* This signals that the group of words is a subsentence. Following are most of the subsentence signal words. Learn to recognize them:

if	when	who	before	although	which
because	whenever	whose	after	as	where
unless	while	whom	since	that	

Most of these words introduce subsentences which answer the questions *when*, *where*, *why*, or *which one*? You can use subsentences to build more meaning into what you write. But you should *not* let subsentences stand alone. Always connect them to a main sentence.

As with the -ing word groups, a subsentence that is added to the beginning of a sentence is followed by a comma:

After it got dark, I went home.

A subsentence that is added to the end of a sentence is *not* preceded by a comma:

I went home after it got dark.

➢ Practice

In the following sentences, put parentheses around each subsentence. Underline the signal word which introduces it. (**Note**: Sometimes a sentence has two subsentences.)

Example: Mr. Dobbs reached the station (<u>after</u> the train had left).

1. When Officer Holmes says something, everyone listens.
2. The witness refused to testify after she was threatened.
3. Before you issue a citation, you should explain why it is being issued.
4. She was caught because the neighbors saw her.
5. Although there were three witnesses, their stories did not agree.
6. Whenever this is the case, a lot more questioning has to be done.
7. Before we can search the apartment, we need a warrant.
8. I will get a warrant if you will watch the apartment while I am gone.

9. As I was making the call, the suspect left.

10. We were able to search anyway since a warrant had been issued.

■ ■ ■ ■ ■ ■ ■ ■ ■ ■ ■ ■ ■ ■ ■ ■

1. (When Officer Holmes says something,) everyone listens.
2. The witness refused to testify (after she was threatened).
3. (Before you issue a citation,) you should explain why it is being issued.
4. She was caught (because the neighbors saw her).
5. (Although there were three witnesses,) their stories did not agree.
6. (Whenever this is the case,) a lot more questioning has to be done.
7. (Before we can search the apartment,) we need a warrant.
8. I will get a warrant (if you will watch the apartment) (while I am gone).
9. (As I was making the call,) the suspect left.
10. We were able to search anyway (since a warrant had been issued).

Sentence fragments cannot stand alone.

➢ More Practice

Eliminate all sentence fragments by attaching them to the appropriate sentence.

1. Officer Jordan bought a farm. After she retired.

2. I responded to an apartment fire. That resulted in the death of Mr. Nye.

3. When the signal is given. We will all move at once.

4. She was told by the victim. That the man was her boyfriend.

5. After the arrest. Narcotics agents were called to the scene.

6. Mr. Goldblum was placing some items in a storage locker. When he heard a hissing sound.

7. When he opened the adjoining locker. He discovered a bomb.

8. Since he knew he was in danger. He called the emergency number.

9. Before the emergency squad arrived. The bomb exploded.

10. Fortunately, Mr. Goldblum had left the store. After he called the emergency squad.

■ ■ ■ ■ ■ ■ ■ ■ ■ ■ ■ ■ ■ ■ ■ ■

1. Officer Jordan bought a farm after she retired.
2. I responded to an apartment fire that resulted in the death of Mr. Nye.
3. When the signal is given, we will all move at once.
4. She was told by the victim that the man was her boyfriend.
5. After the arrest, narcotics agents were called to the scene.
6. Mr. Goldblum was placing some items in a storage locker when he heard a hissing sound.
7. When he opened the adjoining locker, he discovered a bomb.
8. Since he knew he was in danger, he called the emergency number.
9. Before the emergency squad arrived, the bomb exploded.
10. Fortunately, Mr. Goldblum had left the store after he called the emergency squad.

You have now seen the three main kinds of sentence fragments and have learned how they can be corrected.

➢ Practice

Correct any fragments contained in the following sentences. If no corrections are needed, write OK.

1. The victim reports. That on 04-04-20-- at about 1610 hrs. she was driving her '98 Ford Explorer southbound on Wooddale Avenue. Approaching 58th Street.

2. That she became aware of the suspect auto tailgating her vehicle.

3. That because of this she slowed her vehicle. And then again resumed her speed.

4. As she resumed speed. The suspect auto attempted to pass her on the left. But dropped back behind her again.

5. The victim then came to a stop at 58th Street. And started to turn right.

6. As she turned, the suspect followed around the corner. Coming around her left side. Overtaking her and passing her.

7. As he was doing so he cut in on her. And their vehicles collided.

8. The suspect then continued, and she accelerated to follow. And obtain his license number.

9. The suspect then came to a stop at about Clay Lane. The victim came to a stop behind him.

10. The drivers both got out. And exchanged unpleasantries.

■■■■■■■■■■■■■■■■

1. The victim reports that on 04-04-20-- at about 1610 hrs. she was driving her '98 Ford Explorer southbound on Wooddale Avenue approaching 58th Street.
2. She became aware of the suspect auto tailgating her vehicle.

3. Because of this she slowed her vehicle and then again resumed her speed.
4. As she resumed speed, the suspect auto attempted to pass her on the left, but dropped back behind her again.
5. The victim then came to a stop at 58th Street and started to turn right.
6. As she turned, the suspect followed around the corner, coming around her left side, overtaking her, and passing her.
7. As he was doing so he cut in on her and their vehicles collided.
8. The suspect then continued, and she accelerated to follow and obtain his license number.
9. OK
10. The drivers both got out and exchanged unpleasantries.

RUN-ON SENTENCES

A **run-on sentence** contains *two* complete sentences *incorrectly* joined together. For example: "Frank shot the escaped convict and his partner called for help." Notice that this sentence is really two complete sentences, yet the reader doesn't know this until the end is reached. The sentence might be read to come out like this: "Frank shot the escaped convict and his partner." Mistakes like this can happen when two sentences are run together.

Do not confuse run-on sentences with sentences that have a double predicate: "Frank shot the escaped convict and killed him." And do not confuse run-on sentences with those that have a subsentence: "Frank shot the escaped convict who was armed and dangerous."

Do not run sentences together.

Examples:

Wrong:	He caught the suspect_and he arrested him.	
Right:	He caught the suspect,_and he arrested him.	
Right:	He caught the suspect and arrested him.	(double predicate)
Right:	He caught the suspect, who was arrested.	(subsentence)

➢ Identification

Identify the following sentences as correct (OK) or run-on (R).

_____ 1. Pictures of the scene were taken by Officer O'Neill and the debris was brought to the station for evidence.

_____ 2. The police were summoned and I arrived at the home to find the deceased on the floor.

______ 3. John contacted me and told me he could get the gun.

______ 4. He doesn't recall seeing her leave the parking lot and apparently she would have had to drive past him to exit into the street.

______ 5. She had taught at East Elementary School for approximately six months and had been employed with the school system for approximately seven years.

______ 6. On 01-21-20-- the suspect was stopped because of her driving behavior and was charged with driving while under the influence of alcohol.

______ 7. The suspect charged the merchandise and he left the store quickly.

______ 8. The manager became suspicious so he phoned the credit card company.

______ 9. He was told that the card had been reported stolen two weeks earlier.

______ 10. The police department was called and a complaint was filed.

■ ■ ■ ■ ■ ■ ■ ■ ■ ■ ■ ■ ■ ■ ■ ■

1.R, 2.R, 3.OK (the sentence simply has two predicates), 4.R, 5.OK (two predicates), 6.OK (two predicates), 7.R, 8.R, 9.OK (subsentence), 10.R

Now that you can identify sentences that are run-on, what do you do with them? Run-on sentences can be corrected in three ways. Consider, for example, the following run-on sentence:

> Officer Frank chased the suspect and he caught him.

One way to correct this sentence is to make it into two separate sentences:

> Officer Frank chased the suspect. He caught him.

A second way to correct the run-on sentence would be to use a comma before the simple connecting word such as *and, but, or, nor, for, yet, so*:

> Officer Frank chased the suspect, and he caught him.

A third way would be to use a semicolon and a transitional word or *no* connecting word:

> Officer Frank chased the suspect; ultimately he caught him.
> Officer Frank chased the suspect; he caught him.

Run-on sentences can be corrected by:

1. **making them into two separate sentences.**
2. **using a comma before the simple connecting word such as *and, but, or, nor, for, yet, so*.**
3. **using a semicolon and a transitional word or *no* connecting word.**

➢ Practice

Correct any run-on sentences in one of the three ways stated. If no corrections are needed, write OK.

1. At approximately 1335, 02-22-20--, I received a call to proceed to 1875 Claremore Drive and assist Officer Bagley with an attempted suicide.

2. Upon my arrival I met Officer Bagg and two members of the Yachats Fire Department, upon entering I was told by Officer Bagg that the suspect was dead and I saw him in the hallway.

3. Mrs. Sherman, the wife of the victim, was quite upset and I began talking to her and then I called Pastor Hagbarth to the scene to be with her.

4. In a preliminary examination it was found that there were three entrance wounds near the heart area it was also noted that there were powder burns on the pajamas and near the entrance wound.

5. At this time I saw that there was one exit wound but in a later examination by the medical examiner's office it was found to be two exit wounds.

6. Detective Lorenz arrived and we began taking pictures of the scene.

7. I saw that a rifle was laying next to the bed as were two spent .22 caliber cases, there was also one spent case near the bedroom door.

8. A bullet hole in the wall of the bedroom near the bed was noted but we were unable to find the bullet.

9. When the medical examiner's office personnel arrived, there was an examination of the bed where it was apparent that the deceased had been lying.

10. The bedspread was wet and soaked with blood as were several layers of clothing, also visible was an obvious bullet hole an attempt was made to recover this bullet but we were unable to find it.

▪▪▪▪▪▪▪▪▪▪▪▪▪▪▪▪

1. OK
2. Upon my arrival I met Officer Bagg and two members of the Yachats Fire Department. Upon entering I was told by Officer Bagg that the suspect was dead, and I saw him in the hallway.
3. Mrs. Sherman, the wife of the victim, was quite upset, and I began talking to her. Then I called Pastor Hagbarth to the scene to be with her.
4. In a preliminary examination it was found that there were three entrance wounds near the heart area. It was also noted that there were powder burns on the pajamas and near the entrance wound.
5. At this time I saw that there was one exit wound, but in a later examination by the medical examiner's office it was found to be two exit wounds.
6. Detective Lorenz arrived, and we began taking pictures of the scene.
7. I saw that a rifle was laying next to the bed, as were two spent .22 caliber cases. There was also one spent case near the bedroom door.
8. A bullet hole in the wall of the bedroom near the bed was noted, but we were unable to find the bullet.
9. OK
10. The bedspread was wet and soaked with blood, as were several layers of clothing. Also visible was an obvious bullet hole. An attempt was made to recover this bullet, but we were unable to find it.

➢ More Practice

Following are two "stories" with missing punctuation. The sentences all run together. Correct the sentences using the methods you have just learned.

1. A deputy district attorney asked several robbery victims to study a lineup of five people he placed the suspect in the middle and he told each man to step forward and say, "Give me all your money and I need some change in quarters and dimes."

   The first man did it right and the second man did it right but the middle fellow broke the case by blurting, "That isn't what I said."

2. While driving toward Tucson on a nearly deserted freeway at about 2 a.m. I noticed the taillights of a car in the distance the car was weaving slowly from one side of the road to the other considering the hour I reasoned that the driver had just come out of one of the local bars and I began to plan how I could get around him safely.

   I approached very cautiously and was amazed to see that it was the Arizona Highway Patrol but as I passed my confidence was restored just ahead of the patrol sauntered a huge red Hereford steer it was being expertly herded to the nearest off-ramp.

■ ■ ■ ■ ■ ■ ■ ■ ■ ■ ■ ■ ■ ■ ■ ■ ■ ■

1. One possible way to correct this "story" is to add one period and four commas (be sure to capitalize the first word in the new sentence when you add a period):

   > A deputy district attorney asked several robbery victims to study a lineup of five people._He placed the suspect in the middle,_and he told each man to step forward and say, "Give me all your money,_and I need some change in quarters and dimes."

The first man did it right, and the second man did it right, but the middle fellow broke the case by blurting, "That isn't what I said."

2. One possible way to correct this "story" is to add four periods and four commas (again, capitalize the first word in a new sentence created by adding a period):

While driving toward Tucson on a nearly deserted freeway at about 2 a.m., I noticed the taillights of a car in the distance. The car was weaving slowly from one side of the road to the other. Considering the hour, I reasoned that the driver had just come out of one of the local bars, and I began to plan how I could get around him safely.

I approached very cautiously and was amazed to see that it was the Arizona Highway Patrol, but as I passed my confidence was restored. Just ahead of the patrol sauntered a huge red Hereford steer. It was being expertly herded to the nearest off-ramp.

COMBINING SENTENCES

So far you've looked at how to avoid sentence fragments and how to eliminate run-on sentences. Closely related to these two skills is the skill of combining several short sentences into one longer sentence. For example, the following three sentences could be combined:

Jim is a police officer. He is 26 years old. He fired the gun.

Jim, a 26-year-old police officer, fired the gun.

Notice that the second line is less wordy and is also easier to read. Technically, there is nothing wrong with the first line; it does not break any rules, but it is choppy and leaves an impression of immaturity. When you reread your reports, watch for sentences that could be combined. Do *not*, however, make your sentences too long and complicated.

Combine related ideas into a single sentence.

Examples:

Immature: The suspect is 5′ 2″. He is male. He is white.
Mature: The suspect is a 5′ 2″ white male.

Immature: The burglar broke the glass. She opened the window. Then she entered the house. She was quiet.
Mature: The burglar broke the glass, opened the window, and entered the house quietly.

➢ Practice

Improve the following sentences by combining related ideas into single sentences. If no changes are needed, write OK.

1. Mr. Faulkner often sent flowers to Mrs. Jones. The last two occasions were holidays. One occasion was Thanksgiving. One occasion was Christmas.

____

____

2. Mr. Faulkner is an alcoholic. He works for the gas company. Last fall he entered the hospital for rehabilitation.

____

____

3. I received a call from Lorraine Hopkins. She said that she was a friend of Lance LaMonte. Lance LaMonte was a suspect in a robbery.

____

____

4. She wanted to help Lance. She could testify to his whereabouts on the night of the robbery. The robbery took place January 3, 20--.

____

____

5. They had gone to a movie. They saw *Saw*. While they were there they also met some friends.

____

6. After the movie they went to Pete's Pizza Parlor. They had a pizza. And they met two other friends.

____

7. I asked Ms. Hopkins to come to the station. I wanted her to sign a statement. She refused.

____

8. I told her we could not accept her phone call as an alibi. She would have to sign a statement. The statement would contain all the facts.

____

____

■ ■ ■ ■ ■ ■ ■ ■ ■ ■ ■ ■ ■ ■ ■ ■ ■

Several combinations may be correct for each set of sentences. Some samples are given below.

1. Mr. Faulkner, who often sent flowers to Mrs. Jones, sent them on Thanksgiving and Christmas.
2. Mr. Faulkner, an alcoholic who works for the gas company, entered the hospital for rehabilitation last fall.
3. I received a call from Lorraine Hopkins stating that she was a friend of Lance LaMonte, a suspect in a robbery.
4. She wanted to help Lance by testifying to his whereabouts on the night of the robbery, January 3, 20--.
5. They had gone to the movie *Saw* and had met friends there.
6. After the movie they went to Pete's Pizza Parlor for pizza and met two other friends.
7. I asked Ms. Hopkins to come to the station to sign a statement, but she refused.
8. I told her we could not accept her phone call as an alibi and that she would have to sign a statement containing all the facts.

SUMMARY

Write complete sentences. Include both a subject and a predicate. Avoid sentence fragments. Sentence fragments cannot stand alone.

Do not run sentences together. Run-on sentences can be corrected by making them into two separate sentences; using a comma before a simple connecting word such as *and, but, or, nor, for, yet, so*; or using a semicolon and a transitional word or *no* connecting word. Combine related ideas into a single sentence.

You may wish to review this chapter before completing the self-test on p.225.

Chapter Nine

SPELLING AND APOSTROPHES

Do you know:

- How to spell words correctly?
- What to do when you are uncertain of the spelling of a word?
- What the spellings and meanings of the most common homonyms are?
- How to distinguish between commonly confused words?
- When to use apostrophes?

Key terms: homonym, proofreading

Most instructors have had students ask, "Does spelling count?" Spelling *is* important and *always* counts. Consider the following examples (none of which would be caught by a spellcheck):

> He was arrested for a mister meaner.
> He was a drug attic.
> The victim was over rot.
> After the accident he went into a comma.
> He died of a harder tack.
> I called for a toe truck.

Spelling errors can lead your reader to think you're careless or stupid—or both. Correct spelling is important not only for the impression you make on the reader, but also for accuracy. A misspelled name, for example, might cause serious problems in future investigations of the case. You can improve your spelling in several ways:

1. If in doubt about a spelling, look up the word in a dictionary or speller/divider. Most computer programs have a spell-check function on them also.
2. Make a list of your own "trouble words"—words you have to look up frequently. Memorize the spelling of these words.
3. Memorize the spelling of common words with "tricky" spellings.
4. Memorize the spelling of words frequently used in law enforcement.
5. Be careful adding endings to words.
6. Learn to spell words which sound alike but are spelled differently (their, there, they're).
7. Learn to distinguish between words that are commonly confused.
8. Know when to use an apostrophe.
9. **Proofread your writing**.

The first two steps you'll need to do on your own. This chapter concentrates on steps 3-8. After you've mastered them, you'll be ready to do an effective job proofreading your reports.

Note: Use of a speller/divider is highly recommended. These condensed references contain only the spelling of the word and where it divides; consequently they are much smaller than a dictionary. For example, the *New Meriam-Webster Dictionary* is 4″ x 6½″ and has 981 pages. Its companion, *Webster's New World Speller/Divider*, is 4″ by 5½″ and has 331 pages. Speller/dividers are available at most bookstores and are inexpensive (around $5). One page in a speller/divider contains as many words as 20 pages in its comparable dictionary, making looking up words much more efficient. In addition, you do not get distracted reading the various definitions of the word or its history.

COMMON WORDS WITH DIFFICULT SPELLINGS

Following are some common words with difficult spellings. If possible, have someone read the words to you while you write them, or record them and then write them as you play back the recording. This allows you to check your spelling and determine which words you already know and which words you should memorize. Once you know which words give *you* difficulty, write five or ten of them on a card and place it someplace where you will see it often, such as taped to the bathroom mirror. You can work on memorizing spelling words while brushing your teeth.

Memorize common words with difficult spellings.

Do *not* try to learn all the words at once; take five or ten at a time.

accommodate
accumulate
accurate
ache
achievement
acquaintance
across
advantageous
affirmative
again
agreeable
airplane
alcohol
all right (2 words)
a lot (2 words)
although (1 word)
altogether (1 word)
always (1 word)
among
analysis
analyze
annual
apartment
appearance
appropriate
approximately
argument
assistance
athletics
attendance
audible
authentic
authoritative
automatic
auxiliary
awkward
beginning
behavior
believe
benefited
bicycle
breadth
brevity
bulletin
business
calendar
campaign
candidate
cannot (1 word)
carefully
cashier

catastrophe
ceiling
cemetery
chauffeur
circumstances
citizen
collision
column
coming
committed
committee
conscientious
conscious
conspicuous
convenience
cooperate
courteous
criticism
cylinder
deceased
decision
defensive
definite
demonstration
dependent
description
desperate
device
diagonal
die
difference
different
digit
disappear
disastrous
discrepancy
effective
eight
eligible
eliminate
embarrass
enough
equipment
especially
etc.
exaggerate
existence
experience
facilitate
familiar
February
feminine
flexible
forty
fourteen
fulfill
furniture
gauge
genuine
government
grievance
guarantee
hazard
height
humane
imaginary
immediately
imminent
implement
inadequate
indefinite
indicate
inquiry
intelligent
jewelry
judgment
know
knowledge
laboratory
legible
length
lenient
liable
library
license
linoleum
magazine
maintain
maintenance
management
maneuver
mileage
minimum
minority
miscellaneous
necessary
nevertheless (1word)
noticeable
nuisance
obstacle
occasion
occupant
occurred
occurrence
opinion
opponent
opportunity
opposite
pamphlet
perform
permanent
permissible
persecute
personal
pleasant
precede
precise
preferable
prejudice
preliminary
procedure
proceed
proprietor
query
questionnaire
quiet
quite
realize
really
receipt
receive
recognize
recommend
reference
referred
refuse
relieve
remittance

responsibility
restaurant
satisfactory
Saturday
schedule
secretary
separate
several
shriek
signature
similar
specimen
statement
statistics
stopped
subtle
succeed
successful
suffocation
supercede
surely
technique
telephone
thorough
thought
together
tournament
Tuesday
typewriter
unanimous
undoubtedly
urgent
useful
usually
vacancy
variety
vehicle
velocity
vengeance
Wednesday
weighty
weird
welfare
writing
written
yacht
yield
zigzag (1 word)

➢ Practice

Read the following sentences. Correct any misspelled words. If no changes are needed, write OK.

1. Alot of people think it is alright to take ashtrays from aparttments.
2. Alcahol is amoung the magor problems we face.
3. The arguement was ridiculous.
4. In my judgement the vehical is not neccessary.
5. It never occured to him that no one would beleive his story.
6. I can not succede without satisfactery marksmanship.
7. The secretery told the officer her grievence.
8. He made a writen report of all she said.
9. He then recieved a complaint from the managment regarding the report.
10. On this occassion, he undoutedly was right.
11. The canidate stoped at the small town and spoke to the citizins.

12. He made three seperate speaches all together.

13. His words came accross well, and what he said was very usful.

14. I surly recomend that you vote for him if you have the oppertunity.

15. Fourty miles away, a turnament was going on.

16. The witness saw the lisense number clearly.

17. If he had put it in writting immediatly, he would not have forgoten it.

18. Never the less, he was abel to remember the first three digits.

19. It was a goverment plate.

20. There was also a noticable dent in the side of the car.

■ ■ ■ ■ ■ ■ ■ ■ ■ ■ ■ ■ ■ ■ ■

1. A lot, all right, apartments
2. Alcohol, among, major
3. argument
4. judgment, vehicle, necessary
5. occurred, believe
6. cannot, succeed, satisfactory
7. secretary, grievance
8. written
9. received, management
10. occasion, undoubtedly
11. candidate, stopped, citizens
12. separate, speeches, altogether
13. across, useful
14. surely, recommend, opportunity
15. Forty, tournament
16. license
17. writing, immediately, forgotten
18. Nevertheless, able
19. government
20. noticeable

WORDS FREQUENTLY USED IN POLICE REPORTS

As with the commonly used words on the preceding pages, take the following words five or ten at a time and memorize their spellings.

Memorize words frequently used in police reports.

abduction
abrasion
accelerated
accessories
accident
accomplice
acquitted
affidavit
apparatus
arrested
arson
assaulted
bureau
burglary
coercion
commission
complainant
conspiracy
conviction
corpse
counterfeit
criminal
defendant
dispatched
disposition
drunkenness
embezzlement
emergency
evidence
extortion
forcible
fraudulent
headlight
homicide
indict
interrogate
intimidation
intoxication
investigation
juvenile
larceny
legal
lieutenant
misdemeanor
offense
official
patrolling
pedestrian
possession
precinct
premises
prosecute
prostitution
pursuit
resistance
robbery
sabotage
scene
seize
sentence
sergeant
serious
sheriff
statute
strangulation
subpoena
suicide
summons
surrender
surveillance
suspect
suspicion
taillight
testimony
thief
thieves
traffic
trespassing
vagrancy
victim
warrant

➢ Practice

Read the following sentences and correct any incorrectly spelled words. If no corrections are needed, write OK.

1. His drunkeness resulted in an offical complaint.
2. The juvenil offered no resistence during the robbary.
3. The victum of the homoside was the liutenent.
4. He served the subpena on the suspect.
5. Embezzelment is a sereous offence.
6. The criminel was aquited of arsen.
7. The complainent had no real evidance.
8. The sherrif drove him to the wrong presinct.
9. Forceable entry was used during the burglery.

10. Is it legel to interogate this suspict?

■ ■ ■ ■ ■ ■ ■ ■ ■ ■ ■ ■ ■ ■ ■ ■

1. drunkenness, official
2. juvenile, resistance, robbery
3. victim, homicide, lieutenant
4. subpoena
5. embezzlement, serious, offense
6. criminal, acquitted, arson
7. complainant, evidence
8. sheriff, precinct
9. Forcible, burglary
10. legal, interrogate, suspect

Be careful adding endings to words. Use a dictionary or speller/divider if in doubt.

Note: You can always look up in a dictionary or speller/divider the correct way to add endings. Some dictionaries will give you the complete spellings:

occur, occurred, occurring

Others will simply show how the ending should look:

occur, -red, -ring

➢ Practice

Add the endings indicated to the following words.

1. make (ing, s) ______________________________
2. give (s, ing) ______________________________
3. accurate (ly) ______________________________
4. love (s, ed, able, ing) ______________________________
5. drive (s, ing, able) ______________________________
6. sure (ly) ______________________________

7. hope (s, ing, ful) ______________________________

8. compile (s, ed, ing) ______________________________

9. investigate (s, ed, ing) ______________________________

10. interrogate (s, ed, ing) ______________________________

■ ■ ■ ■ ■ ■ ■ ■ ■ ■ ■ ■ ■ ■ ■

1. making, makes
2. gives, giving
3. accurately
4. loves, loved, lovable, loving
5. drives, driving, drivable
6. surely
7. hopes, hoping, hopeful
8. compiles, compiled, compiling
9. investigates, investigated, investigating
10. interrogates, interrogated, interrogating

➢ Practice

Add the endings -s, -ed, and -ing to each of the following words.

Example: refer refers, referred, referring

1. occur ______________________________

2. hop ______________________________

3. hope ______________________________

4. run (can't add -ed) ______________________________

5. stop ______________________________

6. concur ______________________________

7. suspect ______________________________

8. mug ______________________________

9. look ______________________________

■ ■ ■ ■ ■ ■ ■ ■ ■ ■ ■ ■ ■ ■ ■

1. occurs, occurred, occurring
2. hops, hopped, hopping
3. hopes, hoped, hoping
4. runs, running (incidentally, run + -ed = ran)
5. stops, stopped, stopping
6. concurs, concurred, concurring
7. suspects, suspected, suspecting
8. mugs, mugged, mugging
9. looks, looked, looking

To make the plural form of words ending in *y* and preceded by a *vowel* (a,e,i,o,u), add -s. If the *y* is preceded by a *consonant*, change the *y* to *i* and add -es.

➢ Practice

Add the ending -s or -es to make the following words plural.

1. boy ____________________
2. lady ____________________
3. fly ____________________
4. country ____________________
5. burglary ____________________
6. emergency ____________________
7. felony ____________________
8. robbery ____________________
9. key ____________________
10. conspiracy ____________________

■ ■ ■ ■ ■ ■ ■ ■ ■ ■ ■ ■ ■ ■ ■

1. boys, 2. ladies, 3. flies, 4. countries, 5. burglaries, 6. emergencies, 7. felonies, 8. robberies, 9. keys, 10. conspiracies

HOMONYMS

Another way to improve your spelling is to memorize the difference in the homonyms in our language. A **homonym** is a word that sounds like another word but has a different meaning and a different spelling. For example, the words *here* and *hear* are homonyms—they sound the same but they are spelled differently, and they mean different things. A sentence will make sense only if you select the spelling that is correct for what you want to say.

Learn the spellings and meanings of the most common homonyms.

WORD	MEANING	USE IN A SENTENCE
accept	to take, receive, agree to	I *accept* that alibi.
except	to exclude, leave out	It is sound *except* for one point.

WORD	**MEANING**	**USE IN A SENTENCE**
affect	to influence (verb)	How will that *affect* me?
effect	result (noun)	The *effect* is devastating.
all ready	everyone is prepared	The officers are *all ready*.
already	by this time	Is the report *already* written?
ascent	motion upward	Her *ascent* to the top was swift.
assent	consent, agree	Do you *assent* to the conditions?
brake	device for stopping motion	Did the trolley *brake* fail?
break	fracture, interrupt	How did you *break* your arm?
		Let's take a *break*.
capital	money, seat of government	How much *capital* is involved?
capitol	government building	Turn left at the *capitol*.
cite	quote, summon to appear in court	He opted to *cite* the Fifth Amendment.
sight	act of seeing, perception	The *sight* was ghastly.
site	location	She reached the *site* at noon.
council	an assembly	The *council* was in agreement.
counsel	an attorney, advice	His *counsel* gave him *counsel*.
decent	proper, suitable, right	It's the *decent* thing to do.
descent	motion downward	The *descent* from the top was rapid.
dissent	disagreement	The *dissent* caused a strike.
desert	forsake, abandon	I will not *desert* my post.
dessert	course at the end of a meal	She had pie for *dessert*.
forth	onward or forward	He came *forth* upon command.
fourth	numerically number 4	She was *fourth* in line.
hear	perceive by ear, listen to	Did you *hear* him leave?
here	in this place	We got *here* too late to save her.
indict	to charge with an offense	I will *indict* him in the morning.
indite	to compose and write	I will *indite* my thoughts later.
its	owned by "it"	The car lost *its* wheels.
it's	contraction of "it is"	*It's* time for us to go.
knew	past tense of "to know"	Pat *knew* the suspect was guilty.
new	modern, fresh	The *new* car gets good mileage.

WORD	MEANING	USE IN A SENTENCE
lead	a metal	He was hit by a *lead* pipe.
led	past tense of "to lead"	She *led* the procession.
meat	food	I eat *meat* once a day.
meet	encounter, come together	I will *meet* you on the corner.
principal	chief, money, head of a school	He is the *principal* witness.
principle	rule, a fundamental truth	It is a matter of *principle*.
precede	to come before	A *precedes* B in the alphabet.
proceed	to continue, to go on	The investigation will *proceed* later.
right	correct, privilege, direction	She was *right* to go first.
rite	ceremony	It was a religious *rite*.
write	to inscribe by hand	Did you *write* the note?
their	belonging to "they"	It is *their* car.
there	in that place	I went *there* yesterday.
they're	contraction of "they are"	*They're* late, as usual.
threw	past tense of "to throw"	He *threw* the brick at the window.
through	from end to end	She drove *through* the tunnel.
to	toward, in the direction of	He went *to* the store.
too	more than enough, also	I have *too* many *too*.
two	number 2	I have *two* cars.
vary	to change	Her story did not *vary*.
very	extremely, much	He is *very* tired.
whose	belonging to "who"	*Whose* car is this?
who's	contraction of "who is"	*Who's* going to drive it home?
your	belonging to "you"	*Your* car has been stolen.
you're	contraction of "you are"	*You're* going to walk home.

➢ Practice

Select the correct homonyms for each sentence. Underline the word to be used.

1. The lieutenant failed to tell me (whose/who's) assignment had priority this morning.

2. Consequently, the assignment was (to/too/two) late.

3. (Its/It's) extremely inconvenient when an assignment is not covered.

4. (Their/There/They're) (all ready/already) blaming me for the error.

5. (Their/There/They're) were (to/too/two) police officers who could have corrected the error.

6. The captain should keep the lieutenant, (whose/who's) directly responsible for assigning work, more closely informed on (their/there/they're) needs.

7. When the committee has (its/it's) meeting this afternoon, everything will be straightened out.

8. Regardless of (whose/who's) responsible, this mix-up shows that (its/it's) necessary to open up the lines of communication.

9. (Their/There/They're) are probably enough problems to warrant a monthly meeting.

10. The sergeant sent me out (to/too/two) serve a warrant at the (capital/capitol) building.

11. The warrant will (indict/indite) several people.

12. It (cites/sights/sites) names and addresses of several suspects.

13. I (hear/here) that it will cause many people a lot of concern.

14. The (affect/effect) of the warrant on the key suspects could be (vary/very) important.

15. It could (brake/break) up a crime ring (whose/who's) existence thus far has been preserved.

16. We should (precede/proceed) with all due haste in carrying (threw/through) on it.

17. But, if they have good (council/counsel), they may beat the rap.

18. It doesn't seem (right/rite/write) that such a thing could happen.

19. If it did, it would be the (forth/fourth) time in 10 years.

20. I just cannot (accept/except) that the judge might (ascent/assent) to dismissing the case.

21. (Its/It's) highly improbable when such an important (principal/principle) is at stake.

22. We (knew/new) all along, however, that it was a possibility.

23. (Your/You're) going to have to be (vary/very) careful in this case.

24. (Their/There/They're) going to have to prove we're not (right/rite/write).

25. If they do, we'll have to (desert/dessert) the entire case.

■ ■ ■ ■ ■ ■ ■ ■ ■ ■ ■ ■ ■ ■ ■ ■

1. whose; 2. too; 3. It's; 4. They're, already; 5. There, two; 6. who's, their; 7. its; 8. who's, it's; 9. There; 10. to, capitol; 11. indict; 12. cites; 13. hear; 14. effect, very; 15. break, whose; 16. proceed, through; 17. counsel; 18. right; 19. fourth; 20. accept, assent; 21. It's, principle; 22. knew; 23. You're, very; 24. They're, right; 25. desert

As noted earlier, the skills of even the best spellers tend to degenerate rapidly when relying on spellcheckers. But such programs do nothing to correct the choice of the wrong homonym, as illustrated by the following:

My Spellchecker

My pea sea has a spellchecker
Witch four me is something knew.
Its a vary simple matter too run my righting threw.
Weather I report on a cereal killer
Ore a victim whose over rot,
My spellchecker will find miss steaks
Weather eye due ore knot.

The lessen: Do not take you're spellchecker fore granite.

© Kären M. Hess, 2000

COMMONLY CONFUSED WORDS

A cartoon shows two bums talking. The one says, "My mother always wished I'd gone further in life." The other says, "You mean farther, don't you?" The response, "No, I'm sure it was my mother."

Learn to distinguish between words that are commonly confused.

Like the homonyms, another set of words is important because they are frequently confused and will not be identified by a spellcheck program. Following are some of the most frequently used:

WORD	MEANING	EXAMPLE
adapt	to adjust or make suitable	I will *adapt* to working nights.
adopt	select as one's own	I will *adopt* a positive attitude.

WORD	MEANING	EXAMPLE
allusion illusion	casual or indirect reference false idea, unreal image	She made the *allusion* to Plato's work. The mirror created an optical *illusion*.
ante- anti-	before, in front of against, opposite to	We waited in the *ante*room before entering. His *anti*perspirant was not working well.
differ from differ with	to stand apart because of unlikeness to disagree	Boys *differ from* girls biologically. I beg to *differ with* your opinion.
elicit illicit	to bring out or evoke illegal or improper	The trainer's order will *elicit* a response. Marijuana is considered an *illicit* substance.
elude allude	evade, escape notice refer to casually	The suspect managed to *elude* police. He seemed to *allude* to that movie a lot.
fewer less	numbers (how many) amount (how much)	This beer has *fewer* calories. It is also *less* filling.
imply infer	suggest or hint at draw a conclusion	I don't mean to *imply* that you cheated. Based on facts, I *infer* that you cheated.
adjacent contiguous	adjoining in contact	The two friends rented *adjacent* apartments. The *contiguous* United States exclude Alaska and Hawaii.
advise inform	suggest tell	I *advise* you to seek legal counsel. I will *inform* you of our decision later.
amount number	total number (noun) count or enumerate (verb)	I will pay you the full *amount* tomorrow. The tourists here *number* in the thousands.
anxious eager	nervous looking forward to	The witness was anxious about testifying. The convict was eager for parole.
bimonthly semimonthly	every two months twice a month	I fertilize my lawn *bimonthly*. I receive a paycheck *semimonthly*.
credible creditable	believable worthy of praise	The victim's story was *credible*. The officer's actions were *creditable*.
farther further	to a more distant point to a greater extent	Take the bear *farther* out of town. We should question him *further*.

➢ Practice

Select the correct word for each sentence by underlining it.

1. The students were (anxious/eager) for summer break.

2. We didn't think the suspect's alibi was very (credible/creditable).

3. When the K9 handler gives the command, it will (elicit/illicit) the proper response from the dog.

4. When the New Yorker moved to Seattle, she did not (adapt/adopt) well to the new city.

5. When the car next to us rolled backward, it created the (allusion/illusion) that we were moving forward.

■ ■ ■ ■ ■ ■ ■ ■ ■ ■ ■ ■ ■ ■ ■ ■ ■

1. eager, 2.credible, 3. elicit, 4. adapt, 5. illusion

APOSTROPHES

You probably noticed that some of the homonyms were the same except for an apostrophe; for example, *its* and *it's*. Although the apostrophe is only a small punctuation mark, it's a very important one that can change the meaning of a sentence entirely. Consider the following:

A clever dog knows its master.
A clever dog knows it's master.

The butler stood at the door and called the guests names.
The butler stood at the door and called the guests' names.

The apostrophe *is* important, and you need to master the specific purposes for which it is used.

Use an apostrophe to show:

- **omission (contractions).**
- **possession (except for pronouns).**
- **plurals of letters and figures.**

Examples:

- In the word *it's* (meaning "it is"), the *i* of *is* has been omitted.
- In the phrase "the boy's coat," the *'s* shows that the boy owns the coat.
- In the phrase "three A's and two B's," the *'s* shows plurality (more than one).

Sometimes the placement of the apostrophe is very obvious—for example, when letters have been omitted, the apostrophe goes in place of what was omitted:

> *can't* for *cannot* (the *no* has been omitted)
> *you're* for *you are* (the *a* has been omitted)

Notice that *you're* means "you are"—*not* ownership. Do *not* use an apostrophe to show pronoun ownership. The words *yours*, *ours*, *its*, and *whose* are possessive pronouns. They don't need an apostrophe to show possession. If you put an apostrophe in, you change the meaning of the word:

> *you're* means "you are"
> *it's* means "it is"
> *who's* means "who is"
> *they're* means "they are"

For all other words, however, you need an apostrophe and an *s* to show possession. If you simply add an *s*, you make the word plural, as already practiced. The word *boy* is made plural by adding an *s* to make it *boys* (more than one boy). Adding an *'s* makes the word possessive, e.g., the *boy's* coat. If you have a situation in which you have to show *both* plural and possession, then you add *s'*—The two *boys'* coats were stolen.

Knowing where to put the apostrophe to show ownership is made simpler if you think of the meaning of the sentence. The sentence "The boy's coat was stolen" means the same as "The coat of the boy was stolen." Notice that *boy* does not end in *s*, so you simply add *'s*. The sentence "The boys' coats were stolen" means "The coats of the boys were stolen." Notice now that *boys* does end in *s*—to show plural. Therefore, you simply add an apostrophe *after* the *s*.

To summarize:

Adding only *s* makes a word plural.	The *boys* left.
Adding *'s* makes a singular word possessive.	The *boy's* coat was gone.
Adding *s'* makes a word plural and possessive.	The *boys'* coats were gone.

➢ Practice

Add apostrophes where needed in the following sets of sentences. Remember that if the word is only plural, you do *not* use an apostrophe.

1. The books are gone.
2. The books cover is torn.
3. The books jackets are matched.

4. Both suspects excuses were poor.
5. The suspects smile dimmed.
6. We caught the suspects.

7. The mens dinner was late.
8. Men are always late.
9. The mans bus left him.

10. The companies are in competition.
11. My companys plan is good.
12. Other companies plans couldnt compete.

■ ■ ■ ■ ■ ■ ■ ■ ■ ■ ■ ■ ■ ■ ■

1.	books	- no apostrophe—simply plural
2.	book's	- the cover of the *book*—singular, possessive
3.	books'	- the jackets of the *books*—plural, possessive
4.	suspects'	- excuses of the *suspects*—plural, possessive
5.	suspect's	- smile of the *suspect*—singular, possessive
6.	suspects	- no apostrophe—simply plural
7.	men's	- dinner of the *men*—careful: notice there is no *s*, so you add '*s*
8.	men	- no apostrophe—is plural in this form (an irregular English plural)
9.	man's	- bus of the *man*—singular, possessive
10.	companies	- no apostrophe—plural
11.	company's	- plan of my *company*—singular, possessive
12.	companies'	- plan of the *companies*—plural, possessive
	couldn't	- contraction of "could not"

Apostrophes *do* make a difference.

➢ Practice

Add apostrophes where needed in the following sentences. If correct, write OK.

1. All of the victims stated that their attacker was a short man.

2. Theyre going to be called as witnesses in this case.

3. Whos going to recover the victims body?

4. The department has its policy on matters of this sort.

5. Your car was removed to the police garage yesterday.

6. Your daughter is in the juvenile courts custody.

7. Your first two shots hit the targets center.

8. Johns partner, the chiefs son, is a good cop.

9. All efforts to determine the mans identity have failed.

■ ■ ■ ■ ■ ■ ■ ■ ■ ■ ■ ■ ■ ■ ■ ■

1. OK; 2. They're; 3. Who's, victim's; 4. OK; 5. OK; 6. court's; 7. target's; 8. John's, chief's; 9. man's

You should now be able to do a good job of **proofreading** your reports for spelling errors. You should read through every report you write and look at the spelling of each word. Your care in spelling will reflect positively on you as an individual and as a professional.

SUMMARY

Memorize common words with difficult spellings. Memorize words frequently used in police reports. Be careful adding endings to words. Use a dictionary or speller/divider if in doubt.

Learn the spellings and meanings of the most common homonyms. Learn to distinguish between words that are commonly confused.

Use an apostrophe to show omission (contractions), possession (except for pronouns), and plurals of letters and figures. Apostrophes *do* make a difference.

You may wish to review this chapter before taking the self-test on p.227.

Chapter Ten

ABBREVIATIONS, NUMBERS, AND CAPITALIZATION

Do you know:

- When and how to abbreviate?
- When to use figures and when to write the number (2 or two)?
- When to capitalize?

Each of the preceding is an important element in clear, effective writing. Your department may have some special rules of its own regarding abbreviations, use of numbers, and capitalization. Check with your supervisor to make certain none of the rules presented here conflict with your department's policy. If your department uses different rules, learn them! The most important readers of your reports will be individuals within your own department.

ABBREVIATIONS

You've already learned to use abbreviations in notes. They are time-savers and should be used whenever possible, as long as they cannot be misunderstood by your readers. For example, *P.O.* can mean *petty officer*, *post office*, or *postal order*. *A.A.A.* can stand for the *Agricultural Adjustment Administration*, the *Amateur Athletic Association*, or the *American Automobile Association*. Be certain the abbreviations you use cannot be misunderstood.

Find out what abbreviations are commonly used in your department. For example, in many departments *S* is an accepted abbreviation for *suspect* and *V* for *victim*. Appendix C lists some of the most common abbreviations used in law enforcement notes.

In your reports, do not use abbreviations except for titles, addresses, time, speed, and names of agencies usually referred to by initials.

In your *notes*, use accepted abbreviations that cannot be misunderstood.

Examples:

Wrong: *At.* for attention
Right: *Attn.* for attention

Wrong: *S.* for street
Right: *St.* for street

➢ Application

Give the accepted abbreviation for the following words and phrases. If you don't know the abbreviation for a word, look it up in a dictionary. If you don't know the abbreviation for a phrase, take an educated guess. Usually the initials of the main words are used, for example, Federal Bureau of Investigation = FBI.

______ 1. All Points Bulletin

______ 2. Approximately

______ 3. Assault with a Deadly Weapon

______ 4. Avenue

______ 5. Block

______ 6. Boulevard

______ 7. Court

______ 8. Crossing

______ 9. Dead on Arrival

______ 10. Defendant

______ 11. Eastbound

______ 12. Hours

______ 13. Identification

______ 14. Injury

______ 15. Investigation

______ 16. Miles Per Hour

______ 17. Road

______ 18. Signal

______ 19. Speed

______ 20. Street

______ 21. Suspect

______ 22. Temporary

______ 23. Unknown

______ 24. Unmarked

______ 25. Vehicle

______ 26. Victim

______ 27. Witness

■ ■ ■ ■ ■ ■ ■ ■ ■ ■ ■ ■ ■ ■ ■ ■

1. APB, 2. approx., 3. ADW, 4. Ave., 5. blk., 6. Blvd., 7. Ct., 8. X-ing, 9. DOA, 10. Def., 11. E/B, 12. Hrs. (hrs.), 13. ID, 14. Inj., 15. Inv., 16. m.p.h. (mph), 17. Rd., 18. Sig., 19. Spd., 20. St., 21. Susp., 22. Temp., 23. Unk., 24. Unmkd., 25. Veh., 26. Vic., 27. Wit.

How would you respond to reading the following statement in a report?

> At approx. 1000 hrs. I saw def. veh. make a rt turn in hvy trf and go E/B on the rd. past the ct.

You probably would have to take time to "uncode" all the abbreviations. The above statement is perfectly fine for *notes*, but it is *not* acceptable for reports.

In your *reports*, do not use abbreviations except for titles, addresses, time, speed, and names of agencies usually referred to by initials.

Examples:

Wrong: I went <u>E/B</u> on Clark St.
Right: I went <u>eastbound</u> on Clark St.

Wrong: Ms. Smith is the <u>susp</u>. in the case.
Right: Ms. Smith is the <u>suspect</u> in the case

➢ Practice

Read the following sentences. Assume they are in a *report*. If abbreviations are incorrectly used, omit them and write the word(s) which should have been included. If the sentence is correct, write OK.

1. The FBI caught the susp. at the X-ing.
2. I responded to a call at approx. 10 a.m. and answered it in an unmkd. patrol car.
3. Dr. Hawkins lives at 1317 N. Elm Blvd.
4. The veh. drove two blks. at 65/35.

■ ■ ■ ■ ■ ■ ■ ■ ■ ■ ■ ■ ■ ■ ■ ■ ■ ■

1. The FBI caught the <u>suspect</u> at the <u>crossing</u>.
2. I responded to a call at <u>approximately</u> 10 a.m. and answered it in an <u>unmarked</u> patrol car.
3. OK
4. The <u>vehicle</u> drove two <u>blocks</u> at <u>65 m.p.h. in a 35 m.p.h. zone</u>.

Two abbreviations commonly used in writing may be of great use to you. These two abbreviations are *e.g.* and *i.e. E.g.* means "for example"; *i.e.* means "that is." An easy way to remember the difference is to think of "e.g." as "*eg-sample*." Since your reports will contain many details, you probably will have frequent need for these two abbreviations. Note in the examples below that a comma follows each abbreviation (e.g., i.e.,).

Use *e.g.* to show examples.
Use *i.e.* to make an explanation.

Examples:

Many cars are unsafe, *i.e.*, they are frequently involved in accidents.
There are many types of crime, *e.g.*, murder, robbery, arson.

➢ Practice

In the sentences below, add either the abbreviation *e.g.* or *i.e.* between the statement and the example or explanation which follows it.

1. He is a man of action, ______ he gets results.
2. The suspect used abusive language, _____ "pig," "S.O.B."
3. He has been in trouble before, _____ vandalism, shoplifting, auto theft.
4. She should be incarcerated, _____ put in jail.
5. After hitting the tree, the vehicle had a broken radiator, a caved-in roof, and the engine had been ruined, _____ it was a total loss.

▪ ▪ ▪ ▪ ▪ ▪ ▪ ▪ ▪ ▪ ▪ ▪ ▪ ▪ ▪

1\. i.e., 2. e.g., 3. e.g., 4. i.e., 5. i.e.

Look back at the abbreviations on the last few pages. What do you notice about them? Most abbreviations are followed by *periods*. Only those in all capital letters omit the period.

Put a period after all abbreviations
except those that are all in capital letters.

Examples:

Wrong:	Dr Jones removed the bullet.
Right:	Dr. Jones removed the bullet.
Wrong:	CA. (for California)
Right:	CA (for California)

➢ Practice

Add any needed periods to the following abbreviations.

1. a m	4. F B I	7. Ave	10. D O A
2. Mr	5. m p h	8. IL	11. max
3. susp	6. St	9. Ill	12. A S A P

■■■■■■■■■■■■■■■■

1. a.m. 2. Mr. 3. susp. 4. FBI 5. m.p.h. 6. St. 7. Ave. 8. IL 9. Ill. 10. DOA 11. max. 12. ASAP

NUMBERS

Policies vary regarding when numbers are written as figures, e.g., 9, and when they are spelled, e.g., nine. Check with your supervisor to see if your department has a policy on using numbers. The following rules, however, are generally acceptable in most reports.

Write out numbers that are under 10 or that come at the beginning of a sentence.

Use figures for numbers over nine; for a series of numbers; and for dates, street numbers, page numbers, time, and speed.

Be consistent. Do not mix words and figures in the same sentence.

Examples:

Wrong: I have 1 partner.
Right: I have one partner.

Wrong: 187 officers are in our department.
Right: There are 187 officers in our department.

Wrong: He stole three watches, 17 clocks, and 102 rings.
Right: He stole 3 watches, 17 clocks, and 102 rings.

➢ Practice

Correct any numbers that are used incorrectly in the following sentences. If no changes are needed, write OK.

1. The 2 cars were going seventy m.p.h. in a thirty m.p.h. zone.

2. He left at one p.m. for 1309 Walnut St. and arrived at ten p.m.

3. My salary of seventeen thousand five hundred dollars a year is too low.

4. How could the 2 witnesses disagree so much in their descriptions?

5. $10,000 is too much to spend for that piece of equipment.

■ ■ ■ ■ ■ ■ ■ ■ ■ ■ ■ ■ ■ ■ ■ ■

1. The two cars were going 70 m.p.h. in a 30 m.p.h. zone.*
2. He left at 1 p.m. for 1309 Walnut St. and arrived at 10 p.m.
3. My salary of $17,500 a year is too low.
4. How could the two witnesses disagree so much in their descriptions?
5. Ten thousand dollars is too much to spend for that piece of equipment. (*or* The cost, $10,000, is . . .)

* **Note**: Figures are used for speed, even though a number is expressed as a word earlier in the sentence.

CAPITALIZATION

Capitalization should always be used for a reason. Usually this reason is to differentiate between something general and something specific, e.g., street/Oak Street; cow/Flossie.

If you are not sure whether a word should be capitalized, look it up in a dictionary or speller/divider. If the word is capitalized, it will be printed with a capital letter in these references.

Use capital letters for:

- **the first word in a sentence.**
- **names of specific people and members of national, political, racial, regional, or religious groups.**
- **geographical names.**
- **organizations, institutions.**
- **specific streets, buildings, ships, planes, trains, and trademark names.**
- **historical periods, events, and special events.**
- **days of the week, months, and holidays.**
- **titles used before a name.**

Examples:

Wrong: we left yesterday.
Right: We left yesterday.

Wrong: He said that joe, an american, is a lutheran.
Right: He said that Joe, an American, is a Lutheran.

Wrong: The mississippi river runs through minnesota.
Right: The Mississippi River runs through Minnesota.

Wrong: The los angeles police department has many fbi graduates.
Right: The Los Angeles Police Department has many FBI graduates.

Wrong: The mercantile building is on thirtieth street.
Right: The Mercantile Building is on Thirtieth Street.

Wrong: We celebrate christmas on sunday, december 25.
Right: We celebrate Christmas on Sunday, December 25.

Wrong: He gave lieutenant smith a sad story.
Right: He gave Lieutenant Smith a sad story.

➢ Practice

Correct any errors in capitalization in the following sentences. If no changes are needed, write OK.

1. On january 14, 20--, at 0915 hrs., i interviewed mr. jerry Webster, Architect with the firm of Johnson associates.

2. During the Interview, mr. Webster stated the following Facts.

3. on Tuesday, january 13, the Employees in the office of Johnson associates had completed the work for a Local School District and decided to have a little celebration.

4. At approximately 1415 hrs. Champagne was opened and all Employees partied for several hours.

5. At 1715 hrs. they left for the Restaurant where they had dinner.

6. at about 2030 hrs., they left the Restaurant and went to the Apartment of one of the Department Heads, Jim lawson, who lived at 181 third ave.

7. They continued their party until 0130 hrs., then left for a Bar downtown.

▪ ▪ ▪ ▪ ▪ ▪ ▪ ▪ ▪ ▪ ▪ ▪ ▪ ▪ ▪

1. January, I, Mr. Jerry, architect, Associates
2. interview, Mr., facts
3. On, January, employees, Associates, local school district
4. champagne, employees
5. restaurant
6. At, restaurant, apartment, department heads, Lawson, Third Ave.
7. bar

You probably noticed that in the above exercise almost as many errors were caused by capitals being used where they shouldn't be as vice versa. This is also true in report writing. Most errors in capitalization are made in using a capital where it should *not* be used, rather than in forgetting to use a capital letter. If you cannot think of a specific reason for capitalizing a word, do *not* capitalize it.

Do *not* capitalize:

- **general words.**
- **direction.**
- **names of seasons.**
- **course names, unless followed by a number or derived from a proper name.**
- **words showing family relationship preceded by a possessive pronoun.**
- **titles following a name.**

Examples:

Wrong: The Building is new; the time building is old.
Right: The building is new; the Time Building is old.

Wrong: Drive South on Third Street. He lives in the south.
Right: Drive south on Third Street. He lives in the South.

Wrong: I like Summer better than Winter.
Right: I like summer better than winter.

Wrong: I am taking english, History and algebra 1.
Right: I am taking English, history and Algebra 1.

Wrong: I think uncle harry is my favorite Uncle.
Right: I think Uncle Harry is my favorite uncle.

Wrong: Why did the Sergeant return your report?
Right: Why did Sergeant Jones return your report?

➢ Practice

Correct any errors in capitalization in the following sentences. If no changes are needed, write OK.

1. A customer in the dayton's store, Jim Marshall, 1692 ashcroft st., fresno, saw two white males acting suspiciously.
2. The Suspect, Jefferson, stuffed a man's fur coat into a box being held by another Male described as Blond, 170 Lbs.
3. Jefferson then left the Store and walked to a red Pick-up and drove North on Dale street.
4. Marshall obtained the license number and reported it to the Store Manager who notified Security.
5. Security showed a photograph of jefferson to the Witness who said it was the same man; he could be positive because he remembered thinking how much the man looked like his Uncle.
6. A check of the Coat Rack revealed that one fur coat was missing and that the chain running through the coat and up to the Rack had been cut.

7. Security notified the Police Department who immediately sent two Detectives to the Store to investigate.

8. since the coat was made in italy, it cost $550.00; therefore the crime was listed as a Felony.

9. Detective smith and detective Harolds were assigned to the Case.

■ ■ ■ ■ ■ ■ ■ ■ ■ ■ ■ ■ ■ ■ ■

1. Dayton's Store, Ashcroft St., Fresno
2. suspect, male, blond, lbs.
3. store, pick-up, north, Street
4. store manager, security
5. Jefferson, witness, uncle
6. coat rack, rack
7. police department, detectives, store
8. Since, Italy, felony
9. Smith, Detective, case

SUMMARY

In your *notes*, use accepted abbreviations that cannot be misunderstood. In your *reports*, do not use abbreviations except for titles, addresses, time, speed, and names of agencies usually referred to by initials.

Use *e.g.* to show examples. Use *i.e.* to make an explanation.

Put a period after all abbreviations except those that are all in capital letters.

Write out numbers that are under 10 or that come at the beginning of a sentence. Use figures for numbers over nine; for a series of numbers; and for dates, street numbers, page numbers, time, and speed. Be consistent. Do not mix words and figures in the same sentence.

Use capital letters for the first word in a sentence; names of specific people and members of national, political, racial, regional, or religious groups; geographical names; organizations and institutions; specific streets, buildings, ships, planes, trains, and trademark names; historical periods, events, and special events; days of the week, months, and holidays; and titles used before a name.

Do not capitalize general words; direction; names of seasons; course names, unless followed by a number or derived from a proper name; words showing family relationship preceded by a possessive pronoun; and titles following a name.

You may wish to review this chapter before completing the self-test on p.229.

Chapter Eleven

COMMAS

Do you know:

- When to use commas?
- When not to use commas?

Key terms: Harvard comma, interrupters, nonrestrictive, Oxford comma, restrictive, serial comma

Like the apostrophe, the comma is a small punctuation mark, but it can make a big difference in the meaning of a sentence. Consider the following:

> Call me fool if you wish.
> Call me, fool, if you wish.

The comma causes more difficulty than any other punctuation mark. It may be small, but it is extremely important. There are several rules about when to use or *not* to use a comma. Perhaps the best general rule is to use a comma only if it makes the meaning of the sentence clearer.

Punctuation should aid the reader. It is used in place of the normal pauses we use when we speak. A long pause in speech is indicated by a period (.) in writing. It shows the transition from one sentence to another. The comma, on the other hand, shows a short pause within a sentence.

There are four basic rules for use of the comma.

Use a comma:

- **between main clauses joined by *and, but, or, nor, for, yet,* or *so*.**
- **after introductory clauses.**
- **to separate items in a series.**
- **to set off sentence expanders and interrupters.**

Once you have mastered these basic rules, you'll also know when *not* to use a comma.

MAIN CLAUSES

You have already looked at this use of the comma when you learned to correct run-on sentences.

Use a comma between two main clauses joined by the words *and, but, or, nor, for, yet,* or *so*.

Examples:

Wrong:	My boss asked me to come early_but I was late.
Right:	My boss asked me to come early,_but I was late.
Wrong:	Are you free on Friday_or would Thursday be better?
Right:	Are you free on Friday,_or would Thursday be better?

Without the comma between the two main clauses (sentences), the sentence is a run-on sentence. Be careful, however, not to overuse the comma. As you work with commas, be careful that you do *not* use a comma unless there is a specific reason.

- Do *not* use a comma between two predicates.
- Do *not* use a comma between the subject and the predicate.
- Do *not* use a comma between the predicate and object.

Be certain you have two complete sentences on either side of the comma.[1]

Examples:

Wrong:	Our supervisor often gets angry,_and yells at us.
Right:	Our supervisor often gets angry_and yells at us.
Wrong:	Your letter,_has been referred to us.
Right:	Your letter_has been referred to us.
Wrong:	It is imperative,_that the suspect be apprehended.
Right:	It is imperative_that the suspect be apprehended.

(Remember that when a subsentence is attached to the end of a complete sentence, you do *not* put a comma before it.)

---

[1] Two complete sentences (main clauses) joined by a comma *must* have a *conjunction* (and, but, or, nor, for, yet, so) after the comma. The error of using a comma without a conjunction is sometimes called a "comma splice" or "comma fault."

➢ Practice

Correct the following sentences by adding commas where they are needed and omitting unneeded commas. If no changes are needed, write OK.

1. We all know, that supervisors make more money than patrol officers.
2. I will call the witness as soon as possible and I will complete my report.
3. The boys ran up the two steps, and jumped off the platform.
4. Move over there and stand still.
5. The pilot maneuvered his plane through loops and rolls.
6. Your report, has been forwarded for action.
7. The exhibits section of your report was not complete so it has to be returned.
8. It is of the utmost importance, that a police officer be a good marksman.
9. It seems to us, that this is a waste of the taxpayers' money, and a waste of our time.
10. The suspect and her accomplice were transported to police headquarters, after receiving their rights.
11. At this point, Mr. Jones, and a neighbor, made separate attempts to enter the apartment.
12. The suspect did subsequently attempt to perform a breath test, but she was unable to perform it.
13. There was a large desk in this room and its drawers had been opened.
14. Many papers had been strewn around, and the closet door was standing ajar.
15. We took careful notes, and then left.
16. I motioned to my partner to hurry but he didn't see me.
17. The trip to the station was so long, that we were very late.
18. Next time I hope that I have a partner, who is interested in being on time.

■ ■ ■ ■ ■ ■ ■ ■ ■ ■ ■ ■ ■ ■ ■

1. We all know that supervisors make more money than patrol officers.
2. I will call the witness as soon as possible, and I will complete my report.
3. The boys ran up the two steps and jumped off the platform.

4. Move over there, and stand still. (two commands joined by *and*)
5. OK
6. Your report has been forwarded for action.
7. The exhibits section of your report was not complete, so it has to be returned.
8. It is of the utmost importance that a police officer be a good marksman.
9. It seems to us that this is a waste of the taxpayers' money and a waste of our time.
10. The suspect and her accomplice were transported to police headquarters after receiving their rights.
11. At this point Mr. Jones and a neighbor made separate attempts to enter the apartment.
12. OK
13. There was a large desk in this room, and its drawers had been opened.
14. OK
15. We took careful notes and then left.
16. I motioned to my partner to hurry, but he didn't see me.
17. The trip to the station was so long that we were very late.
18. Next time I hope that I have a partner who is interested in being on time.

INTRODUCTORY PHRASES AND CLAUSES

The second use of the comma is to set off introductory words and phrases. Remember you learned earlier about "-ing word groups" and subsentences. If they are attached at the beginning of a sentence, you put a comma after them. If they are attached at the end of a sentence, you do *not* put a comma before them. The only exception to putting a comma *after* introductory material is if it is very short—five words or fewer. In this case the comma is optional. (This will be indicated by an asterisk above the optional comma.)

> **Use a comma *after introductory material*, except when the introductory material is very short, i.e., five words or fewer.**

Examples:

Wrong: At the entrance to the building_I saw a man with a gun.
Right: At the entrance to the building,_I saw a man with a gun.

Wrong: In 2004,_I should get a new car. (a two-word introduction)
Right: In 2004_I should get a new car.

Optional: On 7-7-20-- at 1917 hrs,* his sentence will be over. (* Optional comma)

➢ Practice

Correct the following sentences by adding or removing commas as needed. If no changes are needed, write OK.

1. In the early days of police work education was of little importance for the prospective police officer.
2. After my enlistment is completed I want to work with a civilian law enforcement agency.
3. After 20 years of public life I still am not ready to retire.
4. On 2-6-20-- at 2037 hours Officer Drake saw the suspect's vehicle parked at the curb.
5. After pulling within less than one car length of the patrol car the suspect applied his brakes rapidly.
6. Upon approaching the suspect I immediately noticed her eyes were very red.
7. Upon her arrival to open for business she discovered the loss.
8. Because of the unhealthy condition of the apartment and because the children's mother could not be reached the children were put into protective custody.
9. While on routine patrol through the parking lot at the local bowling alley I saw the above-listed vehicle parked blocking a driving lane.

■ ■ ■ ■ ■ ■ ■ ■ ■ ■ ■ ■ ■ ■ ■

1. In the early days of police work, education . . . .
2. After my enlistment is completed,* I . . . .
3. After 20 years of public life, I . . . .
4. On 2-6-20-- at 2037 hours,* Officer Drake . . . .
5. After pulling within less than one car length of the patrol car, the suspect . . . .
6. Upon approaching the suspect,* I . . . .
7. Upon her arrival to open for business, she . . . .
8. Because of the unhealthy condition of the apartment and because the children's mother could not be reached, the children . . . .
9. While on routine patrol through the parking lot at the local bowling alley, I . . . .

* Optional comma

WORDS IN A SERIES

The third general use of commas is to separate words in a series. This rule applies to several different situations which you should be familiar with.

Use commas between each word in a series of three or more words or phrases.

Use a comma before the *and* preceding the last word or phrase in a series.[2]

Do *not* use a comma after the last word in a series.

The previous edition of this text instructed writers to *not* use a comma before the *and* preceding the last word or phrase in a series. This comma goes by several names—the **Oxford comma**, **Harvard comma**, and **series comma**—and was once considered to be overly academic and too conservative for police reports. However, omitting this comma can reduce the clarity of your report and cause confusion for readers. Consider this sentence which omits the Oxford comma:

Police officers in my family include my parents, Bobby and Phil.

Bobby and Phil happen to be the writer's brothers, but omitting the comma before the *and* in this series could lead the reader to think that the writer's parents are Bobby and Phil. Using the Oxford comma makes the sentence clear.

Examples:

Wrong:	Bill_Harry_Pat and Chris, were assigned the case.
Right:	Bill, Harry, Pat, and Chris_were assigned the case.
Wrong:	Finding the suspect, arresting her_and informing her of her rights are basic duties of the officer.
Right:	Finding the suspect, arresting her, and informing her of her rights are basic duties of the officer.

➢ Practice

Correct the following sentences by adding or deleting commas as needed. If no changes are needed, write OK.

1. The three safeties on automatic pistols are the grip safety safety lock and half cock.
2. The stolen car has power steering power brakes electric door locks electric windows and many other extras.
3. The suspect was placed under arrest for possession of amphetamines possession of marijuana and possession of an alcoholic beverage by a minor.

[2] NOTE TO INSTRUCTORS: This is a key change in content from the previous edition.

4. The suspect's purse contained approximately 1/8 ounce of a substance which appeared to be marijuana and a small bottle containing two small pills marked with a cross on one side.

5. Fourteen unopened cans of 12-ounce Bud beer five unopened cans of Miller Lite beer and two opened cans of Moosehead beer were also found.

■ ■ ■ ■ ■ ■ ■ ■ ■ ■ ■ ■ ■ ■ ■

1. The three safeties on automatic pistols are the grip safety, safety lock, and half cock.
2. The stolen car has power steering, power brakes, electric door locks, electric windows, and many other extras.
3. The suspect was placed under arrest for possession of amphetamines, possession of marijuana, and possession of an alcoholic beverage by a minor.
4. OK (only two objects)
5. Fourteen unopened cans of 12-ounce Bud beer, five unopened cans of Miller Lite beer, and two opened cans of Moosehead beer were also found.

A series of adjectives before a noun should be separated by commas.
Use commas after each adjective before a noun
***except* the one directly before the noun.**

Examples:

Wrong: The tall_lean_lanky_white,_male was arrested.
Right: The tall,_lean,_lanky,_white_male was arrested.

Wrong: The accurate, expensive, automatic,_weapon was stolen.
Right: The accurate, expensive, automatic_weapon was stolen.

Sometimes phrases rather than words are used before a noun. For example, "The Roberto-style, double-breasted, brown-and-black, natural rabbit fur coat was stolen yesterday" contains commas separating *phrases* preceding the noun. The last phrase preceding the noun is "natural rabbit fur"—all three words belong together, so no commas are used. *How* you say the sentence may make a difference in sentences such as this one.

➢ Practice

Correct the following sentences by adding or deleting commas as needed. If no changes are needed, write OK.

1. The tired, angry, nervous, detective swore softly under his breath.

2. The suspect drove away in a late model red compact car.

3. There were three large widely spaced entrance wounds near the heart.

4. The friendly talkative cooperative witness was a big help in the case.

■ ■ ■ ■ ■ ■ ■ ■ ■ ■ ■ ■ ■ ■ ■

1. The tired, angry, nervous detective swore softly under his breath.
2. The suspect drove away in a late model, red compact car.
3. There were three large, widely spaced entrance wounds near the heart. ("wounds" is the noun, "widely spaced" is the word group)
4. The friendly, talkative, cooperative witness was a big help in the case.

Use commas to separate the parts of *dates* and *addresses*.

Examples:

Wrong: On Tuesday_May,_14_20--_he was released.
Right: On Tuesday,_May_14,_20--,_he was released.

Wrong: He lived at 1010 Johnson Street_Minneapolis_Minnesota.
Right: He lived at 1010 Johnson Street,_Minneapolis,_Minnesota.

Wrong: The address of 123,_Ninth Street_Houston_Texas_was given.
Right: The address of 123_Ninth Street,_Houston,_Texas,_was given.

Wrong: On February 26_20--_I arrested the suspect.
Right: On February 26,_20--,_I arrested the suspect. (*no* comma between the month and date)
Right: In February 20--,_I arrested the suspect. (In this situation no commas are needed between the month and year because the *day* is not given. The comma following the date is optional as it is a short introductory phrase.)

➢ Practice

Correct the following sentences by adding or removing commas as needed. If no changes are needed, write OK.

1. On December 21 20-- the suspect was stopped at the intersection of Third Street and Fourth Avenue.

2. The witness lived at 1371 Rogers Avenue Minneapolis Minnesota and the victim at 1821 Hamline Boulevard St. Paul Minnesota.

3. In January, 20-- he moved to Louisville Kentucky with his brother.

4. They stayed there until March 20-- when they moved to New York City.

5. The mountains around Albuquerque New Mexico are quite different from those around Denver Colorado.

■ ■ ■ ■ ■ ■ ■ ■ ■ ■ ■ ■ ■ ■ ■

1. On December 21, 20--, the suspect was stopped at the intersection of Third Street and Fourth Avenue.
2. The witness lived at 1371 Rogers Avenue, Minneapolis, Minnesota, and the victim at 1821 Hamline Boulevard, St. Paul, Minnesota.
3. In January 20--,* he moved to Louisville, Kentucky, with his brother.
4. OK
5. The mountains around Albuquerque, New Mexico, are quite different from those around Denver, Colorado.

* Optional comma.

SENTENCE INTERRUPTERS

You have looked at the first three uses of the comma:

1. Between two main clauses
2. Following introductory phrases and clauses
3. Between items in a series (including dates and addresses)

The fourth use of the comma is to separate words, phrases, and clauses which interrupt the sentence, e.g., "The officer, *who is an expert shot*, fired his pistol only once." There are many different kinds of sentence **interrupters**.

To correctly punctuate sentences with interrupters, take two steps:

1. Find the main sentence.
2. Put commas around anything which interrupts this main sentence (with one exception, which will be explained shortly).

Look at the following sentence:

> "The victim, unfortunately, could not identify her assailant."

The main sentence is: "The victim could not identify her assailant." The word *unfortunately* interrupts this main sentence, so you put commas around it. This helps the reader know what the main sentence is.

Following are the most common types of sentence interrupters:

> My supervisor, Sgt. Wilson, is very fair. (provides additional information, often a name or a title)
>
> My supervisor, who is very fair, is a 20-year veteran. (provides additional information)
>
> My supervisor, not my partner, needs to be informed. (states an exception)
>
> I think, my friends, that we should get an extra day off. (addresses someone)
>
> I also think, however, that we should get paid for that day off. (an aside)

Go back and read the main sentence in each of the preceding examples. Get in the habit of finding the main sentence. If something interrupts the sentence, put commas around that interrupter. If two sentences are joined together, punctuate them to avoid a run-on sentence.

Use commas around sentence interrupters.

Examples:

Wrong: The officer_Sarah Garcia_read the suspect his rights.
Right: The officer,_Sarah Garcia,_read the suspect his rights.

Wrong: My partner_who is not married_doesn't understand family obligations.
Right: My partner,_who is not married,_doesn't understand family obligations.

Wrong: The victim_not the suspect_is probably more believable.
Right: The victim,_not the suspect,_is probably more believable.

Wrong: I think_Sgt. Jones_that you should help us out of here.
Right: I think,_Sgt. Jones,_that you should help us out of here.

Wrong: The witness_understandably_was upset.
Right: The witness,_understandably,_was upset.

If a phrase or clause simply adds additional information or explanation, it is **nonrestrictive** and you should put commas around it, e.g., "Jim, who is over 60 years old, must retire." If, however, the phrase or clause is needed to make the meaning of the sentence explicit, it is called **restrictive**, and you do *not* use commas around it, e.g., "Everyone who is over 60 years old must retire." If you took out the phrase "who is over 60 years old," the sentence would change in meaning. "Everyone must retire." This is not what the original sentence said.

Use commas around any phrases or clauses which can be left out of the sentence without changing its meaning (nonrestrictive phrases and clauses).

Do *not* use commas around phrases and clauses which are needed to make the meaning of the sentence explicit (restrictive phrases and clauses).

Examples:

Wrong: My sergeant_who is a kind man_has few faults.
Right: My sergeant,_who is a kind man,_has few faults. (nonrestrictive)

Wrong: An officer,_who dislikes people,_is in the wrong field.*
Right: An officer_who dislikes people_is in the wrong field. (restrictive)

* **Note**: If you took the interrupter out of the last sentence, it would read "An officer is in the wrong field." The meaning of the sentence has been changed.

➢ Practice

Underline any sentence interrupters. Then correct the sentences by adding or deleting commas as needed. If no changes are needed, write OK.

1. The husband on the other hand felt that the wife was to blame.
2. Mr. Thomas the operations officer called in the report an hour ago.
3. Officers who work for unfriendly superiors are likely to lose their sense of humor.
4. Sergeant Jones a 20-year veteran of the department was promoted last week.
5. Johnson move your car from the no-parking zone.
6. The police patrol car, with the new siren system, is very effective.
7. Often with a large department there are organizational problems.
8. The sergeant it seems to me should listen to the complaint.
9. The witness, who was not married, stated that her husband took her home.

10. General Andrews the post commander is a law-and-order man.

11. I was told by the manager George Wilson that they have a security system.

12. There is no question Smith you are the man we have been looking for.

13. There were however extenuating circumstances in this particular case.

14. As you know Bill police work requires many long hours.

15. The challenge not the money is what makes it all worthwhile.

16. All of the officers even the younger ones in the department know him.

17. Sergeant Jones although he has been with the department for so many years never passes up the opportunity for additional training.

18. The police chief who came on the department with Jones will present him his lieutenant bars.

19. Jones who has had leadership training will take over as shift leader.

20. The suspect not the victim was shot.

21. In law enforcement like everything else we face many challenges.

22. There are I think many reasons for this.

23. According to my records the Jones case, #315-76-0009 was forwarded to your office yesterday.

24. Much of my work day as a special agent is spent at the computer.

25. Everyone who has this much experience should make a good shift leader.

26. Everyone, who has been in the department for 10 years or more, will receive a citation.

27. A sheriff's deputy, who does not like to ride in a car, will have a hard time on patrol.

28. I think Harry that you've done a good job.

29. The witness not the police officer gave the incorrect description.

30. Every man, who is convicted of a crime, deserves to go to jail.

■ ■ ■ ■ ■ ■ ■ ■ ■ ■ ■ ■ ■ ■ ■

1. The husband, on the other hand, felt that the wife was to blame.
2. Mr. Thomas, the operations officer, called in the report an hour ago.
3. OK
4. Sergeant Jones, a 20-year veteran of the department, was promoted last week.
5. Johnson, move your car from the no-parking zone.
6. The police patrol car with the new siren system is very effective.
7. OK
8. The sergeant, it seems to me, should listen to the complaint.
9. OK
10. General Andrews, the post commander, is a law-and-order man.
11. I was told by the manager, George Wilson, that they have a security system.
12. There is no question, Smith, you are the man we have been looking for.
13. There were, however, extenuating circumstances in this particular case.
14. As you know, Bill, police work requires many long hours.
15. The challenge, not the money, is what makes it all worthwhile.
16. All of the officers, even the younger ones in the department, know him.
17. Sergeant Jones, although he has been with the department for so many years, never passes up the opportunity for additional training.
18. The police chief, who came on the department with Jones, will present him his lieutenant bars.
19. Jones, who has had leadership training, will take over as shift leader.
20. The suspect, not the victim, was shot.
21. In law enforcement, like everything else, we face many challenges.
22. There are, I think, many reasons for this.
23. According to my records, the Jones case, #315-76-0009, was forwarded to your office yesterday.
24. OK
25. OK
26. Everyone who has been in the department for 10 years or more will receive a citation.
27. A sheriff's deputy who does not like to ride in a car will have a hard time on patrol.
28. I think, Harry, that you've done a good job.
29. The witness, not the police officer, gave the incorrect description.
30. Every man who is convicted of a crime deserves to go to jail.

REVIEW

You have now looked at the principle uses of the comma—you should have a good idea of when to use commas and when not to use them. Generally, commas are used in the following places:

- Between main clauses joined by a simple conjunction (not between subject and predicate or predicate and object, and not between compound predicates).
- After introductory clauses and phrases.
- To separate items in a series, including adjectives before nouns and parts of dates and addresses.
- To set off sentence interrupters, unless the interrupter is needed—that is, it is *restrictive*—to omit it would change the meaning of the sentence.

As a review, complete the exercise which follows.

➢ Practice

Correct the following sentences by adding commas as needed. If no changes are needed, write OK.

1. Police work requires long hours naturally and devotion to duty.
2. As I was saying Tom you have to put forth some effort into your job in order to get results.
3. His quick efficient professional manner is a credit to him.
4. The accident occurred across the street from 3704 10th Avenue in Denver.
5. The man strong and silent stood alone on the corner.
6. After all the facts of the case have been considered there is only one conclusion we can reach.
7. Eleven jurors felt the man was guilty but one juror insisted he was innocent.
8. The minority not the majority won out in this case.
9. On April 11 1929 the first court precedent was set in Louisville Kentucky in a decisive verdict.
10. The redwood forests of California stately and magnificent left a lasting impression on me.
11. Any police officer who is rude deserves a lecture.
12. After receiving a citation Sergeant Willis the top in her class really thought she was something.
13. The expensive showy gas-gulping Cadillac was a real headache.
14. After I bought the stupid car I realized I had made a mistake and I tried to sell it but was not able to find a buyer.

■ ■ ■ ■ ■ ■ ■ ■ ■ ■ ■ ■ ■ ■ ■

1. Police work requires long hours, naturally, and devotion to duty. (interrupter)
2. As I was saying, Tom, you have to put forth some effort into your job in order to get results. (interrupter)
3. His quick, efficient, professional manner is a credit to him. (adjectives before)
4. OK
5. The man, strong and silent, stood alone on the corner. (adjectives after)
6. After all the facts of the case have been considered, there is only one conclusion we can reach. (introductory)

7. Eleven jurors felt the man was guilty, but one juror insisted he was innocent. (two main clauses)
8. The minority, not the majority, won out in this case. (interrupter)
9. On April 11, 1929, the first court precedent was set in Louisville, Kentucky, in a decisive verdict. (parts of dates and addresses)
10. The redwood forests of California, stately and magnificent, left a lasting impression on me. (adjectives after)
11. OK
12. After receiving a citation, Sergeant Willis, the top in her class, really thought she was something. (introductory and interrupter)
13. The expensive, showy, gas-gulping Cadillac was a real headache. (adjectives before)
14. After I bought the stupid car, I realized I had made a mistake, and I tried to sell it but was not able to find a buyer. (introductory and two main clauses. You should *not* have put a comma between *it* and *but*, as "but was not able to find a buyer" is not a sentence; it is part of a compound predicate.)

SUMMARY

Use a comma between two main clauses joined by the words *and, but, or, nor, for, yet*, or *so*. Use a comma *after introductory material*, except when the introductory material is very short, i.e., five words or fewer.

Use commas between each word in a series of three or more words or phrases. Use a comma before the *and* preceding the last word or phrase in a series. Do *not* use a comma after the last word in a series. A series of adjectives before a noun should be separated by commas. Use commas after each adjective *before a noun* except the one which is directly before the noun.

Use commas to separate the parts of *dates* and *addresses*. Use commas around all *sentence interrupters* if they can be left out of the sentence without changing its meaning (nonrestrictive). Do *not* use commas around interrupters which are needed to make the meaning of the sentence explicit (restrictive).

You may wish to review this chapter before taking the self-test on p.231.

Chapter Twelve

OTHER PUNCTUATION MARKS

Do you know:

- When to use parentheses and dashes?
- When to use slashes/diagonals?
- When to use semicolons?
- When to use colons?
- When to use quotation marks and underlining?
- When to use hyphens?

Key terms: direct quotations, indirect quotations, verbatim

You learned earlier that grammatical errors are usually like felonies—extremely serious. Misusing most of the marks of punctuation contained in the chapter is comparable to a misdemeanor. In fact, many readers will not know the punctuation mark has been misused. Concentrate on the concepts presented in this chapter only after you have mastered those presented in Chapters One through Eleven.

PARENTHESES, DASHES, AND SLASHES/DIAGONALS

In the preceding chapter you learned that sentence interrupters were usually set off from the rest of the sentence by commas. In specific instances, however, these sentence interrupters may be set off by parentheses or dashes. Usually, though, commas are preferred.

Use *parentheses* to enclose figures and to set off supplementary or illustrative matter.

Use *dashes* to mark a sudden break in thought, to set off a summary, or to set off an element that has commas or other marks of punctuation in it.

Use *slashes/diagonals* in certain abbreviations, to express alternatives, to indicate that a person or thing has two functions, and to express dates and fractions.

Examples:

Wrong:	The burglar made three mistakes: 1 he left fingerprints, 2 he dropped a book of matches from a bar he often went to, and 3 he tried to sell the stolen goods to an undercover police officer.
Right:	The burglar made three mistakes: (1) he left fingerprints, (2) he dropped a book of matches from a bar he often went to, and (3) he tried to sell the stolen goods to an undercover police officer.
Wrong:	The car the fastest in the state was caught at the border.
Right:	The car (the fastest in the state) was caught at the border.
Right:	The car, the fastest in the state, was caught at the border.
Wrong:	In fact, she was always right in a way.
Right:	In fact, she was always right—in a way.
Wrong:	He stood up small, frail, and tense looking at the officer.
Right:	He stood up—small, frail, and tense —looking at the officer.
Wrong:	The owner operator of the restaurant was cited.
Right:	The owner/operator of the restaurant was cited.
Wrong:	By 4 6 20-- at least 2-3rds of the violations must be corrected.
Right:	By 4/6/20--* at least 2/3rds of the violations must be corrected.

* **Note**: Hyphens may also be used in dates (4-6-20--).

You see that parentheses, commas, or dashes can be used in the same structure. They affect the tone of the sentence:

Parentheses *whisper* (downplay the information).
Commas provide *normal conversational tone*, which you want to use most often.
Dashes *shout*—which you seldom want to do in your reports.

Note: Both the dash and parentheses should be used sparingly, if at all, in police report writing. The parentheses will most commonly be used to enclose numbers. Dashes will most commonly be used to set off supplementary elements which contain commas or other punctuation.

➢ Practice

Correct the following sentences by adding parentheses or dashes as needed. Often commas could be used, but to gain skill in using parentheses or dashes, please do *not* use commas in this exercise.

1. Officer Fischer saw a large amount of smoke coming from the other side of the apartment east side.

2. The suspect was seen throwing an object through the right side passenger window of the vehicle.

3. The complainant yelled at the suspects, at which time the man kicking at the second vehicle a maroon Cougar ran south on Parklawn Avenue.

4. The latent prints were found on the on off switch.

5. The complainant nervous, angry, and frustrated wanted to sign a statement.

6. These items are marked and are in the property locker evidence locker at the time of the writing of this report.

7. The suspect was traveling at a reduced speed 20 m.p.h. in a 30 m.p.h. zone and was driving primarily on the right shoulder of the roadway.

8. We saw that 1 there were glasses in the sink area, 2 the kitchen door had been broken off its hinges, 3 the back door window had been smashed, and 4 the dog's food dish had been knocked over.

9. He took a true false test.

■ ■ ■ ■ ■ ■ ■ ■ ■ ■ ■ ■ ■ ■ ■ ■ ■

1. Officer Fischer saw a large amount of smoke coming from the other side of the apartment (east side).
2. The suspect was seen throwing an object through the right side (passenger) window of the vehicle.
3. The complainant yelled at the suspects, at which time the man kicking at the second vehicle (a maroon Cougar) ran south on Parklawn Avenue.
4. The latent prints were found on the on/off switch.
5. The complainant—nervous, angry, and frustrated—wanted to sign a statement.
6. These items are marked and are in the property locker (evidence locker) at the time of the writing of this report.
7. The suspect was traveling at a reduced speed (20 m.p.h. in a 30 m.p.h. zone) and was driving primarily on the right shoulder of the roadway.
8. We saw that (1) there were glasses in the sink area, (2) the kitchen door had been broken off its hinges, (3) the back door window had been smashed, and (4) the dog's food dish had been knocked over.
9. He took a true/false test.

SEMICOLONS

You have already seen the main use of the semicolon–~~to~~ separate two main clauses (sentences) not joined by *and, but, or, nor, for, yet*, or *so*. Like the dash, semicolons are sometimes used for clarity when a series of items contains commas. Or they may change the meaning of a sentence entirely as in the following:

> Anne Boleyn kept her head up defiantly an hour after she was executed.
> Anne Boleyn kept her head up defiantly; an hour after, she was executed.

Use a semicolon:

- **between two sentences not joined by a simple conjunction.**
- **to separate items in a series which contain commas.**

Examples:

Wrong:	The officer called for the man to halt, then he fired.
Right:	The officer called for the man to halt; then he fired.
Wrong:	Boston, Massachusetts, Albany, New York, Minneapolis, Minnesota, Austin, Texas, and San Francisco, California, are all nice cities.
Right:	Boston, Massachusetts; Albany, New York; Minneapolis, Minnesota; Austin, Texas; and San Francisco, California, are all nice cities.
Wrong:	The tall, slender, attractive woman smiled, but the short, fat, ugly man turned away.
Right:	The tall, slender, attractive woman smiled; but the short, fat, ugly man turned away.

Note: A semicolon is used between two sentences joined by a simple conjunction when the sentences themselves contain several commas.

➢ Practice

Correct the following sentences by adding commas and semicolons as needed. If already correct, write OK.

1. Six boxes of shells were lying on the floor one box was open but none of the shells was missing.

2. One suspect was described as 4′ 5″ 115 lbs. shoulder-length black hair and olive complexion the other suspect was described as 5′ 2″ 140 lbs. short blond hair and light complexion.

3. The suspect had lived in Oakland California Portland Oregon Denver Colorado and Tempe Arizona since his release from prison.

4. I have lived in Miami Florida but never in Long Beach California.

5. David Strauss 4133 Johnson Lane Dallas Texas was arrested but his accomplice got away.

■ ■ ■ ■ ■ ■ ■ ■ ■ ■ ■ ■ ■ ■ ■ ■

1. Six boxes of shells were lying on the floor; one box was open, but none of the shells was missing.
2. One suspect was described as 4′ 5″, 115 lbs., shoulder-length black hair, and olive complexion; the other suspect was described as 5′ 2″, 140 lbs., short blond hair, and light complexion.
3. The suspect had lived in Oakland, California; Portland, Oregon; Denver, Colorado; and Tempe, Arizona, since his release from prison.
4. I have lived in Miami, Florida, but never in Long Beach, California.
5. David Strauss, 4133 Johnson Lane, Dallas, Texas, was arrested; but his accomplice got away.

COLONS

The colon, too, can change the meaning of a sentence entirely. Consider the following:

Woman without her man is nothing.
Woman: without her, man is nothing.

The colon has three very specific uses.

Use a colon:

- **after the salutation of a business letter.**
- **between the hour and minutes in time (6:10).**
- **to introduce lists or long quotations.**

Examples:

Wrong: Dear Sir,
Right: Dear Sir:

Wrong: He left at 9-15 a.m.
Right: He left at 9:15 a.m.

Wrong: There are three uses of the colon,_after the salutation of a business letter, between the hour and minutes in time, and to introduce lists or long quotations.

Right: There are three uses of the colon:_after the salutation of a business letter, between the hour and minutes in time, and to introduce lists or long quotations.

Do *not* use a colon if you are using the 24-hour clock.

Do *not* use a colon before a simple list following the verb. Use nothing.

Example:

Wrong: The most important witnesses are:_Smith, Anders, and Wu.

Right: The most important witnesses are_Smith, Anders, and Wu.

If, however, the sentence contains a phrase between the verb and the list announcing that a list is coming, use a colon. Such phrases include *the following* and *as follows*.

Example:

Wrong: The most important witnesses are the following,_Smith, Anders, and Wu.

Right: The most important witnesses are the following:_Smith, Anders, and Wu.

➢ Practice

Correct the following sentences by adding colons as needed. If no correction is needed, write OK.

1. Mrs. Duncan described four possible suspects (1) a white male customer, (2) a white female customer, (3) a teenage boy, and (4) a Mexican-American woman.

2. Gentlemen

3. The following items were stolen 1 pair pants, size 4, style 975; 1 pair pants, size 6, style 978.

4. The witness described the suspect as follows "A mean, leering old man with foul breath who was obviously drunk."

5. My car needs three improvements new tires, new windshield wipers, and new shocks.

6. Dear Commissioner

7. I believe the man is guilty for the following reasons discovered during the interview. Each reason has been fully documented.

8. I received the call at 10 15 a.m. but was not able to respond until 11 00 a.m.

9. He was described as being 6′ 2″ tall and weighing 210 pounds.

■ ■ ■ ■ ■ ■ ■ ■ ■ ■ ■ ■ ■ ■ ■ ■

1. Mrs. Duncan described four possible suspects: . . .
2. Gentlemen:
3. The following items were stolen: . . .
4. The witness described the suspect as follows: . . .
5. My car needs three improvements: . . .
6. Dear Commissioner:
7. OK
8. I received the call at 10:15 a.m. but was not able to respond until 11:00 a.m.
9. OK

QUOTATION MARKS

Knowing when to use quotation marks is only "half the battle." You also need to know how to use other marks of punctuation in conjunction with quotation marks.

First look at when quotation marks are used.

Use quotation marks:

- **to set off all actual words spoken.**
- **to set off titles of short stories, short poems, songs, and magazine articles.**
- **to set off words used in a special way, e.g., slang words.**

Examples:

Wrong:	Bill said_Shut the door.
Right:	Bill said, "Shut the door." (actual words spoken)
Wrong:	The robbery occurred during the singing of_The Star-Spangled Banner.
Right:	The robbery occurred during the singing of "The Star-Spangled Banner."
Wrong:	I told him to_chill out.
Right:	I told him to "chill out." (slang words)

Before you practice using quotation marks, look at how other marks of punctuation are used with quotation marks.

- **Periods and commas always go *inside* the final quotation mark.**
- **Colons and semicolons always go *outside* the final quotation mark.**
- **Dashes, question marks, and exclamation points go inside the final quotation mark when they apply to the quoted matter; they go outside when they refer to the whole sentence.**

Examples:

Wrong:	Bill said, “Shut the door”.
Right:	Bill said, “Shut the door.” (period inside)
Wrong:	Bill said, “Shut the door”, and then he left.
Right:	Bill said, “Shut the door,” and then he left. (comma inside)
Wrong:	Bill said, “Shut the door;” then he left.
Right:	Bill said, “Shut the door”; then he left. (semicolon outside)
Wrong:	Bill said, “Can we go”?
Right:	Bill said, “Can we go?” (the quoted matter is a question)
Wrong:	Did Bill say, “You can go?”
Right:	Did Bill say, “You can go”? (the whole sentence is a question)

Officers often question when it is necessary to quote someone, that is, to use their exact words. The general rule of thumb is that if it shows a subject’s state of mind and avoids conclusionary language, use **direct quotations**. Recall from Chapter Two Rutledge’s example of how directly quoting a suspect saved the case. You may want to review the list of conclusionary language presented in Table 2-1 where you should include **verbatim**, that is, a word-for-word statement of what a subject said. When you quote directly, use quotation marks.

Most of your report, however, will consist of **indirect quotations**, that is, simply stating in your own words the general information you were told. For example, the victim told me he had been robbed. No need to quote.

Example:

Wrong:	The victim said, “He worked for Bloomingdale’s.”
Right:	The victim said that he worked for Bloomingdale’s.

Be especially careful when using direct or indirect quotes that you select the correct pronoun. Use *I* with direct quotes, *he* or *she* with indirect quotes.

Example:

Indirect quote: The suspect said that he hit him only once, with an open fist.
Direct quote: The suspect said, "I hit him only once, with an open fist."

➢ Practice

Correct the following sentences by adding the needed punctuation. If no changes are needed, write OK.

1. Upon questioning, the suspect stated I was not in the store at the time of the robbery.

2. In his letter the chief said I am proud of the performance of all members of this department however I don't think he really meant it.

3. The saying Better late than never has been truc for mc scvcral times.

4. The hit song Why Did You Leave Me has sold a million copies.

5. I read Tourist Attacks on the Rise in *Law Enforcement News*.

6. The victim said she wanted to press charges against her assailant.

■ ■ ■ ■ ■ ■ ■ ■ ■ ■ ■ ■ ■ ■ ■ ■

1. Upon questioning, the suspect stated, "I was not in the store at the time of the robbery."
2. In his letter the chief said, "I am proud of the performance of all members of this department"; however, I don't think he really meant it.
3. The saying "Better late than never" has been true for me several times.
4. The hit song "Why Did You Leave Me?" has sold a million copies.
5. I read "Tourist Attacks on the Rise" in *Law Enforcement News*.
6. OK

➢ More Practice

Punctuate the following stories by adding commas and quotation marks as needed.

1. The police officer pulled a car over on the freeway. The driver asked What's the matter, Officer?

   The officer replied Your wife fell out of your car three miles down the road.

   Oh, thank goodness! the driver exclaimed. I thought I was going deaf.

2. The disability claims department adjuster was interviewing a man who wanted disability benefits. Tell me, Mr. Jones the adjuster began When did your impairment first begin to affect you?

    When I fell off the loading dock Mr. Jones replied.

    To which the adjuster asked At what point did your condition become severe enough to prevent you from doing your job?

    And Mr. Jones replied When I hit the ground.

▪ ▪ ▪ ▪ ▪ ▪ ▪ ▪ ▪ ▪ ▪ ▪ ▪ ▪ ▪ ▪

1. The police officer pulled a car over on the freeway. The driver asked, "What's the matter, Officer?"
   The officer replied, "Your wife fell out of your car three miles down the road."
   "Oh, thank goodness!" the driver exclaimed. "I thought I was going deaf."

2. The disability claims department adjuster was interviewing a man who wanted disability benefits. "Tell me, Mr. Jones," the adjuster began. "When did your impairment first begin to affect you?"
   "When I fell off the loading dock," Mr. Jones replied.
   To which the adjuster asked, "At what point did your condition become severe enough to prevent you from doing your job?"
   And Mr. Jones replied, "When I hit the ground."

UNDERLINING (ITALICS)

When you hand-write a report, it is not possible to italicize, and it is equally difficult with most typewriters. What would be *italicized* in a book is indicated by underlining in written reports.

Underline:

- **titles of books, magazines, newspapers, movies, and TV shows.**
- **names of works of art.**
- **names of planes, trains, and ships.**
- **foreign words and words spoken of as words or terms.**

Examples:

Wrong:	The boy stole a copy of "Playboy" from the newsstand.
Right:	The boy stole a copy of Playboy from the newsstand.
Wrong:	The incident occurred at the showing of "Aliens."
Right:	The incident occurred at the showing of Aliens.

Wrong: The vandalism to the "Mona Lisa" was reported today.
Right: The vandalism to the Mona Lisa was reported today.

Wrong: The captain of the "Flying Cloud" was arrested.
Right: The captain of the Flying Cloud was arrested.

Wrong: The witness used the word "stupid" in his description.
Right: The witness used the word stupid in his description.

➢ Practice

Correct the following sentences by adding underlining and commas, or quotation marks and commas, as needed. If no changes are needed, write OK.

1. The gang had gotten the idea from watching The A Team on TV.

2. The recent article Our Heroes in Blue in USA Today was well written.

3. The words helter skelter had been written in blood.

4. Upon questioning, the suspect said I was not in the store at the time of the robbery.

5. The newspaper referred to the murderer as cold-blooded ruthless and dangerous.

6. The sergeant won a cruise on the Mardi Gras in a sweepstakes.

7. The suspect was carrying an issue of Time under his left arm and a bag with his right hand.

8. Mr. Jefferson said that we should send a police officer out because, in his words we have a dead broad in the bathroom.

9. The suspect said that he and a friend had spent the evening at the local theater where they had sat through two showings of Die Hard.

■ ■ ■ ■ ■ ■ ■ ■ ■ ■ ■ ■ ■ ■ ■ ■

1. The gang had gotten the idea from watching The A Team on TV.
2. The recent article "Our Heroes in Blue" in USA Today was well written.
3. The words helter skelter had been written in blood.
4. Upon questioning, the suspect said, "I was not in the store at the time of the robbery."
5. The newspaper referred to the murderer as "cold-blooded," "ruthless," and "dangerous."
6. The sergeant won a cruise on the Mardi Gras in a sweepstakes.
7. The suspect was carrying an issue of Time under his left arm and a bag with his right hand.
8. Mr. Jefferson said that we should send a police officer out because, in his words, "We have a dead broad in the bathroom."
9. The suspect said that he and a friend had spent the evening at the local theater where they had sat through two showings of Die Hard.

HYPHENS

A hyphenated word may be a new word created by a writer to avoid confusion, or it may be two words which are in the process of becoming one word, e.g., *basketball* used to be written *basket-ball*. Like other marks of punctuation, hyphens can change the meaning of a sentence entirely, as in the following:

He saw a man eating lobster.
He saw a man-eating lobster.

Use a hyphen:

- **with compound numbers from 20 to 99 (ninety-nine), dates, and phone numbers.**
- **to avoid ambiguity.**
- **to express a unit idea.**
- **with the prefixes *ex-*, *self-*, *all-*, and the suffix *-elect*.**
- **in place of the word *to*.**
- **when dividing a word at the end of a line.**

Note: Use of the hyphen is often a matter of individual style.

Examples:

Wrong:	Thirty_seven threats had been made.
Right:	Thirty-seven threats had been made.
Wrong:	His recreation of the crime scene was helpful.
Right:	His re-creation of the crime scene was helpful.
Wrong:	The suspect had a know_it_all attitude.
Right:	The suspect had a know-it-all attitude.
Wrong:	The exconvict was noted entering the store.
Right:	The ex-convict was noted entering the store.
Wrong:	He had a 5--6 minute start.
Right:	He had a 5-6 minute start.

Be careful when dividing a word at the end of a sentence. You may write an unintentionally humorous sentence such as the following:

The officer felt that the suspect was bi-
ased.

She gave him a come hit-
her look.

At every opportunity, the police chaplin pre-
ached.

➢ Practice

Correct the following sentences by adding hyphens where needed. If no changes are needed, write OK.

1. On 02 17 20-- I called for a back up unit to meet me at the church.
2. The suspect was described as approximately thirty five (35) years of age, wearing a blue green shirt, and driving a top of the line Cadillac.
3. The sergeant will re enlist tomorrow.
4. Our job was to guard the president elect.
5. He was Gerald Peterson, D.O.B. 9 10 64, of 6076 Forty third Avenue, telephone 801 555 9574.
6. He recovered the stolen property the next day.

■ ■ ■ ■ ■ ■ ■ ■ ■ ■ ■ ■ ■ ■ ■ ■

1. On 02-17-20--* I called for a back-up unit to meet me at the church.
2. The suspect was described as approximately thirty-five (35) years of age, wearing a blue-green shirt, and driving a top-of-the-line Cadillac.
3. The sergeant will re-enlist tomorrow. (*reenlist* is difficult to read)
4. Our job was to guard the president-elect.
5. He was Gerald Peterson, D.O.B. 9-10-64,* of 6076 Forty-third Avenue, telephone 801-555-9574.
6. OK (but he re-covered the roof)

* Slashes may also be used for dates: 02/17/20--.

➢ More Practice

The following story gives you a chance to practice using a variety of punctuation marks, including hyphens, apostrophes, commas, and quotation marks. Add punctuation as needed.

One burden of the small town mayor was his brother in law, a fellow who liked to throw his in laws weight around. The mayor instructed the police officers and other city officials to simply ignore this mans demands.

One day the brother in law got a parking ticket. He came raging into police headquarters, waving the ticket Hey you cops he shrieked do you know who I am?

The desk sergeant gazed at him calmly, then picked up his phone and called the mayors office. Tell the mayor he said to the operator that his brother in law is down at the station and cant remember his name.

■ ■ ■ ■ ■ ■ ■ ■ ■ ■ ■ ■ ■ ■ ■ ■

One burden of the small-town mayor was his brother-in-law, a fellow who liked to throw his in-law's weight around. The mayor instructed the police officers and other city officials to simply ignore this man's demands.

One day the brother-in-law got a parking ticket. He came raging into police headquarters, waving the ticket. "Hey, you cops," he shrieked, "do you know who I am?"

The desk sergeant gazed at him calmly, then picked up his phone and called the mayor's office. "Tell the mayor," he said to the operator, "that his brother-in-law is down at the station and can't remember his name."

SUMMARY

Use *parentheses* to enclose figures and to set off supplementary or illustrative matter. Use *dashes* to mark a sudden break in thought, to set off a summary, or to set off an element that has commas or other marks of punctuation in it. Use *slashes/diagonals* in certain abbreviations, to express alternatives, to indicate that a person or thing has two functions, and to express dates and fractions.

Use a semicolon between two sentences not joined by a simple conjunction and to separate items in a series which contain commas. Use a colon after the salutation of a business letter, between the hour and minutes in time (6:10), and to introduce lists or long quotations. Use quotation marks to set off all actual words spoken; to set off titles of short stories, short poems, songs, and magazine articles; and to set off words used in a special way, e.g., slang words.

Periods and commas always go *inside* the final quotation mark. Colons and semicolons always go *outside* the final quotation mark. Dashes, question marks, and exclamation points go inside the final quotation mark when they apply to the quoted matter; they go outside when they refer to the whole sentence.

Underline titles of books, magazines, newspapers, movies, and TV shows; names of works of art; names of planes, trains, and ships; foreign words; and words spoken of as words or terms.

Use a hyphen with compound numbers from 20 to 99 (ninety-nine), dates, and phone numbers; to avoid ambiguity; to express a unit idea; with the prefixes *ex-*, *self-*, *all-*, and the suffix *-elect*; in place of the word *to*; and when dividing a word at the end of a line. Use of the hyphen is often a matter of individual style.

You may wish to review this chapter before taking the self-test on p.234.

REVIEW

The following pages contain a summary of the most important concepts presented in this text.

CHAPTER ONE—AN INTRODUCTION TO REPORTS AND REPORT WRITING

A report is a permanent written record which communicates important facts to be used in the future. An administrative report deals with the routine functioning of the department or agency, whereas an operational report deals with the activities of law enforcement officers.

Reports are used to examine the past, keep other police officers informed, continue investigations, prepare court cases, provide the courts with relevant facts, coordinate law enforcement activities, plan for future law enforcement services, and evaluate law enforcement officers' performance.

Reports are read and used by other officers, supervisors, attorneys and judges, jurors, city officials, reporters, and citizens. Reader-friendly writing avoids police jargon and abbreviations and communicates in plain, simple language. It is written as it would be spoken, and it considers its audience. Reader-friendly reports avoid referring the reader "above."

Among the common problems in police reports are confusing or unclear sentences, conclusions and assumptions, extreme wordiness and overuse of police jargon and abbreviations, missing or incomplete information, misspelled words, grammatical/mechanical errors, and referring to "above" information.

Well-written reports can save the department time and expense and result in better police work and more convictions. Well-written reports can reduce legal liability for both the officer and the officer's department. Well-written reports reflect positively on your education, your competence, and your professionalism.

CHAPTER TWO—CHARACTERISTICS OF A WELL-WRITTEN REPORT: CONTENT

Content and form are equally important. The content of a well-written report is factual, accurate, objective, and complete.

A well-written report is *factual*. It does *not* contain opinions. Avoid conclusionary language in police reports. A well-written report is *accurate*; it is specific. Details of a report should be both factual and accurate. A well-written report is *objective*, meaning it is nonopinionated, fair, and impartial. You can assure objectivity in your reports by avoiding words with emotional overtones and including all relevant facts. A well-written report is *complete*. It answers the questions Who? What? Where? When? How? Why? A report should give as full an account as possible.

A complete criminal report addresses the elements of the crime, conditions that must exist and be proven to exist for an act to be called a specific kind of crime. Successful prosecution of a criminal case requires each element to exist and be documented by the reporting officer.

CHAPTER THREE—CHARACTERISTICS OF A WELL-WRITTEN REPORT: FORM

The form of a well-written report is concise, clear, mechanically correct, written in standard English, legible, and on time.

A well-written report is *concise*. Conciseness means you make every word count without leaving out important facts. A well-written report is *clear*. A well-written report states details clearly. A well-written report is *mechanically correct*—that is, it follows the rules for spelling, capitalization, and punctuation. A mechanically incorrect report leaves a poor impression of its writer. A well-written report is written *in standard English*. A report in nonstandard English leaves a poor impression of its writer. A well-written report is *legible*. It must also be *on time*.

CHAPTER FOUR—STEPS IN REPORT WRITING

The five basic steps in writing a report are gathering the facts (investigate, interview, interrogate), recording the facts immediately (take notes), organizing the facts, writing the report, and evaluating the report (edit and proofread; revise if necessary).

To gather information, observe and listen. Record all relevant information legibly, in ink, in a notebook. Felt-tip or ball-point pens are acceptable. Good notes have many of the same characteristics of good reports. Good notes are clear, complete, concise, accurate, and objective. Good notes are a prerequisite for a good report. Good notes include all relevant facts.

Organize your information. Report it in chronologically arranged paragraphs. The opening paragraph of a police report states the time, date, type of incident, and how you became involved. The next paragraph contains what you were told by the victim(s) or witness(es). For each person talked to, use a separate paragraph. Next record what you did based on the information you received. The final paragraph states the disposition of the case.

When using names and courtesy titles in a report, remember to use a person's full name the first time; after that, use only the last name unless more than one person with the same last name is included in the report. If two or more individuals having the same last name are included in the report, use their first initial and last name. Do not keep repeating the person's name; use pronouns. Also, do not use courtesy titles unless there is a specific reason.

Do *not* include in your report the questions asked to victims, witnesses, or suspects. Remember to stay in the past tense throughout a police report. Finally, edit and proofread your reports.

CHAPTER FIVE—PRINCIPLES OF CLEAR WRITING

Use the first person to refer to yourself. If the subject performs the action, the sentence is in the active voice. If the subject does *not* perform the action, the sentence is in the passive voice. Use the active voice. Statements are usually clearer in the active voice. The active voice is preferable, unless there is a specific reason to use the passive voice.

Place modifiers as close as possible to the words they modify. Misplaced modifiers may confuse the reader. Modifiers should clearly modify only one word or phrase. Placement of the modifier can determine the meaning of a sentence. Place modifiers so they refer clearly and directly to a word or phrase in the sentence. Dangling modifiers are puzzling to the reader. Correct modification can do much to make your writing clear. When you edit your reports, pay careful attention to your modifiers. Be certain they are as close as possible to the word(s) they modify.

Pronouns should clearly refer to only one person or object. An unclear pronoun reference leaves a question in the reader's mind. When in doubt, use the proper name, not a pronoun. Finally, word similar ideas in similar ways. The use of parallelism results in smoother sentences.

CHAPTER SIX—CHOOSING THE RIGHT WORDS

Choosing the right words is a critical step in report writing. Use common words, but avoid slang. Reports should be straightforward and factual. Police reports should use a serious, objective tone. Do not be redundant. Eliminating unnecessary words makes your reports more effective. In concise writing, every word counts.

CHAPTER SEVEN—GRAMMAR

If the pronoun is the subject of the sentence, use *I, we, you, he, she, it, they, who*, *whoever, whosoever*. If the pronoun is the object of the sentence, use *me, us, you, him, her, it, them, whom*, *whomever, whomsoever*. If the pronoun is used to show possession, use *my, mine, our, ours, your, yours, his, her, hers, its, their, theirs, whose, whosoever*. Note: Possessive pronouns do *not* have an apostrophe.

Use the pronoun *myself* only after having used the pronoun *I* or *me*. Use the pronoun *whom* following prepositions. Use the pronoun *who* or *whom* to refer to people. Do *not* use the pronoun *that* to refer to people.

Subject and verb should agree. Pick out the subject and verb of the sentence and say them together to determine if they agree. For singular subjects joined by *and*, use a plural verb. For singular subjects joined by *or*, make the verb agree with the closer subject. *One*, *everybody*, *someone*, and *each* take a singular verb. Periods of time, amounts of money, weights, and measures are usually singular. These are collective nouns—they refer to a single unit.

Use adjectives to modify nouns. Use adverbs to modify all other words. *Good* is an adjective; *well* is an adverb. *Real* is an adjective; *really* is an adverb. Do *not* use double comparatives. Avoid double negatives. Do not leave out *a*, *an*, or *the* in your reports. Use *a* before words beginning with a consonant sound; use *an* before words beginning with a vowel sound.

CHAPTER EIGHT—SENTENCES THAT MAKE SENSE

Write complete sentences. Include both a subject and a predicate. Avoid sentence fragments. Sentence fragments cannot stand alone. Do not run sentences together. Run-on sentences can be corrected by making them into two separate sentences; using a comma and simple connecting word such as *and, but, or, nor, for, yet, so*; or using a semicolon and a transitional word or *no* connecting word. Combine related ideas into a single sentence.

CHAPTER NINE—SPELLING AND APOSTROPHES

Memorize common words with difficult spellings. Memorize words frequently used in police reports. Be careful adding endings to words. Use a dictionary or speller/divider if in doubt. Learn the spellings and meanings of the most common homonyms. Learn to distinguish between words that are commonly confused. Use an apostrophe to show omission (contractions), possession (except for pronouns), and plurals of letters and figures. Apostrophes *do* make a difference.

CHAPTER TEN—ABBREVIATIONS, NUMBERS, AND CAPITALIZATION

In your *notes*, use accepted abbreviations that cannot be misunderstood. In your *reports*, do not use abbreviations except for titles, addresses, time, speed, and names of agencies usually referred to by initials. Use *e.g.* to show examples. Use *i.e.* to make an explanation. Put a period after all abbreviations except those that are all in capital letters.

Write out numbers that are under 10 or that come at the beginning of a sentence. Use figures for numbers over nine; for a series of numbers; and for dates, street numbers, page numbers, time, and speed. Be consistent. Do not mix words and figures in the same sentence.

Use capital letters for the first word in a sentence; names of specific people and members of national, political, racial, regional, or religious groups; geographical names; organizations and institutions; specific streets, buildings, ships, planes, trains, and trademark names; historical periods, events, and special events; days of the week, months, and holidays; and titles used before a name.

Do not capitalize general words; direction; names of seasons; course names, unless followed by a number or derived from a proper name; words showing family relationship preceded by a possessive pronoun; and titles following a name.

CHAPTER ELEVEN—COMMAS

Use a comma between two main clauses joined by the words *and, but, or, nor, for, yet*, or *so*. Use a comma *after introductory material*, except when the introductory material is very short, i.e., five words or fewer.

Use commas between each word in a series of three or more words or phrases. Use a comma before the *and* preceding the last word or phrase in a series. Do *not* use a comma after the last word in a series. A series of adjectives before a noun should be separated by commas. Use commas after each adjective before a noun *except* the one which is directly before the noun.

Use commas to separate the parts of *dates* and *addresses*. Use commas around all *sentence interrupters* if they can be left out of the sentence without changing its meaning (nonrestrictive). Do *not* use commas around interrupters which are needed to make the meaning of the sentence explicit (restrictive).

CHAPTER TWELVE—OTHER PUNCTUATION MARKS

Use *parentheses* to enclose figures and to set off supplementary or illustrative matter. Use *dashes* to mark a sudden break in thought, to set off a summary, or to set off an element that has commas or other marks of punctuation in it. Use *slashes/diagonals* in certain abbreviations, to express alternatives, to indicate that a person or thing has two functions, and to express dates and fractions.

Use a semicolon between two sentences not joined by a simple conjunction and to separate items in a series which contain commas. Use a colon after the salutation of a business letter, between the hour and minutes in time (6:10), and to introduce lists or long quotations. Use quotation marks to set off all actual words spoken; to set off titles of short stories, short poems, songs, and magazine articles; and to set off words used in a special way, e.g., slang words.

Periods and commas always go *inside* the final quotation mark. Colons and semicolons always go *outside* the final quotation mark. Dashes, question marks, and exclamation points go inside the final quotation mark when they apply to the quoted matter; they go outside when they refer to the whole sentence.

Underline titles of books, magazines, newspapers, movies, and TV shows; names of works of art; names of planes, trains, and ships; foreign words; and words spoken of as words or terms.

Use a hyphen with compound numbers from 20 to 99 (ninety-nine), dates, and phone numbers; to avoid ambiguity; to express a unit idea; with the prefixes *ex-, self-, all-*, and the suffix *-elect*; in place of the word *to*; and when dividing a word at the end of a line. Use of the hyphen is often a matter of individual style.

A FINAL WORD

You should now be well on your way to writing effective police reports. Remember, however, that like any other skill, skill in report writing can continuously be improved by concentration and practice or can slowly deteriorate through carelessness or lack of practice.

If you continue to apply the principles you've learned in this text, your report-writing skill *will* continue to develop. You can do it on your own by simply evaluating each report you write, proofreading and revising as needed.

**Professional abilities are not pushed in one big shove,
but by daily nudges at their limits.**

EVALUATION CHECKLIST FOR REPORTS

➔ **Is the report**:
- factual?
- accurate?
- objective?
- complete?
- chronological?
- concise?
- clear?
- mechanically correct?
- written in standard English?

➔ **Does the report use**:
- first person?
- active voice?
- past tense?
- correct modification?
- correct pronoun reference?
- parallel sentence structure?
- paragraphs?

➔ **Are the sentences effective with**:
- no fragments?
- no run-on sentences?
- similar ideas combined into single sentences?

➔ **Are the sentences mechanically correct in terms of**:
- spelling?
- use of apostrophes?
- abbreviations?
- numbers?
- capitalization?
- punctuation?

➔ **Are the sentences grammatically correct in terms of**:
- correct use of pronouns?
- agreement of subject and verb?
- correct use of adjectives and adverbs?
- correct use of negation?
- correct use of articles?

➔ **Does the report allow the reader to visualize what happened**?

END-OF-CHAPTER

SELF-TESTS

In each of the self-tests which follow, answer the questions as completely as possible. Each question is followed by the points for a correct response. When you have completed each test, check your answers against those given on the page listed at the end of the test.

CHAPTER ONE SELF-TEST
(30 points)

---

1. What is a report? (7 points)

   ____

   ____

2. What are the two major types of reports? (2 points)

   a. ______________________________

   b. ______________________________

3. Which type of report deals with the activities of law enforcement officers? (1 point)

   ____

4. Which type of report deals with the routine functioning of the law enforcement department or agency? (1 point)

   ____

5. What are at least four uses of reports? (4 points)

   a. ______________________________

   b. ______________________________

   c. ______________________________

   d. ______________________________

6. Name the positions of at least three people who might read your report? (3 points)

   a. ______________________ c. ______________________

   b. ______________________

7. What are at least three ways to make your writing reader friendly? (3 points)

   a. ____________________

   b. ____________________

   c. ____________________

8. What are five common problems in many police reports? (5 points)

   a. ____________________

   b. ____________________

   c. ____________________

   d. ____________________

   e. ____________________

9. Why should your reports be well written? (4 points)

   a. ____________________

   b. ____________________

   c. ____________________

   d. ____________________

Check your answers with those on pp.239-240 and calculate your score: ______ out of a possible 30 points. You should have scored at least 24 points. If you did not, review the pages indicated on the answer sheet.

CHAPTER TWO SELF-TEST
(36 points)

1. Which is more important: content or form? (2 points)

____

2. *What is said* is a report's (circle one; 1 point): content form

3. *How it is said* is a report's (circle one; 1 point): content form

4. What are four characteristics of the content of a well-written report? (4 points)

   a. ______________________ c. ______________________

   b. ______________________ d. ______________________

5. Identify the term being defined in each of the following statements: (3 points)

   A personal belief: ______________________

   A conclusion based on reasoning: ______________________

   A statement that can be proven: ______________________

6. Of the three types of statements in Question 5, which one should make up the majority of statements in a police report? (1 point)

____

7. An effective report answers which six basic questions? (6 points)

   a. ______________________ d. ______________________

   b. ______________________ e. ______________________

   c. ______________________ f. ______________________

8. "The driver could not touch her nose with her finger" is an example of ________________________ language. (1 point)

9. The statement in Question 8 is also a/an (circle one; 1 point): fact inference opinion

10. One way to make a report more accurate is to use ___________________ language rather than vague, general language. (1 point)

11. Another word for nonopinionated, fair, and impartial is ________________________. (1 point)

12. Words which have emotional overtones are ______________________ words. (1 point)

13. Words which are objective in their meaning are _______________________ words. (1 point)

14. The ___________________________________ are conditions that must exist and be proven to exist for an act to be called a specific kind of crime. (1 point)

----

15. Evaluate the *content* of the following report. Underline any words or phrases that violate the rules you learned in Chapter Two regarding the characteristics of the content of a well-written report. (11 points)

    In the latter part of October, Jerry Hindley (Stanton Ave.) called me at the police station. He was nervous and told me he had some information on some Uzi machine guns. Uzis are very cool. Gerry Hindly, a person whom I have known for many years and who has given me good information in the past, said that a broad named Barb Wilkins had approached him about purchasing some Uzi machine guns. Barb Wilkins' brother, Jeff Wilkins, lived with a guy named Joe who apparently had some guns for sale. Immediately after the conversation with Ms. Wilkins, Jerry contacted me. I told him to try and get a look at the guns and then contact me again. A few days later, Jerry did go down to Jeff Wilkins' apartment complex. He is probably a druggie since his apartment is located in a bad part of town. At that location, Jerry met a man named Joe and was shown two Uzi's by Joe.

Check your answers with those on *pp.240-241* *and calculate your score: ______ out of a possible 36 points. You should have scored at least 28 points. If you did not, review the pages indicated on the answer sheet.*

CHAPTER THREE SELF-TEST
(30 points)

---

1. List six characteristics of the form of a well-written report and briefly explain each. (6 points)

   a. ______________________________

   b. ______________________________

   c. ______________________________

   d. ______________________________

   e. ______________________________

   f. ______________________________

2. Check the more effective sentence in each pair. In the space below each pair of sentences, indicate which of the six characteristics of form is at issue (which element makes your selection more effective). (10 points)

   a. _____ (1) Due to the fact that the driver was weaving from one side of the road to the other, the officer signaled for the driver of the car to pull over.
   _____ (2) Since the car was weaving from one side of the road to the other, the officer pulled the driver over.
   Why is your selection more effective? ______________________________

   b. _____ (1) It wasn't the first time that store had been broken into.
   _____ (2) It weren't the first time that store had been broked into.
   Why is your selection more effective? ______________________________

   c. _____ (1) The officer ran past the witness while he drew his weapon.
   _____ (2) The officer, drawing his weapon, ran past the witness.
   Why is your selection more effective? ______________________________

   d. _____ (1) The witness believes the red car did not have any license tags on it.
   _____ (2) It is the opinion of the witness that the car, which was red in color, was void of the presence of any license tags on it.
   Why is your selection more effective? ______________________________

   e. _____ (1) When I arrived at the scene, the suspect was running east on Maryland Blvd.
   _____ (2) When I arrived at the scene, the suspict was running east on maryland blvd
   Why is your selection more effective? ______________________________

⇒ *Questions 3-10 are worth 1 point each.*

3. Using diagrams and sketches only adds confusion to a complex report. True False

4. Longer sentences are preferable to shorter sentences. True False

5. Using common abbreviations is acceptable. True False

6. An illegible report reflects poorly on the writer. True False

7. Ideally, reports should be handwritten. True False

8. Being brief is not necessarily the same as being concise. True False

9. In a report, it is acceptable to leave out words such as *a*, *an*, and *the* to reduce wordiness. True False

10. The standards for spoken and written English are the same. True False

----

11. Read the following report, and be prepared to evaluate it.

BURGLARY

On June 16, 20--, at about 2237 hours, Officer Joyce Clay and I were dispatched to a reported burglary in progress at 2441 Riverside Road. The information we received from dispatch was that the next-door neighbor, William Ramirez, had reported the incident. Ramirez was watching his neighbor's house who had gone on vacation and had seen lights in the house and a strange car, an older-model Ford LTD, green in color, parked in front of the house.

Upon arrival at about 2242 hours, we observed the car described by Ramirez still parked in front of the house at 2441 Riverside Road, and we observed a light in the front part of the house which appeared to be a flashlight. The lights from our patrol unit were turned off, and we parked behind the suspict vehical.

As we exited our patrol unit, I observed a male adult walk out the front door with a television set in his hands. He was ordered to freeze, which he did. He was detained by Officer Clay. At this point in time sergeant walters arrived, and he and I entered the house through the open front door to search for other suspects. None were found.

At this point in time, Ramirez came out of his house at 2443 Riverside Road and approached us. He looked at the suspect and told us he did not recognize him as the occupant, or any friend or relative of the occupant, who lived at 2441 Riverside Road. Ramirez also looked at the television set which had been in the suspect's hands which he said he recognized as belonging to Avery Cepeda, the occupant at 2441 Riverside Road.

At this point, the suspect, who identified himself as John Thomas Quirk, was placed under arrest. Sergeant Walters and Officer Clay remained at the scene to conduct witness interviews and complete the scene investigation while I transported Quirk to headquarters.

At headquarters, I interviewed Quirk, reading him his Miranda Rights, as follows:

(1) You have the right to remain silent.
(2) Anything you say can and will be used against you in a court of law.
(3) You have the right to talk with an attorney and to have an attorney present before and during questioning.
(4) If you cannot afford an attorney, one will be appointed free of charge to represent you before and during questioning, if you desire.
(5) You can decide at any time to exercise these rights and not answer any questions or make any statements.

I asked Quirk whether he understood his constitutional rights, and he said, "Yea, sure." I asked him if he would talk with me, having those rights in mind. He told me, "Hell, no." I did not question him. He was booked into the county jail.

➢ EVALUATION

Evaluate the report by answering the following questions. For any negative response, give at least one example to support your evaluation. (6 points)

a. Is the report concise? ______________________________

____

b. Is the report clear? ______________________________

____

c. Is the report mechanically correct? ______________________________

____

d. Is the report written in standard English? ______________________________

____

e. What do you consider the greatest strength of this report? ______________________________

____

f. What do you consider the greatest weakness of this report? ______________________________

____

Check your answers with those on pp.241-242 and calculate your score: ______ out of a possible 30 points. You should have scored at least 24 points. If you did not, review the pages indicated on the answer sheet.

CHAPTER FOUR SELF-TEST
(31 points)

1. List the five basic steps in writing a police report. (5 points)

   a. ______

   b. ______

   c. ______

   d. ______

   e. ______

2. List at least four factors to consider when interviewing a subject. (4 points)

   a. ______

   b. ______

   c. ______

   d. ______

3. List at least two ways to encourage conversation with a subject. (2 points)

   a. ______

   b. ______

4. List at least four procedures to be followed in taking notes. (4 points)

   a. ______

   b. ______

   c. ______

   d. ______

5. List three ways to improve the organization of your report. (3 points)

   a. ______________________________

   b. ______________________________

   c. ______________________________

6. Number 1-4 the proper sequence for structuring the narrative of a police report. (4 points)

   _____ a. Record what you did based on the information you received.

   _____ b. State the time, date, type of incident, and how you became involved.

   _____ c. State the disposition of the case.

   _____ d. State what you were told by the victim(s) or witness(es).

⇒ *Questions 7-11 are worth 1 point each.*

7. A police report should always be written in present tense.	True	False
8. The sentence "The car has a smashed windshield" is in which tense?	Past	Present
9. The sentence "The suspect had red hair and a beard" is in which tense?	Past	Present
10. It is acceptable to devise your own shorthand for your notes.	True	False
11. Do not use courtesy titles unless there is a specific reason.	True	False

12. Name the two procedures to use in evaluating your reports and briefly explain each. (4 points)

   a. ______________________________

   b. ______________________________

Check your answers with those on pp.242-243 and calculate your score: ______ out of a possible 31 points. You should have scored at least 25 points. If you did not, review the pages indicated on the answer sheet.

CHAPTER FIVE SELF-TEST
(35 points)

---

1. Improve the following sentences by using the principles of clear writing. If no changes are needed, write OK. (5 points)

   a. This officer read the suspect the Miranda warning.

   ____

   b. The car was broken into and stolen by the thief.

   ____

   c. I was summoned to the office by the hotel manager.

   ____

   d. The sergeant told the deputy that he needed a shave.

   ____

   e. To protect the public and also ensuring his appearance in court, the suspect belongs in jail.

   ____

2. Note whether each sentence is active (A) or passive (P). (5 points)

   ____ a. The gun was found by the K-9 unit.

   ____ b. The suspect called her attorney.

   ____ c. The arsonist set three fires last night.

   ____ d. Three fires were set by the arsonist last night.

   ____ e. The captain disciplined the two officers.

3. Note whether each sentence is written in the first person (F) or third person (T). (5 points)

   _____ a. I enjoy detective work immensely.

   _____ b. This officer responded to the call at 0930 hours.

   _____ c. The undersigned officer testified in court yesterday.

   _____ d. This reporting officer took aim at the suspect and fired.

   _____ e. I advised the victim to change the locks on his doors.

4. Note whether the modification in each sentence is correct (C) or incorrect (I). (5 points)

   ______ a. The guard dog bit the intruder with sharp, pointy teeth.

   ______ b. I saw the suspect running toward the shop owner with a gun.

   ______ c. The statement the witness made suddenly did not fit the rest of his story.

   ______ d. At that instant she decided to run for cover.

   ______ e. After leaving the building, the bomb went off.

⇒ *Questions 5-9 are worth 1 point each.*

5. If the subject does not perform the action, the sentence is passive. True False

6. Use the first person to refer to yourself. True False

7. Statements are usually clearer in the passive voice. True False

8. A passive sentence is acceptable if the doer of the action is unknown. True False

9. When in doubt, use a pronoun, not the proper name. True False

----

10. Read the following report and evaluate its clarity. Identify instances of third person, unnecessary use of passive voice, improper modification, unclear pronoun reference, and lack of parallelism. (10 points)

PROPERTY DAMAGE REPORT

At 0800 hours on March 3, 20--, this officer was dispatched to Acme Hardware, 1005 Main Street, to investigate property damage. Upon arrival at 0810 hours, Mr. Hill, the owner and manager of the store, met this officer.

Hill said he left the store last night at about 2100 hours and did return this morning at about 0730 hours. He discovered the damage at that time. The wall and window had been sprayed with green paint. A can of Ward's green paint was found by Hill in the alley that looked like the same color.

This officer went to the alley and looked at the damage. This reporting officer found one can of Ward's green spray paint in the alley that was bagged and kept as evidence. Hill said he thought that a recently fired part-time employee, John Johnson, may have been involved. Hill said he had to let him go, and he was not happy about it.

Case pending.

Check your answers with those on pp.243-245 and calculate your score: ______ out of a possible 35 points. You should have scored at least 28 points. If you did not, review the pages indicated on the answer sheet.

CHAPTER SIX SELF-TEST
(35 points)

1. Make the following sentences more concise by eliminating unnecessary words. If no changes are needed, write OK. (8 points)

   a. I proceeded to conduct an interview with subject John Doe.

   ____

   b. At this point in time I made an effort to impede his forward motion.

   ____

   c. There are three suspects who I have interviewed in this case.

   ____

   d. There has been no progress made on the case.

   ____

   e. The establishment of guidelines was an important first step.

   ____

   f. Partners are dependent on each other.

   ____

   g. The chief provided assistance to the two officers in the settlement of their disagreement.

   ____

   h. The suspect was observed to have a gun.

   ____

⇒ *Questions 2-7 are worth 1 point each.*

2. Police reports should use a relaxed, subjective tone. True False

3. Redundancy is acceptable since it drives home the points the writer is making. True False

4. You can write concisely by using positive statements. True False

5. You should avoid frequent use of *there is* and *there are.* True False

6. You can write concisely by using the active voice. True False

7. You can write concisely by writing with nouns, not verbs. True False

8. Replace each wordy phrase with a more concise alternative. (8 points)

WORDY	CONCISE
a. all of a sudden	a. ____________________
b. during the time that	b. ____________________
c. exhibited a tendency to	c. ____________________
d. in close proximity to	d. ____________________
e. in the event that	e. ____________________
f. subsequent to	f. ____________________
g. upon an individual basis	g. ____________________
h. in spite of the fact that	h. ____________________

----

9. Read the following report. Find examples of wordiness and replace them with more concise words or phrases. Sometimes a word can be eliminated without replacing it. The wordy version of the report contains 272 words. Try to get the total down to 230 words (eliminate 40 or more words). (13 points)

At about 0930 hours on 06-15-20--, I was dispatched to 1375 Bantam Drive to investigate a reported home burglary. When I arrived, I was met by the victim, Sara Kruse.

Ms. Kruse communicated verbally that she had returned from the grocery store and found the back door to her house unlocked, despite the fact that she was absolutely certain she had locked it prior to leaving. Upon entering the house, she saw a kitchen chair overturned and several kitchen drawers pulled open. In light of the fact that she had a teenage son, Ms. Kruse initially was of the opinion that her son had returned home from school, left the door unlocked, and caused the disarray. She then discovered, however, that the house was empty and that several items were missing. Ms. Kruse made a note of the fact that the television in the living room was missing as was the stereo in her son's bedroom. At that point in time, she checked her bedroom for the purpose of determining if anything else was missing and found that her jewelry box and 35mm camera were also gone. At that time, she called the police.

She estimated she was gone a combined total of 45 minutes. None of the neighbors reported seeing anything, although one neighbor made mention of the fact that this was the third break-in he had heard of happening in that neighborhood during the month of June.

I informed Ms. Kruse that in the majority of instances, such stolen property is not recovered, but that if we located anything matching the description of her property we would call her.

Check your answers with those on pp.245-246 and calculate your score: ______ out of a possible 35 points. You should have scored at least 28 points. If you did not, review the pages indicated on the answer sheet.

CHAPTER SEVEN SELF-TEST
(60 points)

---

1. Correct any errors in use of pronouns, subject and verb agreement, adjectives, adverbs, negation, or articles. If no changes are needed, write OK. (24 points)

   a. The victim discovered that a real old coin collection and stamp collection was missing from bedroom desk.

   b. House was full of valuable antiques, jewelry, and a portable color TV, none of which were disturbed by the burglar.

   c. A neighbor that was coming home late said that he didn't see nothing suspicious.

   d. He had just came home from work and was real tired, so his statement couldn't hardly be completely reliable.

   e. Me and another officer then questioned the neighbors on the other side of victim's house.

   f. One neighbor said that there was several strange sounds around midnight.

   g. Another neighbor across the street come out of her house and said she seen a orange van drive by around midnight with no lights on.

   h. Complete list of missing items will be furnished by victim after she has a chance to go through her valuables.

   i. Officer Harris and myself conducted preliminary investigation, but case will be handled from here by detectives.

   j. There is currently no leads on identity of burglar.

2. Correct all errors in the following report. (31 points)

At approximately 0338 hours on 01-23-20--, police and fire units responded to a apartment fire at 5179 Fairway Drive, Apt. 104. Mr. Arnold Millsap, resident manager, contacted police dispatcher by phone and said the above apartment was on fire and that an invalid, Mary Foster, lived there.

Upon arrival, Officer Manos and myself did not see no visible flames; however, we did see large amount of smoke coming from other side (east side) of the apartment. Officer Manos was able to open the outer entry door and crawl a short distance on the floor, but he could not reach the door to victim's apartment due to the real dense smoke. The Humboldt Fire Department arrived on scene at 0343, and they was able to gain entrance into the apartment using face masks. Victim's body was discovered in living room by firefighters. The body, nude except for a pair of panty hose, was located in front of a serving bar with the head against the south wall and approximately 15 feet from east side of apartment. Body was on its right side with the front portion facing the glass sliding door. The entire body had a brown, baked appearance.

Coroner arrived and took pictures of the body. Victim's purse and contents were turned over to coroner. Identification was made through driver's license and other identification within the purse. It was observed by myself that bedside clock had stopped at 0332 hrs. Further interviews with adjoining tenants and resident manager revealed the following information: victim had worked for local school district for two years; she was a "loner"; she had hardly no visitors. No one had no personal contact with her. Resident manager said victim had a daughter that did come to visit sometimes, but her name and address was unknown.

3. How would you rate the above report? (1 point) ______________________________

____

4. What are its strengths? (2 points) ______________________________

____

5. What are its weaknesses? (2 points) ______________________________

____

Check your answers with those on pp.246-247 and calculate your score: ______ out of a possible 60 points. You should have scored at least 48 points. If you did not, review the pages indicated on the answer sheet.

CHAPTER EIGHT SELF-TEST
(30 points)

---

1. Correct any errors in sentence structure. Improve any choppy sentences by combining related ideas into single sentences. If no changes are needed, write OK. (5 points)

   a. John is a good shot he often fires in the grand-master class.

   b. Because he is such a good shot. We rely on him to carry some of our weaker teams.

   c. Since there will be a briefing tomorrow afternoon. All shift leaders will report one-half hour early.

   d. All officers will have their riot equipment with them. This includes tear gas. It includes gas masks. And it includes rifles with scopes.

   e. The officer called to the suspect to halt. She radioed for a backup unit. She again called for the suspect to halt. She finally pursued the suspect. She caught him in an alley two blocks away.

2. A complete sentence includes both a ____________________ and a ____________________. (2 points)

3. The ____________________ part of a sentence *tells*. (1 point)

4. The ____________________ part of a sentence *names*. (1 point)

5. If a sentence does not include both elements given in Question 2, it is called a sentence ____________________________. (1 point)

6. Two or more complete sentences incorrectly joined together are known as ________________________ sentences. (1 point)

7. It is acceptable to combine related ideas into a single sentence. True False (1 point)

----

8. Read the following report. Correct any errors in sentence structure, wordiness, or lack of clarity. (18 points)

On 06-16-20-- at approximately 1738 hrs., Officer Madsen and I saw a 2000 red Chevrolet. It was parked at the yellow curb in front of the First National Bank. The Chevrolet was occupied by two people. One was sitting in the driver's seat the second person was sitting in the right rear seat. On seeing the vehicle and occupants at that location. It appeared suspicious and we turned our vehicle around to watch the Chevrolet.

At this time we saw a young male running eastbound on the sidewalk of the shopping center toward the red Chevrolet. He was later identified as Ray Shipley. The suspect was carrying a brass clock and he was being pursued by a female. She was later identified as Mary Chase.

As the suspect approached the vehicle. The right door was opened to allow him to enter however he ran past and around the east end of the building and headed south. At this time the Chevrolet began moving. Out of the parking lot onto York Avenue southbound. Officer Madsen gave chase on foot after the suspect. The suspect dropped the above-described clock. And continued running south through an open field. Officer Madsen caught the suspect on the south side of the apartments. He placed him under arrest.

Check your answers with those on pp.247-248 and calculate your score: ______ out of a possible 30 points. You should have scored at least 24 points. If you did not, review the pages indicated on the answer sheet.

CHAPTER NINE SELF-TEST
(75 points)

---

1. Correct any spelling or apostrophe errors in the following sentences. Also be aware of homonyms and "confused" words and replace them with more appropriate words. If no changes are needed, write OK. (Note: There are spelling errors in words you have not studied specifically.) (30 points)

   a. Before questionning begins, the officer must read the suspicts rites to him.

   b. The departments polisy on the use of firearms is vary clear.

   c. Youre going to need a lawyer for youre son.

   d. They too have an interest in bringing the case to court.

   e. He had to go two the city attornies office.

   f. Once again, the armed robber managed to allude authoritys.

   g. The affect of this nieghborhood on young people is very strong.

   h. Alot of people think that its alright to take towels from hotels.

   i. Their are alot of things I can not do.

   j. He was arested for posession of narcatics.

   k. The warrent was youre responsability.

   l. The principle of the school was gilty, and he new it.

2. Correct all errors in the following report (spelling, use of the apostrophe, sentence structure, wordiness, or lack of clarity). (45 points)

    On this date at about 0125 hours. I saw the suspect driving south on Normandale Road. At a vary slow speed. Suspects vehicle, a 1993 Buick, blue in color, Michigan plate #DWI222, was traveling aproximately 10 m.p.h. in a 50 m.p.h. zone between West 50th Street and County Road 62. I attempted too stop suspect four about three blocks. Using my red lights and siren while directly behind and alongside him. Suspect eventually stopped at the Normandale Road and West 66th Street intersection. I approached suspects car as he was attempting to get out. Suspect fell on his face when I was about 15 feet from him. At the time I saw suspect fall. I heard glass breaking near his vehicle. I rushed to his assistence. The suspect was sobbing. And asking for help. I assisted suspect to his feet. And could smell a strong odor of alcaholic beverage on suspects breath and clothing. I asked suspect about his condition. He said he was dead drunk, had been drinking for too days, and wanted to dye. I told suspect that I was arresting him. And informed him of the Implied Consent Law. Suspect told me he wanted to have the blood test and requested permision to stay in the hospital for treatment after the test. A broken quart bottle of skotch was found where the suspect had fell.

    Suspects vehicle was toed. And impounded by Southport Garage. I transported suspect to Mercy Hospital wear Nurse Sarah Connors drew a blood sample while in the presence of myself. I marked the blood container with the date, case number, suspects name, and my initials. I gave the suspect a notice to appear, including the charges and court date, and releesed him to his doctors care. The remnants of the skotch bottle were booked into evidense.

Check your answers with those on pp.248-249 and calculate your score: ______ out of a possible 75 points. You should have scored at least 60 points. If you did not, review the pages indicated on the answer sheet.

CHAPTER TEN SELF-TEST
(75 points)

1. Correct any errors in abbreviations, numbers, or capitalization in the following sentences. If no changes are needed, write OK. (26 points)

   a. The comp. reports the theft of 1 tec-lite electronic demonstrator unit contained in a samsonite suitcase.

   b. The Device was taken from the rear seat of his 4-door 1998 mercedes benz while in the Parking lt. of 5009 Washington Av.

   c. The Complainant says he is unsure of where the theft occurred; Therefore he is reporting the incident to both the ashville and brownston police departments.

   d. attached to this rept. is a pic. of the Stolen Item.

   e. sgt. smyth will return to work after 3 more days at the hosp.

2. Correct any errors in abbreviations, numbers, or capitalization in the following report. (25 points)

   1 Typewriter, IBM selectric #2, ser. #1401679, was removed from the sect. desk in the front office of the early American life insurance co. the machine was last seen about five pm on 12-24-20--, when ms. Everson, Head Secretary, left the office. a box of Typewriter Ribbons for the machine was removed from the storage closet shelf and left on the desk. 1 plastic spray bottle of klenzo, such as used by Janitors, was left sitting close to where the mach. was last seen. The off. door was found unlocked with no indication of Force or Damage.

3. Using the facts given below, write a report of the incident using your own paper. (24 points)

When: Today's date; 1630 hours

Where: Assault: 2800 Dakota Avenue; victim taken to City Medical Center

Who: *Victim*: Michael David, 14 years old, 2800 Dakota Ave., 555-4631
Suspects: Three 17- or 18-year-old boys, wearing blue windbreakers, jeans, and tennis shoes. Described as "really big," but no specifics. None wore glasses. One called Joe.
Neighbor: Mrs. Helen Chaplin, 2802 Dakota Ave., 555-6061

What: Michael David was playing basketball by garage in own backyard. Suspects walked through alley, took basketball. Mike tried to get it back, but they pushed him down and kicked him, then ran back down the alley, heading north. They left the ball. Mike went to his neighbor's for help. She called police, but she had seen nothing of the incident. Mike required seven stitches for cut in back of head received when he was pushed. Interviewed victim and neighbor at City Medical Center. Parents were not home at time of incident.

Check your answers with those on pp.249-251 and calculate your score: ______ out of a possible 75 points. You should have scored at least 60 points. If you did not, review the pages indicated on the answer sheet.

CHAPTER ELEVEN SELF-TEST
(79 points)

1. Correct the following sentences by adding commas where needed. If no changes are needed, write OK. (17 points)

    a. This car is a sporty roomy economical vehicle.

    b. Shift work I think is one of the things a new officer must get used to.

    c. Williams Johnson Harrison you three move into position.

    d. Any buyer who does not read the warranty card deserves what he gets.

    e. The body bloody and battered had been thrown from the speeding car.

    f. The court hearing held on June 3 20-- was indecisive.

    g. My partner however would rather patrol a beat than talk to people.

    h. Public relations necessarily is an important part of each officer's tour of duty and it is not to be taken lightly.

2. Correct any comma errors in the following report. (38 points)

    On April 27 20-- at approximately 1405 hrs. two Caucasian males dressed identically and armed entered the south entrance of the First National Bank 1515 Third Street and ordered all customers to lie down on the floor. The four tellers were visited by Suspect No. 1 and the money was collected in an old brown tattered gunny sack. Suspect No. 2 held the rest of the building's occupants on the floor. Eyewitness No. 1 who was directly in front of Suspect No. 2 had been standing in the center of the lobby. After having visited all the tellers the two suspects left the building through the same door they had entered and drove off heading north.

Suspect No. 1 was described as a white male 5′ 8″ 140 pounds between 23 and 28 years old and carrying a long-barreled pistol. Suspect No. 2 was described as a white male 5′ 11″ 160 pounds between 25 and 30 years old and carrying a machine gun. Both suspects according to witnesses were wearing Budweiser beer caps black stockings on their faces navy blue jeans army-green shirts with rolled-up sleeves and boots.

The suspect's car located in the parking lot of Ship-Shape Seafood 6686 Bellvue Blvd. was examined by Henry Mayfield and pictures were taken at the scene of the recovery by Officer Andrews. The FBI verified that the car a blue Accord was hot-wired and stolen from the Sears employees' parking lot on April 26 20--. The car was released to James Flint the owner on May 25 20--.

3. Using the facts given below, write a report of the incident using your own paper. (24 points)

Date:	Today's date	**Time of Dispatch**:	0650
Location:	Downtown Marina	**Time of Arrival**:	0700

Officer: Good morning. Police Dispatch called me and said you have a theft report to give me.

Victim: Yes, I came out to the marina this morning, and my boat was gone, with my motor.

Officer: Where were your boat and motor?

Victim: In the water, tied up here, inside this covered dock.

Officer: What is your home address?

Victim: 2925 Lake Drive.

Officer: Can you give me a description of the boat? Do you have any serial numbers?

Victim: The serial number is 31621978, and the model number is 316-D.

Officer: I see here from your registration card this is a 1998 Aluma-craft; it's a 14-footer; it's this state's license plate number CA-1336-AZ. Are there any identifying things about the boat itself?

Victim: Well, it's aluminum in color; it has red padded seats and green oar-locks. And my license number is painted in purple on the oar-locks.

Officer: When did you notice these items missing?

Victim: At about 6:30 this morning. I came down to get some ski ropes out of my boat, and it was gone.

Officer: When was the last time you noticed these things intact?

Victim: They were there last night at 7:30.

Officer: OK. I'm going to have to get the crime lab technician because I noticed the rear window of your covered dock was broken and the door was jimmied open. Were there any other thefts here?

Victim: No, I didn't notice anything else.

Officer: What would you say the value of the boat is?

Victim: $280.

Officer: And the motor?

Victim: $500.

Officer: OK. That would be a $780 loss. Your insurance company is?

Victim: Intramarine Insurance.

Officer: Do you have a representative there?

Victim: Yes. Don George.

Officer: OK. I'll call in for a crime lab tech to come out here and take some fingerprints and take pictures of the damage to your covered dock. There's one thing I have to have here, a description of your motor. Do you have your identification card for your motor?

Victim: Yes.

Officer: I see here it's a 22-horsepower Johnson outboard motor. It's white and gold in color, and the shaft is green in color. It's a 1998 model. Serial number is 1461723; model number is J-1672. Is that correct?

Victim: Yes.

Officer: You're Mrs. Jackie Lundgren? I want to make sure I get this all right; I'll copy it right off your owner's title card here. You live at 2925 Lake Drive, your home phone number is 555-6542, and your business number is 555-9729. Is that correct?

Victim: Yes, it is.

Officer: Thank you. What is your business address?

Victim: It's 6500 Pacific Ave. I manage the McDonald's there.

Officer: Thank you. I'll call all this in now.

Check your answers with those on pp.251-253 and calculate your score: ______ out of a possible 79 points. You should have scored at least 63 points. If you did not, review the pages indicated on the answer sheet.

CHAPTER TWELVE SELF-TEST
(202 points)

---

1. Correct the errors in the following sentences by adding commas, parentheses, dashes, quotation marks, colons, semicolons, underlining, and hyphens as needed. If no changes are needed, write OK. (24 points)

   a. On 06 28 20-- at approximately 11 14 pm I was dispatched to Black Road and Markey Drive to check on a slumper a person slumped over a vehicle steering wheel.

   b. The two men from the rescue squad Charles Myre and Harold Veron said they had called for a back up unit.

   c. Shortly thereafter the suspect shouted No cop is going to get me out of this car.

   d. A search of the suspect revealed the following 1 a switchblade knife 2 a small revolver 3 a bottle of pills and 4 a map of a neighboring town.

   e. The Chronicle carried the entire story and it was mentioned in Time Magazine in an article entitled Small Town Suffers Large Loss.

2. Correct the following report by adding commas, parentheses, dashes, colons, semicolons, quotation marks, underlining, and hyphens as needed. (20 points)

   The complainant reported that on 08 08 20-- at approximately 2 10 pm she answered a knock at her apartment door Apartment #6. Upon opening the door she was struck on the left side of the head by a white male adult Suspect #1 with a revolver he was holding in his right hand. Suspect #1 was accompanied by a second white male adult Suspect #2. The complainant screamed Help! Help! and both suspects fled. Neither suspect spoke to the complainant. See follow up case in file.

   Suspect #1 white male adult late 30's early 40's light brown crew cut hair blue gray sport coat.

   The complainant did not get a good look at Suspect #2 although she says it might have been her ex husband.

3. Correct the following report for *all* errors. (82 points)

The suspect was seen Northbound on H. 299 at approximately 1 30 am on 07 04 20--. Suspect appearred to be traveling at a speed above the posted limit 50 mph and he was traveling with his bright lites on. The suspect was observed meeting 3 oncoming cars without diming his bright lites. After the susp. passed by this officer's squad car this officer began to follow him he continued North on hwy 299. At a pt. approx. 50 ft. North of Denton Avenue the suspect weaved accross the center line by approx. 2 feet. At this point I attempted to stop him with my red lights and horn but I was unable to do so. By using my siren the suspect was finally stopped in the 5300 block.

After I finally managed to stop the vehical I approached the suspect told him why he was being stopped and asked to see his drivers lisence. It took suspect approx. 2 minutes to find and remove his lisence. I saw that the suspects eyes was blood shot and there was a strong oder of an alcaholic beverage on the suspects breth. When I asked the suspect if he had been drinking he answered No. I then asked the suspect to step out of his vehicle to preform field sobreity tests. On the heel to toe test the suspect had considerable difficulty maintaining his ballance he stumbled 1 time swayed continuously thruout the distance of the test and compleatly lost his balance at 1 point. On the finger to nose test the suspect completely missed with his right arm striking his upper lip not his nose. With his left arm. the suspect touched the nostril's rather than the tip of his nose. After having completed these feild sobreity tests I again asked the suspect if he had been drinking and he again stated no. I placed suspect under arrest and transported him to county jail.

4. What strengths does the above report have? (2 points) ____________________________________

____

5. What weaknesses does the above report have? (2 points) __________________________________

____

6. Using the facts given below, you will take notes and the write a report of the incident. Use your own paper for this exercise. (72 points)

Date: Today's date
Time: 2000 hours (dispatched); 2010 hours (arrived)

Officer: Hello, sir. You phoned about a burglary of your residence?

Victim: Yes, I did. I came home from work, and I found that my house had been broken into and ransacked. But the only things I could determine missing after checking the house over was my Panasonic color television and my wife's diamond ring. It was on the bedroom dresser.

Officer: OK. I have a regular form here that I fill out. Could I start by asking you your name?

Victim: Yes, my name is John Edward Gordon. G-O-R-D-O-N.

Officer: And your age, sir?

Victim: I'm 28. I was born July 23rd.

Officer: And may I have your business address and phone number?

Victim: 5200 Washington Street, and the phone number is 555-8400.

Officer: And this is 8142 Norman Drive. And what is the phone number here at your residence?

Victim: 555-4440.

Officer: Now, I'll just list the items that you have found that you lost. You say one is a TV?

Victim: Yes, I just bought it a month ago. I've got the registration and sales slip with the serial number on it.

Officer: OK. Could you give that to me, sir?

Victim: Yeah, the serial number is 14832. And it's a 19-inch, color, black and silver cabinet, portable model, and the model number is LS42. I paid $550.00 for it.

Officer: OK, I'll list that. And then you state you also lost a diamond ring?

Victim: Right, my wife's diamond ring. She'd left it on the dresser. It was a one-third carat stone and a 14-karat gold band. And a simple setting.

Officer: Were there any initials engraved on it?

Victim: Yes, her initials, R.S.G., were engraved on the metal band.

Officer: Do you recall the value of that ring?

Victim: Yes, we had it appraised recently for $675.00.

Officer: You said the ring was in the bedroom on the dresser. Where was the TV in the house?

Victim: In the living room.

Officer: In the living room. Then that would probably be this portable stand I see where there obviously is a TV missing.

Victim: Right.

Officer: I noticed the glass was broken in the door as I entered here. That appears to be the point of entry.

Victim: Yes. I left for work this morning at about eight o'clock, and I got home about seven-thirty, and the front door was broken, the window in the front door was broken, and when I went inside I could see that it had been forced. I looked around and right away I could see that the TV was gone. I called my wife, and she asked me to check for the ring right away because she had forgotten it this morning as she was running out the door for work. So I looked on the dresser where she keeps it, and that was gone, and several other items were moved and left in kind of a mess. But that's the only thing I can determine was taken at this time.

Officer: First thing I'll do, Mr. Gordon, is take in a few of these items to the detective division to see if they can dust for prints. You say so far the only two items missing are the TV and the ring.

Victim: I checked with my neighbors on both sides of me, and they didn't see anything unusual during the day when I was gone.

Officer: And your wife had left before you did? You say you left at eight in the morning. Your wife was already gone for work?

Victim: Yes, she left a few minutes before I did.

Officer: OK, Mr. Gordon, did you find out how or where they left your home?

Victim: I always make sure I lock the doors when I leave for work. I think they must have gone out the front door because the back door was still locked, and it doesn't look like it was opened.

Officer: I see here around the door, I can see this pry mark, so apparently that's how the door was forced. They must have used some type of pry tool. I'm glad to see that you did have the type of locks that weren't accessible by just breaking out the window, but of course, in a situation like this, they still get in. All right, Mr. Gordon, I'll just take a couple of these articles, like I said, for dusting to headquarters. What I would advise you to do is to notify your insurance company. Then, if you find any further loss, please notify us, and we'll add it to our list here.

Victim: Well, like I said, at this point I've only noticed those two items missing, but when my wife gets home, she might discover something else.

Officer: OK, Mr. Gordon. I'll be turning this case over to the detective division, and they'll probably be contacting you soon. Thank you.

⇒ Take notes of the facts presented in the above dialogue. Use your own paper. Then, using your notes, write your report, again using your own paper.

Check your answers with those on pp.254-257 and calculate your score: _____ out of a possible 202 points. You should have scored at least 162 points. If you did not, review the pages indicated on the answer sheet.

SELF-TEST

ANSWERS

Check your self-test answers against those that follow. Each answer is followed by page references to review if your answer was incorrect.

CHAPTER ONE SELF-TEST ANSWERS

1. A report is a permanent written record which communicates important facts to be used in the future. [p.2]

- 3 points for "permanent written record" or something similar
- 2 points for "communicates important facts" or something similar
- 2 points for "to be used in the future" or something similar

2. Administrative and operational (1 point each) [p.3]
3. Operational reports [p.3]
4. Administrative reports [p.3]

5. Reports are used to (any four answers; 1 point each):
   - examine the past.
   - keep other police officers informed.
   - continue investigations.
   - prepare court cases.
   - provide the court with relevant facts.
   - coordinate law enforcement activities.
   - plan for future law enforcement services.
   - evaluate law enforcement officers' performances. [p.4]

6. Reports are read and used by (any three answers; 1 point each):
   - other officers.
   - supervisors.
   - attorneys and judges.
   - jurors.
   - city officials.
   - reporters.
   - citizens. [p.6]

7. Reader-friendly writing (any three answers; 1 point each):
   - avoids police jargon and abbreviations.
   - communicates in plain, simple language.
   - is written as it would be spoken.
   - considers its audience. [p.7]

8. Common problems in many police reports include (any five answers; 1 point each):
   - confusing or unclear sentences.
   - conclusions and assumptions.
   - extreme wordiness.
   - overuse of police jargon.
   - overuse of abbreviations.
   - missing or incomplete information.
   - misspelled words.
   - grammatical/mechanical errors.
   - referring to "above" information. [p.9]

(Self-Test One, continued)

9. Well-written reports (any four answers; 1 point each):
   - save the department time and expense.
   - result in better police work and more convictions.
   - reduce legal liability for the officer and the department.
   - communicate better.
   - reflect positively on the writer. [pp.10-11]

CHAPTER TWO SELF-TEST ANSWERS

1. Content and form are equally important. [p.14]
2. content [p.14]
3. form [p.14]

4. The content of a well-written report is:
   - factual.
   - accurate.
   - objective.
   - complete. [p.14]

5. opinion
   inference
   fact [p.15]

6. facts [p.15]
7. Who? What? Where? When? Why? How? [pp.25-27]
8. conclusionary [pp.17-18]
9. inference [p.15]
10. specific [p.19]
11. objective [p.21]
12. connotative [p.22]
13. denotative [p.22]
14. elements of the crime [p.30]

15. (1 point for each underlined word or phrase)

    In the latter part of October, Jerry Hindley (Stanton Ave.) called me at the police station. He was nervous and told me he had some information on some Uzi machine guns. Uzis are very cool. Gerry Hindly, a person whom I have known for many years and who has given me good information in the past, said that a broad named Barb Wilkins had approached him about purchasing some Uzi machine guns. Barb Wilkins' brother, Jeff Wilkins, lived with a guy named Joe who apparently had some guns for sale. Immediately after the conversation with Ms. Wilkins, Jerry contacted me. I told him to try and get a look at the guns and then contact me again. A few days later, Jerry did go down to Jeff Wilkins' apartment complex. He is probably a druggie since his apartment is located in a bad part of town. At that location, Jerry met a man named Joe and was shown two Uzi's by Joe.

(Self-Test Two, continued)

a. "latter part of October" - vague, not accurate. Give the date.
b. "Stanton Ave." - incomplete address, does not provide phone number.
c. "He was nervous" - conclusionary.
d. "Uzis are very cool." - opinion.
e. "Gerry Hindly" - spelled differently from the first time, inaccurate.
f. "many years" - vague, not accurate.
g. "broad" - not objective, has negative connotations. "Woman" would be better.
h. "contacted" - how? Called on the phone? Came in person? Sent an e-mail?
i. "few days" - not accurate. How many days specifically?
j. "He is probably a druggie since his apartment is located in a bad part of town." - not factual, inference made, and no address given.
k. Finally, the report is not complete. It doesn't say what happened. It's unfinished.

CHAPTER THREE SELF-TEST ANSWERS

1. The form of a well-written report is (in any order):
   - concise: not wordy.
   - clear: short sentences, common abbreviations, correct modifications.
   - mechanically correct: correct spelling, capitalization, and punctuation.
   - written in standard English: follows the rules of English grammar.
   - legible: readable.
   - on time: punctual. [p.40]

2. a. 2 - concise (less wordy) [pp.40-43]
   b. 1 - written in standard English [pp.49-50]
   c. 2 - clear (who drew the weapon?) [pp.44-47]
   d. 1 - concise [pp.40-43]
   e. 1 - mechanically correct [pp.47-49]

3. False [p.44]
4. False [p.45]
5. True [p.45]
6. True [p.51]
7. False [p.51]
8. True [p.42]
9. False [p.40]
10. False [p.49]

11. a. No, the report is not concise–it is wordy and repetitious. [pp.40-43]
    b. No, the report is not clear–modifiers are not always close to the words they describe. For example: ". . . we observed a light in the front part of the house which appeared to be a flashlight." [pp.44-47]

(Self-Test Three, continued)

c. No, the report is not mechanically correct–there are misspelled words and words which should be capitalized but are not. For example: "suspict vehical" should be "suspect vehicle." [pp.47-49]
d. Yes, the report is written in standard English. [pp.49-50]
e. The greatest strength of this report is its attention to specific facts and details.
f. The greatest weakness of this report is its wordiness. It could have been written in half as many words and still included all important facts. For example, stating exactly what was said during the Miranda warning is unnecessary and space-consuming. You can simply write: I read the suspect his Miranda rights, using the Miranda Warning card.

CHAPTER FOUR SELF-TEST ANSWERS

1. The five basic steps in writing a police report are:
   a. Gather the facts.
   b. Record the facts (take notes).
   c. Organize the facts.
   d. Write the report.
   e. Evaluate the report. [p.54]

2. Some factors to consider when interviewing a subject are (any four of the following):
   - Prepare for each interview in advance.
   - Obtain your information as soon after an incident as possible.
   - Be considerate of the subject's feelings.
   - Be friendly.
   - Use a private setting if possible.
   - Eliminate physical barriers.
   - Encourage conversation.
   - Ask simple questions.
   - Ask one question at a time.
   - Listen to what is said and how.
   - Watch for indications of tension, surprise, guilt, etc.
   - Establish the reliability of the subject.
   - Be objective and controlled. [pp.55-56]

3. Some ways to encourage conversation with a subject are (any two of the following):
   - Keep your own talking to a minimum.
   - Use open-ended questions.
   - Avoid "yes/no" type questions.
   - Allow long pauses. [p.56]

4. Procedures to be followed in taking notes are (any four of the following):
   - Use a notebook–not scraps of paper.
   - Use ink.
   - Write legibly.
   - Identify the notes with your name, the date, and the case number.

(Self-Test Four, continued)

- Record all relevant facts as you get them.
- Check spelling, numbers, and dates as you record them.
- Use freehand sketches if the situation calls for it.
- Omit words such as *a, an*, and *the*, and use common abbreviations. [p.58]

5. Ways to improve the organization of your reports are (any three of the following):
   - Organize your field notebook.
   - Make an outline or report plan.
   - Use paragraphs.
   - Use chronological order.
   - Establish a format for the introductory sentence. [pp.61-63]

6. a. 3
   b. 1
   c. 4
   d. 2 [p.65]

7. False [p.70]
8. Present [p.70]
9. Past [p.70]
10. False [p.59]
11. True [pp.67-68]

12. The two procedures to use in evaluating reports are (1 point each for naming the two procedures; 1 point for each brief explanation):
    a. Editing: rewriting to improve the content of the report.
    b. Proofreading: improving the form of the report by correcting any errors in spelling, capitalization, and punctuation. [pp.71-72]

CHAPTER FIVE SELF-TEST ANSWERS

1. a. I read the suspect the Miranda warning. [pp.75-76]
   b. The thief broke into and stole the car. [pp.77-79]
   c. The hotel manager summoned me to the office. [pp.77-79]
   d. The sergeant told the deputy that the deputy needed a shave. *or* The sergeant told the deputy that the sergeant needed a shave. [pp.93-95]
   e. To protect the public and ensure his appearance in court, the suspect belongs in jail. [pp.96-97]

2. a. P
   b. A
   c. A
   d. P
   e. A [pp.77-79]

(Self-Test Five, continued)

3. a. F
   b. T
   c. T
   d. T
   e. F [pp.75-76]

4. a. I
   b. I
   c. I
   d. C
   e. I [pp.83-92]

5. True [pp.77-79]
6. True [pp.75-76]
7. False [pp.77-79]
8. True [pp.77-79]
9. False [pp.93-95]

10. (1 point for each underlined word or phrase)

PROPERTY DAMAGE REPORT

At 0800 hours on March 3, 1996, this officer[1] was dispatched to Acme Hardware, 1005 Main Street, to investigate property damage. Upon arrival at 0810 hours, Mr. Hill[2], the owner and manager of the store, met this officer[3].

Hill said he left the store last night at about 2100 hours and did return[4] this morning at about 0730 hours. He discovered the damage at that time. The wall and window had been sprayed with green paint.* A can of Ward's green paint was found by Hill[5] in the alley that looked like the same color[6].

This officer[7] went to the alley and looked at the damage. This reporting officer[8] found one can of Ward's green spray paint in the alley that was bagged and kept as evidence[9]. Hill said he thought that a recently fired part-time employee, John Johnson, may have been involved. Hill said he had to let him go, and he[10] was not happy about it.

Case pending.

Score one point for each of the following you identified:

1. "This officer" is in third person. Should be in first person: "I." [pp.75-76]
2. Mr. Hill did not arrive at 0810; incorrect modification. [p.89]
3. "this officer" (third person) should be "I" (first person). [pp.75-76]
4. "did return" should be "returned" to be parallel with "left." [pp.96-97]
5. Written passive; should be active: "Hill found a can of Ward's green paint . . ." [pp.77-79]

(Self-Test Five, continued)

6. The alley didn't look like the same color, the can of paint did; incorrect modification. [p.87]
7. Again, third person should be first person "I." [pp.75-76]
8. "This reporting officer" (third person) should be "I" (first person). [pp.75-76]
9. The alley wasn't bagged and kept as evidence; incorrect modification. [pp.83-84]
10. "he" could be either Hill or the fired employee; incorrect modification. [pp.83-84]

* Recall when the doer of the action is unknown, it is appropriate to use the passive voice. This is better than "Person or persons unknown had sprayed the wall and window with green paint."

CHAPTER SIX SELF-TEST ANSWERS

1. a. I proceeded to interview John Doe. [pp.105-113]
   b. I tried to stop his progress. [pp.99-102]
   c. I have interviewed three suspects in this case. [p.108]
   d. No progress has been made on the case. [p.108]
   e. Establishing guidelines was an important first step. [p.108]
   f. Partners depend on each other. [p.108]
   g. The chief helped the two officers settle their disagreement. [p.108]
   h. I saw the suspect had a gun. [p.107]

2. False [p.103]
3. False [p.105]
4. True [p.108]
5. True [p.108]
6. True [p.107]
7. False [p.108]

8. a. suddenly
   b. while
   c. tended to
   d. near
   e. if
   f. after
   g. individually
   h. although [pp.109-110]

9. (Score 1 point for each underlined word or phrase)

   At about 0930 hours on 06-15-20--, I was dispatched to 1375 Bantam Drive to investigate a reported home burglary. When I arrived, I was met by the victim, Sara Kruse.

   Ms. Kruse said[1] that she had returned from the grocery store and found the back door to her house unlocked, although[2] she was (omit "absolutely")[3] certain she had locked it before[4] leaving. Upon entering the house, she saw a kitchen chair overturned and several kitchen drawers pulled open.

(Self-Test Six, continued)

Because (*or* Since)[5] she had a teenage son, Ms. Kruse initially thought[6] her son had returned home from school, left the door unlocked, and caused the disarray. She then discovered, however, that the house was empty and that several items were missing. Ms. Kruse noted[7] that the television in the living room was missing, as was the stereo in her son's bedroom. Then[8], she checked her bedroom to see[9] if anything else was missing and found that her jewelry box and 35mm camera were also gone. At that time, she called the police.

She estimated she was gone (omit "a combined total of")[10] 45 minutes. None of the neighbors reported seeing anything, although one neighbor mentioned[11] that this was the third break-in he had heard of happening in that neighborhood during (omit "the month of")[12] June.

I informed Ms. Kruse that usually[13], such stolen property is not recovered, but that if we located anything matching the description of her property we would call her.

CHAPTER SEVEN SELF-TEST ANSWERS

1. Score 1 point for each underlined item:

   a. The victim discovered that a very (*or* really) old coin collection and stamp collection were missing from the bedroom desk.

   b. The house was full of valuable antiques, jewelry, and a portable color TV, none of which was disturbed by the burglar.

   c. A neighbor who was coming home late said that he didn't see anything suspicious. (*or* he saw nothing suspicious)

   d. He had just come home from work and was very (*or* really) tired, so his statement could hardly be completely reliable.

   e. Another officer and I then questioned the neighbors on the other side of the victim's house.

   f. One neighbor said that there were several strange sounds around midnight.

   g. Another neighbor across the street came out of her house and said she had (*or* saw) seen an orange van drive by around midnight with no lights on.

   h. A complete list of missing items will be furnished by the victim after she has a chance to go through her valuables.

   i. Officer Harris and I conducted the (*or* a) preliminary investigation, but the case will be handled from here by detectives.

   j. There are currently no leads on the identity of the burglar. [pp.115-128]

(Self-Test Seven, continued)

2. Score 1 point for each underlined item:

   At approximately 0338 hours on 01-23-20--, police and fire units responded to an apartment fire at 5179 Fairway Drive, Apt. 104. Mr. Arnold Millsap, resident manager, contacted the police dispatcher by phone and said the above apartment was on fire and that an invalid, Mary Foster, lived there.

   Upon arrival, Officer Manos and I did not see any visible flames; however, we did see a large amount of smoke coming from the other side (east side) of the apartment. Officer Manos was able to open the outer entry door and crawl a short distance on the floor, but he could not reach the door to the victim's apartment due to the very dense smoke. The Humboldt Fire Department arrived on the scene at 0343, and they were able to gain entrance into the apartment using face masks. The victim's body was discovered in the living room by the firefighters. The body, nude except for a pair of panty hose, was located in front of a serving bar with the head against the south wall and approximately 15 feet from the east side of the apartment. The body was on its right side with the front portion facing the glass sliding door. The entire body had a brown, baked appearance.

   The coroner arrived and took pictures of the body. The victim's purse and contents were turned over to the coroner. Identification was made through her (*or* a) driver's license and other identification within the purse. I saw that the bedside clock had stopped at 0332 hrs. Further interviews with adjoining tenants and the resident manager revealed the following information: the victim had worked for the local school district for two years; she was a "loner"; she had hardly any visitors. No one had any personal contact with her. The resident manager said the victim had a daughter who did come to visit sometimes, but her name and address were (*or* are) unknown. [pp.115-128]

3. This report conveys much information, but it also has several errors.
4. Strengths: It is well organized and contains specific details relevant to the case.
5. Weaknesses: Numerous errors, wordy, use of passive voice.

CHAPTER EIGHT SELF-TEST ANSWERS

1. Your answers may vary slightly from those given below.

   a. John is a good shot. He often fires in the grand-master class. (*or* Since John is a good shot, he often fires in the grand-master class.)

   b. Because he is such a good shot, we rely on him to carry some of our weaker teams.

   c. Since there will be a briefing tomorrow afternoon, all shift leaders will report one-half hour early.

(Self-Test Eight, continued)

d. All officers will have their riot equipment with them, including tear gas, gas masks, and rifles with scopes.

e. The officer called to the suspect to halt, radioed for backup, and again called for the suspect to halt. She finally pursued the suspect and caught him in an alley two blocks away. [pp.129-143]

2. subject, predicate [pp.129-130]
3. predicate [p.129]
4. subject [p.129]
5. fragment [p.133]
6. run-on [pp.139-141]
7. True [p.143]

8. Again, your answers may vary slightly from those given below. Score 1 point for each underlined item. Note some of the items simply denote that words have been removed.

    On 06-16-20-- at approximately 1738 hrs., Officer Madsen and I saw a 2000 red Chevrolet parked[1] at the yellow curb in front of the First National Bank. The Chevrolet was occupied by two people, one in[2] the driver's seat and one[3] in the right rear seat. The vehicle and occupants looked suspicious, so[4] we turned our vehicle around to watch the Chevrolet.

    We[5] saw a young male running eastbound on the sidewalk of the shopping center toward the red Chevrolet. The suspect, later[6] identified as Ray Shipley, was carrying a brass clock and was[7] being pursued by a female, later[8] identified as Mary Chase.

    As the suspect approached the vehicle, the[9] right door was opened for[10] him;[11] however,[12] he ran past and around the east end of the building and headed south. The Chevrolet then[13] began moving out[14] of the parking lot onto York Avenue southbound. Officer Madsen pursued[15] on foot. The suspect dropped the clock[16] and[17] continued running south through an open field. Officer Madsen caught the suspect on the south side of the apartments and placed[18] him under arrest. [pp.129-143]

CHAPTER NINE SELF-TEST ANSWERS

1. Score 1 point for each word or group of words you found and corrected:

    a. questioning, suspect's, rights
    b. department's, policy, very
    c. You're, your
    d. OK (1 point for this)
    e. to, attorney's
    f. elude, authorities
    g. effect, neighborhood
    h. A lot, it's, all right
    i. There, a lot, cannot
    j. arrested, possession, narcotics
    k. warrant, your, responsibility
    l. principal, guilty, knew [pp.147-162]

(Self-Test Nine, continued)

2. Score 1 point for each identified item:

On this date at about 0125 hours, I[1] saw the suspect driving south on Normandale Road very slowly.[2] The[3] suspect's[4] vehicle, a 1993 blue[5] Buick, Michigan plate #DWI222, was traveling approximately[6] 10 m.p.h. in a 50 m.p.h. zone between West 50th Street and County Road 62. I attempted to[7] stop the[8] suspect for[9] about three blocks, using[10] my red lights and siren while directly behind and alongside him. The[11] suspect eventually stopped at the Normandale Road and West 66th Street intersection. I approached the[12] suspect's[13] car as he was attempting to get out. The[14] suspect fell on his face when I was about 15 feet from him. At the time I saw the[15] suspect fall, I[16] heard glass breaking near his vehicle. I rushed to his assistance.[17] The suspect was sobbing and[18] asking for help. I assisted him[19] to his feet and[20] could smell a strong odor of alcoholic[21] beverage on the[22] suspect's[23] breath and clothing. I asked him[24] about his condition. He said he was dead drunk, had been drinking for two[25] days, and wanted to die.[26] I told the[27] suspect that I was arresting him and[28] informed him of the Implied Consent Law. The[29] suspect told me he wanted to have the blood test and requested permission[30] to stay in the hospital for treatment after the test. I found[31] a broken quart bottle of scotch[32] where the suspect had fallen.[33] (*or* " . . . where the suspect fell.")

The[34] suspect's[35] vehicle was towed[36] and[37] impounded by Southport Garage. I transported the[38] suspect to Mercy Hospital where[39] Nurse Sarah Connors drew a blood sample in my presence.[40] I marked the blood container with the date, case number, suspect's[41] name, and my initials. I gave the suspect a notice to appear, including the charges and court date, and released[42] him to his doctor's[43] care. The remnants of the scotch[44] bottle were booked into evidence.[45]

CHAPTER TEN SELF-TEST ANSWERS

1. Score 1 point for each underlined item. Total points for each sentence are given at the end in ( ).

   a. The complainant reports the theft of one Tec-lite electronic demonstrator unit contained in a Samsonite suitcase. (4)

   b. The device was taken from the rear seat of his four-door 1998 Mercedes Benz while in the parking lot of 5009 Washington Ave. (7)

   c. The complainant says he is unsure of where the theft occurred; therefore he is reporting the incident to both the Ashville and Brownston Police Departments. (6)

   d. Attached to this report is a picture of the stolen item. (5)

   e. Sgt. Smyth will return to work after three more days at the hospital. (4) [pp.164-171]

(Self-Test Ten, continued)

2. Score 1 point for each identified item:

   One[1] typewriter,[2] IBM Selectric[3] #2, serial[4] #1401679, was removed from the secretary's[5] desk in the front office of the Early[6] American Life[7] Insurance[8] Co.[9] The[10] machine was last seen about 5[11] p.m.[12] on 12-24-20--, when Ms.[13] Everson, head[14] secretary,[15] left the office. A[16] box of typewriter[17] ribbons[18] for the machine was removed from the storage closet shelf and left on the desk. One[19] plastic spray bottle of Klenzo,[20] such as used by janitors,[21] was left sitting close to where the machine[22] was last seen. The office[23] door was found unlocked with no indication of force[24] or damage.[25]

3. Compare your report with this sample report. Many differences may occur; however, points are based on your answers to the questions which follow the report.

ASSAULT REPORT

On (today's date), at approximately 1630 hours, I was dispatched to City Medical Center to investigate the report of an assault. Upon arrival, I talked to the 14-year-old victim, Michael David; his neighbor, Mrs. Helen Chaplin; and Michael's physician, Dr. Johnson.

Michael related that about 1530 hours he was home alone and had been playing basketball by his garage when three white males who he had never seen before came down the alley and took his ball away. He described the males as 17 or 18 years old, wearing blue windbreakers, jeans, and tennis shoes. He said they were "really big," but he had no idea of their height or weight. One of them was called "Joe."

When Michael tried to get his ball back, the three boys knocked him down and kicked him in the back. The back of his head was cut when he fell. The males dropped the ball and ran down the alley, heading north. Michael went to his neighbor, Mrs. Chaplin, for help.

Mrs. Chaplin related that Michael came to her home and told her three older boys knocked him to the ground and kicked him. When she saw his head injury, she drove him to City Medical Center for treatment. She did not see the assault.

Dr. Johnson related that Michael required seven stitches to close the cut in the back of his head. He also had several bruises on his back.

I radioed the description of the suspects to other patrol units.

Case suspended pending further leads.

(Self-Test Ten, continued)

⇒ Evaluate your report for clarity by checking the following (score 2 points for each "Yes"):

Have you:			
	used the active voice?	_____ Yes	_____ No
	used correct modification?	_____ Yes	_____ No
	used proper pronoun reference?	_____ Yes	_____ No
	used parallelism?	_____ Yes	_____ No
	used common words?	_____ Yes	_____ No
	been concise?	_____ Yes	_____ No

⇒ Now, evaluate your report for these characteristics (score 2 points for each "Yes"):

Is your report:			
	factual?	_____ Yes	_____ No
	accurate?	_____ Yes	_____ No
	objective?	_____ Yes	_____ No
	complete?	_____ Yes	_____ No
	chronological?	_____ Yes	_____ No
	written in standard English?	_____ Yes	_____ No

CHAPTER ELEVEN SELF-TEST ANSWERS

1. Score 1 point for each comma added. Total points for each sentence are given at the end in ( ).

    a. This car is a sporty, roomy, economical vehicle. (2)

    b. Shift work, I think, is one of the things a new officer must get used to. (2)

    c. Williams, Johnson, Harrison, you three move into position. (3)

    d. OK (score 1 point if you marked this restrictive sentence as "OK"; otherwise score 0)

    e. The body, bloody and battered, had been thrown from the speeding car. (2)

    f. The court hearing held on June 3, 20--, was indecisive. (2)

    g. My partner, however, would rather patrol a beat than talk to people. (2)

    h. Public relations, necessarily, is an important part of each officer's tour of duty, and it is not to be taken lightly. (3) [pp.174-186]

(Self-Test Eleven, continued)

2. Score 1 point for each comma added:

   On April 27, 20--, at approximately 1405 hrs., two Caucasian males, dressed identically and armed, entered the south entrance of the First National Bank, 1515 Third Street, and ordered all customers to lie down on the floor. The four tellers were visited by Suspect No. 1, and the money was collected in an old, brown, tattered gunny sack. Suspect No. 2 held the rest of the building's occupants on the floor. Eyewitness No. 1, who was directly in front of Suspect No. 2, had been standing in the center of the lobby. After having visited all the tellers, the two suspects left the building through the same door they had entered and drove off, heading north.

   Suspect No. 1 was described as a white male, 5′ 8″, 140 pounds, between 23 and 28 years old, and carrying a long-barreled pistol. Suspect No. 2 was described as a white male, 5′ 11″, 160 pounds, between 25 and 30 years old, and carrying a machine gun. Both suspects, according to witnesses, were wearing Budweiser beer caps, black stockings on their faces, navy blue jeans, army-green shirts with rolled-up sleeves, and boots.

   The suspect's car, located in the parking lot of Ship-Shape Seafood, 6686 Bellvue Blvd., was examined by Henry Mayfield, and pictures were taken at the scene of the recovery by Officer Andrews. The FBI verified that the car, a blue Accord, was hot-wired and stolen from the Sears employees' parking lot on April 26, 20--. The car was released to James Flint, the owner, on May 25, 20--.

3. Compare your report with this sample report. Many differences may occur; however, points are based on your answers to the questions which follow the report.

   THEFT REPORT

   On (this date) at 0650 hours, I was dispatched to the Downtown Marina regarding the report of a felony theft. Upon arrival at about 0700, I talked to the victim, Jackie Lundgren, who told me the following:

   She arrived at the Downtown Marina at about 0630 hours to retrieve some ski ropes from her boat. When she went to her covered boat dock, she discovered the dock's door was open and her boat and motor were missing. She did not go inside the dock but immediately phoned the police. She had locked the door the night before at about 1930 hours when she left the dock. The boat and motor were in the dock at that time. She saw no other person around the dock when she left. She had no idea how the boat or motor were taken. (See property loss section below for full description.)

   I checked the door and saw that it appeared to have been jimmied. I radioed for a crime lab technician to come to the scene and process it for physical evidence. Refer to her supplemental report for further information.

   Case referred to the Detective Division for follow-up.

(Self-Test Eleven, continued)

PROPERTY LOSS:

Item	Description	Value
1	Boat, 1998 - 14′ Aluma-craft Model 316-D, Serial No. 31621978, with red padded seats, State License No. CA-1336-AZ on both sides near the stern.	$280.00
2	Motor, 1998 - 22 HP Johnson Outboard, Model No. J-1672, Serial No. 1461723, white and gold with a green shaft.	$500.00
	TOTAL LOSS (Owner's Estimate)	$780.00

Note: You may have to put the description and value of the boat and motor as the third paragraph. To include in the second paragraph would make the paragraph too long.

⇒ Evaluate your report for clarity by checking the following (score 2 points for each "Yes"):

Have you:			
	used the active voice?	_____ Yes	_____ No
	used correct modification?	_____ Yes	_____ No
	used proper pronoun reference?	_____ Yes	_____ No
	used parallelism?	_____ Yes	_____ No
	used common words?	_____ Yes	_____ No
	been concise?	_____ Yes	_____ No

⇒ Now, evaluate your report for these characteristics (score 2 points for each "Yes"):

Is your report:			
	factual?	_____ Yes	_____ No
	accurate?	_____ Yes	_____ No
	objective?	_____ Yes	_____ No
	complete?	_____ Yes	_____ No
	chronological?	_____ Yes	_____ No
	written in standard English?	_____ Yes	_____ No

CHAPTER TWELVE SELF-TEST ANSWERS

1. Score 1 point for each correction made. Total points for each sentence are given at the end in ( ). (**Note**: Periods added to the abbreviations "a.m." and "p.m." count as one correction, not two; similarly, a set of quotation marks " " and a set of parentheses ( ) counts as one correction, not two).

   a. On 06-28-20-- at approximately 11:14 p.m., I was dispatched to Black Road and Markey Drive to check on a "slumper"– a person slumped over a vehicle steering wheel. (You may also use parentheses around the definition of *slumper*.) (7)

   b. The two men from the rescue squad, Charles Myre and Harold Veron, said they had called for a back-up unit. (You may also put parentheses around the names in place of the commas.) (3)

   c. Shortly thereafter the suspect shouted, "No cop is going to get me out of this car." (2)

   d. A search of the suspect revealed the following: (1) a switchblade knife, (2) a small revolver, (3) a bottle of pills, and (4) a map of a neighboring town. (8)

   e. The Chronicle carried the entire story, and it was mentioned in Time Magazine in an article entitled "Small Town Suffers Large Loss." (4) [pp.189-201]

2. Score 1 point for each correction made.

   The complainant reported that on 08-08-20--[1,2] at approximately 2:10[3] p.m.[4] she answered a knock at her apartment door (Apartment #6).[5] Upon opening the door she was struck on the left side of the head by a white male adult (Suspect #1)[6] with a revolver he was holding in his right hand. Suspect #1 was accompanied by a second white male adult (Suspect #2).[7] The complainant screamed,[8] "Help! Help!"[9] and both suspects fled. Neither suspect spoke to the complainant. (See follow-up[10] case in file.)[11]

   Suspect #1:[12] white male adult,[13] late 30's-early 40's,[14,15] light brown crew-cut hair,[16,17] blue-gray[18] sport coat.

   The complainant did not get a good look at Suspect #2;[19] although she says it might have been her ex-husband.[20]

3. Score 1 point for each correction made.

   The suspect was seen northbound[1] on Hwy.[2] 299 at approximately 1:30[3] a.m.[4] on 07-04-20--.[5,6] The[7] suspect appeared[8] to be traveling at a speed above the posted limit (50 m.p.h.),[9,10,11] and he was traveling with his bright lights[12] on. The suspect was observed meeting three[13] oncoming cars without dimming[14] his bright lights.[15] After the suspect[16] passed by my[17] squad car,[18] I[19] began to follow him.[20] He[21] continued north[22] on Hwy.[23,24] 299. At a point[25] approximately[26] 50 ft. north[27] of Denton Avenue,[28] the suspect weaved across[29] the center line by approximately[30] 2 ft.[31] At this point I attempted to stop him with my red lights and horn,[32] but I was unable to do so. By using my siren,[33] I finally stopped the suspect[34] [rewrote passive to be active] in the 5300 block.

(Self-Test Twelve, continued)

I[35] [deleted first eight words of original report] approached the suspect,[36] told him why he was being stopped,[37] and asked to see his driver's[38] license.[39] It took the[40] suspect approximately[41] two[42] minutes to find and remove his license.[43] I saw that the suspect's[44] eyes were[45] blood-[46] shot,[47] and there was a strong odor[48] of an alcoholic[49] beverage on the suspect's[50] breath.[51] When I asked the suspect if he had been drinking,[52] he answered,[53] "No."[54] I then asked the suspect to step out of his vehicle to perform[55] field sobriety[56] tests. On the heel-to-toe[57,58] test,[59] the suspect had considerable difficulty maintaining his balance[60];[61] he stumbled one[62] time,[63] swayed continuously throughout[64] the distance of the test,[65] and completely[66] lost his balance at one[67] point. On the finger-to-nose[68,69] test,[70] the suspect completely missed with his right arm striking his upper lip,[71] not his nose. With his left arm[72] the suspect touched the nostrils[73] rather than the tip of his nose. After having completed these field[74] sobriety[75] tests,[76] I again asked the suspect if he had been drinking,[77] and he again stated,[78] "No."[79,80] I placed the[81] suspect under arrest and transported him to the[82] county jail.

4. Strengths: It is well organized and contains specific details relevant to the case.
5. Weaknesses: There are numerous errors; it is wordy; is uses the passive voice.

6. Your notes and report may vary from the samples shown below. Points, however, are based on your answers to the questions which follow the notes and report.

NOTES

Today's date

2000 hours dispatched to 8142 Norman Drive–burglary

Victim: John Edward Gordon, owner of residence

Said he and wife had been gone since 0800 hours that day. When he returned home at 1930 hours found house had been broken into, and color television missing from its stand in living room. He phoned wife, who told him to check on their dresser for her diamond ring. When he looked on dresser, he saw ring was gone and several items moved and in disarray.

Vict. described television as Panasonic, 19″color set in black and silver cabinet, port. model LS42, ser. #14832, valued at $550.00. The ring was lady's diamond ring, 1/3-carat diamond stone, 14-karat gold setting, with initials R.S.G. inside the band, valued at $675.00.

Vict. said he had talked to neighbors who said they hadn't noticed anything unusual during day.

Entry to house probably made through front door. Window in door broken, but apparently because of dead-bolt locks, suspect had to further pry door to get in. Back door was still locked, so suspect probably exited back out front door.

I collected a few of items which Vict. said had been moved from original location on dresser. Advised Vict. to contact his insurance company; asked him to phone the department if discovered that other items were missing; informed him that his case would be turned over to detective unit.

(Self-Test Twelve, continued)

⇒ Evaluate your notes using the following criteria (score 2 points for each "Yes"):

Did you:			
	use ink?	_____ Yes	_____ No
	write legibly?	_____ Yes	_____ No
	identify your notes with your name, date, and case number?	_____ Yes	_____ No
	record all the relevant facts as you got them?	_____ Yes	_____ No
	check spelling, numbers, and dates as you recorded them?	_____ Yes	_____ No
	omit words such as *a, an*, and *the*, and use common abbreviations?	_____ Yes	_____ No

BURGLARY REPORT

On (today's date) at 2000 hours I was dispatched to 8142 Norman Drive regarding a burglary report.

Upon my arrival, the victim, John Edward Gordon, told me the following:

His wife and he left for work at about 0800 hours on (today's date). When he returned home at 1930 hours, he discovered his house had been broken into, and his color television was missing from its stand in the living room. He then phoned his wife, who told him to check on their dresser for her diamond ring. When he looked on the dresser, he saw that the ring was gone, and several items were moved and in disarray.

He described the television as a Panasonic, 19″color set in a black and silver cabinet, portable model LS42, serial number 14832, valued at $550.00. The ring was a lady's diamond ring, 1/3-carat diamond stone, 14-karat gold setting, with the initials R.S.G. inside the band, valued at $675.00.

He said he talked to his neighbors, who said they hadn't noticed anything unusual during the day.

I noted that entry to the house was apparently made through the front door. The window in the door had been broken, but apparently because of the dead-bolt locks, the suspect had to further pry the door to get in. The back door was still locked, so it appears the suspect went back out the front door.

I collected a few of the items which Gordon said had been moved from their original location on the dresser (see attached evidence list for description and disposition). I advised Gordon to contact his insurance company. I asked him to phone the department if he discovered that other items were missing. And I informed him that his case would be turned over to the detective unit.

Case forwarded to the detective division for follow-up.

⇒ Evaluate your report using the Evaluation Checklist for Reports on p.208. Score 2 points for each "Yes" checked among the 30 items on the checklist.

Appendix A

INVESTIGATIVE STEPS AND TIPS FOR MAJOR CRIMINAL OFFENSES

This appendix is intended to assist you in investigating and reporting those offenses which are more complex or which require specific actions on your part to be performed and reported if the case is to successfully weather the criminal court process. The listed offenses include murder, rape, robbery, burglary, larceny or theft, arson, and assault.

MURDER ▪ defined as the killing of one person by another with malice aforethought (i.e., deliberate, willful, and with preformed intent).

❖ Investigative Steps

A. First arriving officer:

- ❑ Do not contaminate scene if at all possible. If scene is outside, consider leaving one marked trail to body for others to follow.
- ❑ Protect the entire scene. Keep unauthorized persons (including non-involved supervisors) out.
- ❑ Start a log: Note times/persons in scene/persons around area.
- ❑ Consider immediate photos if scene or evidence perishable.
- ❑ Notify supervisor. Protect scene until arrival.

B. If you are incident commander/investigator in charge:

- ❑ Limit entry to scene investigators only.
- ❑ Ensure decedent and scene are photographed.
- ❑ Ensure scene is diagrammed.
- ❑ Consider videotaping the scene.
- ❑ Ensure complete search for physical evidence.
- ❑ If scene is room, be sure to look up at ceiling, get down on floor, etc.
- ❑ Isolate witnesses. Interview separately
- ❑ Be prepared to collect or have proper technician collect trace evidence such as fibers, etc.

❖ Tips

- Conduct your investigation as if: a) nothing is ever as it seems, and b) no one ever tells the truth (until you learn otherwise).
- Remember, in over 70 percent of all homicide cases, the victim and the suspect knew each other.
- Never prejudge anything. Be prepared to revise your thinking as you learn new information.
- Remember, motive and opportunity are key issues.
- Be sure to get a homicide scene search warrant, if necessary.
- For eyewitnesses, hostile witnesses, suspects: Consider obtaining their word-for-word account (written or tape recorded).

RAPE ▪ defined as the unlawful carnal knowledge (sexual intercourse) of a person by force and against their will.

❖ Investigative Steps

A. In General (feminine pronouns are used, as most rape victims are female):

- ❑ Find out and note how the rape was reported.
- ❑ Interview the victim with a female present (preferably a support person, such as a rape crisis team member).
- ❑ Ensure the victim is medically examined.
- ❑ Ensure you have a sexual assault evidence collection kit available for the doctor's use.
- ❑ Ensure that adequate samples are collected of victim's and suspect's blood, pubic hairs, head hairs, saliva, fingernail scraping, etc.
- ❑ Ensure you retrieve and properly store the victim's clothing (especially underclothing).
- ❑ If you locate the suspect, be sure to retrieve his clothing, have him stand on a clean white sheet, and retain the sheet for trace evidence.
- ❑ Ensure you maintain a proper chain of custody.
- ❑ Ensure the victim and injuries are photographed.
- ❑ Ensure the scene, the vehicle, and the suspect are adequately searched and photographed.
- ❑ Consider a videotape/aerial photographs of the scene.
- ❑ Consider a photo/physical/voice lineup.
- ❑ Consider taking victim back to scene for proper ID, etc. Note tire tracks, remoteness of area, etc.

B. With the victim:

- ❑ Let her first tell her story from beginning to end without interruption, then a second time with notes, or formal recorded statement, etc.
- ❑ Complete physical description of suspect (including shaven, tattoos, scars, unique or hidden features, etc.).
- ❑ What did he say? (Exact quotes, if possible, for later voice lineup.) Alcohol or drugs involved?
- ❑ What force/fear used? (Each and every use is important to document.)
- ❑ Did he have an erection? Did he penetrate? Oral, anal, vaginal penetration? Did he ejaculate?
- ❑ Any possible witnesses? People close by?
- ❑ Did she tell anyone right after the event? Who? (Admissible as evidence of fresh complaint.)
- ❑ Who was the last person she talked to before the event?
- ❑ Did the suspect take anything with him?
- ❑ Did she bite or scratch him? Where? Results?
- ❑ Did she yell? Scream? Cry out? Specify.
- ❑ Her recollection of crime scene (lighted, dark, been there before, etc.).
- ❑ Complete description of any vehicle involved (including interior and items inside).
- ❑ How did he leave? Did she get away?

C. With the suspect:

- ❑ Protect his rights (Miranda).
- ❑ Interview him alone in a controlled setting. Let him talk.
- ❑ If he gives a statement, pin him down as to dates, times, places, threats, amount of force, friends, employer, etc.
- ❑ Consider taking him to scene. Have him describe what happened, show you where things happened, etc.

❖ Tips

- Remember that the following defenses are always possible, so structure your investigation from beginning to end with them in mind:

  Alibi
  "I didn't do it."
  Consent
  Diminished capacity (drunk, took drugs, etc.)
  "It never happened."

- Always treat the victim with care, compassion, and consideration for the emotional and physical trauma she's experienced.
- An objective and considerate approach toward the suspect will more likely reap the statement you want.
- Remember, a statement full of lies (which can be disproved) is better than no statement at all.
- Be sure to obtain proper consent signatures (medical release/consent to search, etc.).

ROBBERY ▪ defined as the felonious taking of the personal property from the person of another against his will by the means of force or fear.

❖ Investigative Steps

- ❑ Note time call received, when you arrived, etc. (Response time could become an issue later.)
- ❑ As soon as you have determined that a robbery has occurred, obtain initial suspect information for a Be-On-The-Lookout (BOLO) radio broadcast to other units.
- ❑ Secure scene immediately. Limit entry.
- ❑ Interview victim for complete details of event.
- ❑ Separate witnesses. Interview away from others.
- ❑ Obtain complete description of suspect(s), vehicle(s), property taken, etc.
- ❑ Note injuries to victim. Photograph. Obtain medical release for emergency room (ER) treatment info., etc.
- ❑ Obtain exact quotes of suspect's words, if possible.
- ❑ Process scene completely for physical evidence, including fingerprints, trace evidence, etc.
- ❑ Photograph/videotape scene.
- ❑ When interviewing the suspect(s), be sure you obtain complete statements including alibis.
- ❑ Consider doing a photo/physical/voice lineup.

BURGLARY ▪ defined as the breaking into and entry of the dwelling house of another in the nighttime with the intent to commit a crime therein. (Note: "in the nighttime" may not apply in your state.)

❖ Investigative Steps

- ❑ Interview victim. Obtain complete statement, to include the following information: When was last time he/she saw the structure or vehicle intact? When did he/she discover the burglary? How was entry made? Was it forced?
- ❑ Obtain complete description of property loss, including amount, brand names, manufacturers, model numbers, serial numbers, color, size, personal identifiers, unique marks, estimated value, etc.
- ❑ Secure/protect scene, if appropriate.
- ❑ Conduct thorough scene investigation, including search for fingerprints, pry marks, trace evidence, etc.
- ❑ Photograph scene.
- ❑ Attempt to determine point of entry and point of exit. Thoroughly examine those areas for physical evidence.
- ❑ Diagram the scene, if appropriate.
- ❑ Establish pattern/M.O. (Method of Operation/Modus Operandi) information for possible similars in same area, etc.
- ❑ Search outside area around burglary scene for footprints, tire prints, other physical evidence.
- ❑ Talk to neighbors. Check the area. Attempt to locate witnesses.
- ❑ Interview all witnesses separately.
- ❑ If you have a suspect, interview him/her after Mirandizing.
- ❑ Obtain a complete statement, including any alibis.

LARCENY or THEFT ▪ defined as the felonious taking by trespass of the personal property of another with the intent to permanently deprive that person of the property.

❖ Investigative Steps

- ❑ Interview victim. Obtain complete statement, to include the following information: When did he/she last see the property? When was it discovered missing? What were the conditions of the loss?
- ❑ Obtain complete description of property loss, including amount, brand names, manufacturers, model numbers, serial numbers, color, sizes, personal identifiers, unique marks, estimated value, etc.

- ❑ Secure/protect scene, if appropriate.
- ❑ Conduct thorough scene investigation, including search for fingerprints, trace evidence, etc.
- ❑ Photograph/diagram scene, if appropriate.
- ❑ Establish pattern/Modus Operandi of theft.
- ❑ Search area for footprints, tire prints, other physical evidence.
- ❑ Attempt to locate witnesses.
- ❑ Interview all witnesses separately.
- ❑ If you have a suspect, interview him/her after Mirandizing. Obtain a complete statement, including any alibis.

ARSON ▪ defined as the willful and malicious burning of the dwelling of another. (In most states, arson now extends to the property and lands of another.)

❖ Investigative Steps

NOTE: In many ways, an arson investigation is as complex as a homicide investigation (and, in certain instances, homicide may also be involved). This especially is true of the scene investigation. One of the most difficult tasks faced by the first arriving officer is continuous protection of the scene.

A. First arriving officer:

- ❑ Before arrival, ensure that a continuous presence at the scene is maintained by firefighters. If the scene is left unattended for any length of time, a search warrant (or consent) will be required before reentry.
- ❑ Ensure the entire scene is secure and cordoned off. Keep unauthorized persons (including non-involved supervisors) out. Use firefighters to assist in protecting the scene.
- ❑ A fire scene is potentially very toxic. Consider wearing face and eye protection even though the fire is out.
- ❑ Start a log: Note times/persons in scene/persons around area.
- ❑ Interview firefighters for fire scene observations/witnesses/possible suspects.
- ❑ Notify supervisor/specialists. Protect scene until arrival.
- ❑ Consider immediate photos/videotape.

B. If you are investigator in charge:

- ❑ Establish a plan of action. Ensure you have adequate personnel available for the scene search.
- ❑ Ensure scene is diagrammed/photographed/videotaped, etc.
- ❑ Ensure a complete search for evidence. (Note: fire scenes are best searched through a grid search method, using sifting screens.)
- ❑ Isolate witnesses/interview separately.
- ❑ Interview victim(s)/owner extensively regarding circumstances surrounding fire, loss, insurance, etc.
- ❑ Ensure a thorough fire/arson origin-and-cause investigation is completed (charring, burn patterns, etc.)

❖ Tips

- Conduct your investigation as if: a) nothing is ever as it seems, and b) no one ever tells the truth (until you learn otherwise).
- Never prejudge anything. Be prepared to revise your thinking as you learn new information.
- Remember, motive and opportunity are key issues.
- Often, arson investigations require a showing of a "negative corpus" (i.e., the fire wasn't caused by a natural occurrence [such as lightning], spontaneous ignition/combustion, electrical short, etc., leaving arson as the only remaining cause). Ensure your fire/arson investigator includes this information in his/her report.
- For eyewitnesses, hostile witnesses, suspects: Consider obtaining their word-for-word account (written or tape recorded).

ASSAULT ▪ defined, in most jurisdictions, as an unlawful attempt, coupled with the present ability, to commit a violent injury upon the person of another.

However, the degrees and forms of assault vary widely from state to state. For example, assault can vary in degree from *simple assault* or *assault and battery* (the completed act) to *assault with a deadly weapon* or *assault with great bodily injury*. It can vary in form from *simple assault of another* to *spousal abuse*, *child abuse*, or *elder abuse*.

For the purposes of demonstration, only the simplest degree and form of assault will be discussed in this appendix.

❖ Investigative Steps

- ❑ Interview victim for complete details of event.
- ❑ Note injuries to victim. Obtain photos/medical release, E.R. treatment info, etc.
- ❑ If weapon involved, consider photographing in place.
- ❑ Obtain complete description of suspect, vehicle, weapon, etc.
- ❑ Ensure you have clear understanding of circumstances of assault, i.e., was there provocation, escalation, etc.
- ❑ Separate witnesses. Interview away from others.
- ❑ Locate and interview suspect. Get his/her side of the story. Mirandize, if you conduct your interview in custody or with arrest in mind. Note any alibis. Photograph, if appropriate.

❖ Tips

- Denial or self-defense are common defenses.
- Many external injuries, such as black eyes, do not show up well until 2-3 days after the assault. Consider photographing the victim then.
- In spousal abuse and child abuse cases, evidence of "fresh complaint" (i.e., what the victim said to the first person he or she told about the assault) can prove important.
- In assault cases of any nature—and in any other crimes involving specific intent—the defense of *diminished capacity* (i.e., under the influence of alcohol, drugs, etc.) may become an issue, regardless of whether or not your state allows such a defense. Consider obtaining a blood and/or urine sample from the suspect in any case involving specific intent.

Appendix B

ARREST REPORTS AND "THE BUILDING BLOCKS OF PROBABLE CAUSE"

To arrest a person, you must have probable cause (reasonable cause to believe) that a crime occurred and that the person you are arresting is the one who committed it. After the arrest, you must explain in writing what you did. Your arrest report must clearly show the reader, step-by-step, how you came to form your belief and what actions you took. And, you must clearly show the reader that you did not violate the arrested person's constitutional rights in the process. Since each event in the step-by-step probable cause process builds upon the preceding event until the arrest occurs, the process might be referred to as "the building blocks of probable cause."

For example, read the following arrest report:

> On 11-20-20-- at about 2230 hours, I was driving south on Main Street, between First and Second Streets, when I saw a late model, red Camaro, license #ABC123, traveling south about one block ahead of me. The Camaro was traveling slower than the flow of traffic, and it occasionally weaved from the number one lane into a portion of the number two lane and back.
>
> I followed the Camaro for about three blocks. It continued to weave from lane to lane as it traveled at about 20 m.p.h. In the belief that the driver was either experiencing medical problems or had been drinking, I activated my emergency lights to stop the Camaro. However, it continued on for two more blocks before finally stopping near the intersection of Main and Seventh Streets.
>
> I stopped my patrol unit behind the Camaro and approached it on the driver's side. The driver and sole occupant, Mark Phipps, asked me if there was a problem. As he spoke, I could smell the strong odor of an alcoholic beverage on his breath. I shined my flashlight in the car and saw that his face was flushed and his eyes were red and watery.
>
> I instructed Phipps to get out of the car. As he stepped out, he staggered and leaned on the door to keep his balance.
>
> I asked him for his driver's license; his hands fumbled as he attempted to retrieve it from his wallet.
>
> After Phipps gave me his driver's license, I instructed him to step to the sidewalk under the street light to perform field sobriety tests. I asked him if he had any physical problems with his back, hips, or legs. He answered, "No." I demonstrated each test to him before instructing him to perform it. The following is the result of those tests:
>
> - Finger Count—Fail: Phipps did not complete this test. He counted, "1,2,3,4,5. . . . 5, uh. . . . . I can't do the rest."
> - Recite Alphabet—Fail: Phipps did not continue past the letter M.
> - One-Leg Stand—Fail: Phipps did not keep one leg off the sidewalk for more than five seconds at a time.
> - Write Alphabet—Fail: Phipps' printing was nearly illegible. He did not write past the letter P, and he repeated the letter N twice.
> - Walk and Turn, Heel-Toe—Fail: Phipps staggered as he walked; his heels and toes never touched; he stopped halfway through the test and said he could not continue.

Because Phipps failed five of five field sobriety tests, I arrested him for driving while intoxicated and placed him in my patrol unit. I locked his car, then I transported him to County Jail.

At the jail, I read Phipps the admonishment forms and offered him a blood, urine, or breathalyzer test. He requested a breathalyzer test. The results were .19/.20. (copy of test results attached—original form with the casefile). I read Phipps his Miranda Rights. He waived his rights by saying, "Yeah, I understand them," and "Yeah, I'll talk to you." Phipps said that he drank four martinis at the Downtown Bar just before I stopped him.

Deputy Jones booked Phipps into jail.

Case forwarded to the Prosecuting Attorney's Office for action.

Now, let's break the narrative down into its separate building blocks of probable cause:

FIRST EVENT (How you came to be involved in the investigation—and your observations):

On 11-20-20-- at about 2230 hours, I was driving south on Main Street, between First and Second Streets, when I saw a late model, red Camaro, license #ABC123, traveling south about one block ahead of me. The Camaro was traveling slower than the flow of traffic, and it occasionally weaved from the number one lane into a portion of the number two lane and back.

NEXT EVENT (What you did about what you saw):

I followed the Camaro for about three blocks.

NEXT EVENT (What you saw):

It continued to weave from lane to lane as it traveled at about 20 m.p.h.

NEXT EVENT (You formed an opinion and acted on that opinion, i.e., you had reasonable cause to believe you were observing a crime in progress (drunk driving). But, as any reasonable person would do, you weren't ruling out the possibility of innocent behavior):

In the belief that the driver was either experiencing medical problems or had been drinking, I activated my emergency lights to stop the Camaro.

NEXT EVENT (What you saw. The driver's slowness to respond to your emergency lights added to your probable cause):

However, it continued on for two more blocks before finally stopping near the intersection of Main and Seventh Streets.

NEXT EVENT (What you did.)

I stopped my patrol unit behind the Camaro and approached it on the driver's side.

NEXT EVENT (Your observations, which now include initial confirmation of your probable cause to believe the driver committed a crime by driving while under the influence):

The driver and sole occupant, Mark Phipps, asked me if there was a problem. As he spoke, I could smell the strong odor of an alcoholic beverage on his breath. I shined my flashlight in the car and saw that his face was flushed and his eyes were red and watery.

NEXT EVENT (What you did about what you observed—and his reactions —which tended to confirm your original opinion):

I instructed Phipps to get out of the car. As he stepped out, he staggered and leaned on the door to keep his balance.

I asked him for his driver's license; his hands fumbled as he attempted to retrieve it from his wallet.

NEXT EVENT (What you did—a clear showing that you reacted reasonably and properly):

After Phipps gave me his driver's license, I instructed him to step to the sidewalk under the street light to perform field sobriety tests. I asked him if he had any physical problems with his back, hips, or legs. He answered, "No." I demonstrated each test to him before instructing him to perform it. The following is the result of those tests:

NEXT EVENT (Your observations about what he did—and now sufficient probable cause to make your arrest):

- Finger Count—Fail: Phipps did not complete this test. He counted, "1,2,3,4,5. . . . 5, uh. . . . . I can't do the rest."
- Recite Alphabet—Fail: Phipps did not continue past the letter M.
- One-Leg Stand—Fail: Phipps did not keep one leg off the sidewalk for more than five seconds at a time.
- Write Alphabet—Fail: Phipps' printing was nearly illegible.
- He did not write past the letter P, and he repeated the letter N twice.
- Walk and Turn, Heel-Toe—Fail: Phipps staggered as he walked; his heels and toes never touched; he stopped halfway through the test and said he could not continue.

NEXT EVENT (You explain to the reader how you came to form your belief and what you did to effect the arrest):

Because Phipps failed five of five field sobriety tests, I arrested him for driving while intoxicated and placed him in my patrol unit. I locked his car, then I transported him to County Jail.

FINAL EVENTS (Your completion of the arrest and booking process—done while continuing to protect the suspect's constitutional rights):

> At the jail, I read Phipps the admonishment forms and offered him a blood, urine, or breathalyzer test. He requested a breathalyzer test. The results were .19/.20. (copy of test results attached—original form with the casefile). I read Phipps his Miranda Rights. He waived his rights by saying, "Yeah, I understand them," and "Yeah, I'll talk to you." Phipps said that he drank four martinis at the Downtown Bar just before I stopped him.
>
> Deputy Jones booked Phipps into jail.
>
> Case forwarded to the Prosecuting Attorney's Office for action.

As you can see, a properly written arrest report will clearly show the reader that you acted in a reasonable and prudent manner throughout the process—a process which will be closely scrutinized at every level.

NOTE: The above sample report is for *example purposes only*. The required report content and forms associated with an arrest of this nature vary from state to state. Refer to your own state's reporting system for exact requirements.

Appendix C

COMMON ABBREVIATIONS USED IN LAW ENFORCEMENT NOTES

Abbreviation	Meaning
A&A	Assisted and advised
AKA	Also known as (alias)
A/O	Arresting Officer
APB	All points bulletin
Arr.	Arrest
Asst.	Assistant
Att.	Attempt
BAC	Blood alcohol content
BOLO	Be on the Lookout
Capt.	Captain
CBA	Cleared by arrest
CJRS	Criminal justice reporting system
Co.	County
Comp.	Complainant
Def.	Defendant
Dept.	Department
Dist.	District
DMV	Department of Motor Vehicles
DOA	Dead on arrival
DOB	Date of birth
DOT	Direction of travel
DUI	Driving under the influence of alcohol
DWI	Driving while intoxicated
E/B	Eastbound
GOA	Gone on arrival
Hdqtrs.	Headquarters
HWY	Highway
I.D.	Identification
Inf.	Informant
Insp.	Inspector
Juv.	Juvenile
L/F	Left front
Lic.	License
L/R	Left rear
Lt.	Lieutenant
Memo	Memorandum
M.O.	Modus operandi
NATB	National Automobile Theft Bureau
N/B	Northbound
NCIC	National Crime Information Center
NFD	No further description
NMN	No middle name
OID	Operation Identification
OLN	Operator License Number
P.C.	Penal Code
PIN	Personal Identification number
Rec'd	Received
R/F	Right front
R/O	Reporting Officer
ROA	Referred to other agency
R/R	Right rear
S/B	Southbound
Sgt.	Sergeant
Subj.	Subject
Susp.	Suspect
S/w	Station wagon
UCR	Uniform Crimc Rcports
UTL	Unable lo locate
V.	Victim
Vict.	Victim
VIN	Vehicle Identification Number
Viol.	Violation
W&R	Warned and released
W/B	Westbound
Wit.	Witness
WFA*	White female adult
WMJ*	While male juvenile
2drHT	Two-door hardtop

* The "W" indicates race. It is also appropriate to substitute "B" for Black, "H" for Hispanic, "A" for Asian, "NA" for Native American.

GLOSSARY

The number in ( ) at the end of each term denotes the primary chapter in which that term is discussed.

active (voice) ▪ the subject performs the action. (5)

adjective ▪ a word that modifies a noun. (7)

administrative report ▪ deals with the routine functioning of the department or agency. (1)

adverb ▪ a word that modifies a verb, an adjective, or other adverb. (7)

article ▪ a word used with a noun to make it more specific; English has three articles: *a, an*, and *the*. (7)

chronological ▪ going in time from the beginning to the end. (4)

concise ▪ leaving out unnecessary words; making every word count without leaving out important facts. (3)

conclusionary language ▪ also referred to as inferences. (2)

connotative ▪ words which have an emotional effect; the connotative meaning of a word is its positive or negative overtones. (2)

content ▪ what is said. (2)

dangling modifier ▪ a group of words that does not refer clearly and logically to any word in the sentence. (5)

denotative ▪ words which have little emotional effect; the denotative meaning of a word is its *objective* meaning. (2)

direct quotations ▪ shows a subject's state of mind and avoids conclusionary language; repeats exactly what a subject said and places quotations marks around the statement. (12)

edit ▪ to evaluate the content of a report. (4)

elements of the crime ▪ conditions that must exist and be proven to exist for an act to be called a specific kind of crime. (2)

fact ▪ a statement that can be proven. (2)

first person ▪ referring to yourself as "I"; direct. (5)

form ▪ how something is written. (2)

grammar ▪ the rules for how words change and combine to form sentences. (7)

Harvard comma ▪ the comma between the next to the last word in the series and the *and*; also called the *Oxford comma* or *serial comma*. (11)

homonym ▪ a word that sounds like another word but has a different meaning and a different spelling, for example, the words *here* and *hear*. (9)

imperative ▪ a command, such as "Close the window," where it is acceptable to leave out the subject of a sentence. (8)

indirect quotations ▪ simply stating in your own words the general information you were told by a subject; uses no quotation marks. (12)

inference ▪ a conclusion based on reasoning. (2)

-ing word group ▪ a type of sentence fragment that cannot stand alone and must be attached to a sentence. (8)

interrupters ▪ phrases and clauses which interrupt the sentence. (11)

mechanically correct ▪ follows the rules for spelling, capitalization, and punctuation. (3)

mechanics ▪ translating ideas and spoken words into written words. (3)

modifiers ▪ words which describe other words. (5)

narrative ▪ a technical report structured in chronological order describing a sequence of events. (4)

nonrestrictive ▪ a phrase or clause which simply adds additional information or explanation; separated from the main sentence by commas. (11)

objective ▪ nonopinionated, fair, and impartial. (2)

operational report ▪ deals with the activities of law enforcement officers. (1)

opinion ▪ a personal belief. (2)

Oxford comma ▪ the comma between the next to the last word in the series and the *and*; also called the *Harvard comma* or *serial comma*. (11)

parallelism ▪ using the same type of structure for similar parts of a sentence. (5)

passive (voice) ▪ the subject does *not* perform the action. (5)

predicate ▪ the part of a sentence that *tells* something about the subject. (8)

pronoun ▪ a word used in place of a noun. (5)

proofreading ▪ evaluating the form of a report. (4,9)

redundant ▪ words which repeat themselves. (6)

report ▪ a permanent written record which communicates important facts to be used in the future. (1)

restrictive ▪ a phrase or clause needed to make the meaning of the sentence explicit; no commas are placed around it. (11)

run-on sentence ▪ contains *two* complete sentences *incorrectly* joined together. Not to be confused with sentences that have a double predicate or with those that have a subsentence. (8)

sentence fragment ▪ a group of words that does not have both a subject and a predicate. (8)

serial comma ▪ the comma between the next to the last word in the series and the *and*; also called the *Harvard comma* or *Oxford comma.* (11)

slanting ▪ including only one side of a story or only facts that tend to prove or support a theory. (2)

split predicate ▪ a type of sentence fragment where one sentence contains the subject and half of the predicate. Then the last part of the predicate is put into a sentence of its own—a fragment. (8)

squinting modifier ▪ a word or phrase could modify both the word it follows and the word it precedes, resulting in two possible meanings for the sentence. (5)

subject ▪ tells *who.* (5,8)

subsentence ▪ a type of sentence fragment that does have a subject and a predicate but still cannot stand alone. It depends on a main sentence for its meaning. Subsentences tell *what kind, why, which, when*, or *where.* (8)

tense (verb) ▪ used to show time. Verbs may be in the present (I see), past (I saw) or future (I will see). (4)

third person ▪ referring to yourself as "this person" or "this officer"; indirect. (5)

tone ▪ refers to how the writer relates to the reader, that is the "tone of voice" used to present information; may be described as friendly, serious, distant, angry, bitter, sarcastic, argumentative, or objective. (6)

verb ▪ tells *what.* (5)

verbatim ▪ a word-for-word statement of what a subject said; has quotation marks around it. (12)

INDEX